A Dictionary of Theological Terms

From Joyce
christmas 1997

A Dictionary of Theological Terms

M. E. Manton

General Editor H. J. Appleby

Grace Publications

GRACE PUBLICATIONS TRUST
139 Grosvenor Avenue
London   N5 2NH
England

Joint Managing Editors:
    H. J. Appleby
    J. P. Arthur M.A.

ISBN 0 946462-40-2

Distributed by
EVANGELICAL PRESS
12 Wooler Street
Darlington
Co. Durham   DL1 1RQ
England

Printed in Great Britain at the Bath Press, Avon

Cover design by Leverpress/Insight Ltd, Ipswich, Suffolk

FOREWORD

I am pleased to write a few words to underline the importance and usefulness of this handbook.

Every intellectual discipline has its own technical terms. Without an understanding of these, a working grasp of that subject will be effectively hindered. This applies as much to the study of theology as to other (less) important sciences e.g. computer technology and its particular jargon.

This little volume is, as its title indicates, a dictionary. It explains words and expressions — theological ones. It lists them in alphabetical order with a cross reference system where necessary. The terms listed are chosen because they occur as shorthand expressions in biblical, historical and doctrinal literature. To have the meaning of these terms defined succinctly is a real advantage when one begins to read theology.

Such a service is all the more important when the terms in question are neither used in English speech nor are they found in dictionaries nor are they introduced in classes where English is taught as a foreign language. This handbook will therefore be of immense value to non-European students of theology. But, in addition, students from the United Kingdom will find it valuable because the study and proper use of words is not given the attention which it used to have and Latin (and Greek) are no longer taught in our secondary schools. Many of these theological terms are anglicized versions of classical (Latin and Greek) words. Where this is so, the author indicates the word or words in the original languages.

Margaret Manton has devoted much of her life to the study and teaching of theology. Her first degree was in modern languages and she followed this with a degree in theology and a qualification for teaching. She taught at the London Bible College, Ridgelands Bible College and for eleven years at the Bible College of Singapore. Her qualifications to write such a book as this are impeccable and one wishes it a far wider circulation than was perhaps at first envisaged. The need exists: the work has been done. May the Lord of truth use this book in educating generations of his servants!

Hywel R. Jones
London Theological Seminary

The Dictionary

* marking a word indicates that word is explained in a
separate entry in the relevant alphabetical section.

cf	=	'compare'
e.g.	=	'for example'
et al	=	'and elsewhere'
lit	=	'literally'

Absolution (Latin 'absolvo' — to set free)

The forgiveness of sins. The Roman Catholic Church uses this word to describe the forgiveness which, they say, comes to any people through the priest to whom they confess their sin.

The Bible teaches that only God can forgive sins. In protestant *evangelical churches the preacher declares that God is able and willing to forgive sins if a *repentant sinner confesses to God alone and trusts in what Christ has done for sinners on the cross.

Active obedience of Christ

When Jesus Christ was on earth, he lived a life which was in every way obedient to his Father's will. God now gives to believers the merit of that active obedience to count as their own.

See Passive Obedience of Christ. See also Imputation.

Adiaphora (Greek 'adiaphoros' — lit. 'not different'; so not a thing of importance)

Note: The letter 'a' before several words in Greek and English makes that word negative. E.g. a-gnostic, a-diaphora (indifferent), a-moral (without morals).

A word used by some Protestants after the *Reformation to describe anything considered helpful done or used in worship which is neither commanded nor forbidden by Scripture — e.g. ceremonies, robes, statues, sign of the cross, etc. The only **essential** truth was thought to be faith in Christ for salvation.

Other Protestants (the Puritans) held that only those things should be done or used in church worship which are actually commanded in Scripture. They argued that obedience to all Bible truth — and only to that — was essential to obedience to the Lordship of Christ, and that permissible adiaphora are limited only to those things of no moral or spiritual significance which do not conflict with Scripture teaching or with the glory of God, e.g. the materials used for building construction, the times and arrangement of meetings, etc. which are to be decided by using common sense.

See Regulative Principle

Adoption

One of the acts of God in the salvation of believers, distinct from his
*calling them, *regenerating them and *justifying them, by which
he adopts them as his children (John 1:12).

See a Bible Dictionary.

Adoptionism

One of the false teachings or heresies which arose in the early
*church. It said that Christ was only a man, but was 'adopted' as
God's Son because of his obedient life. That is to say, he was a man
who became God.

Advent (Latin 'adventus' — coming)

This word is used to describe both comings of Christ — his first
coming (the *incarnation) and his second coming (second advent).
   In the Anglican Church calendar the word 'advent' is used for the
month of December up to Christmas Day (e.g. the first/second
Sunday in Advent).

Agnosticism (Greek 'a-ginosko' — not to know)

Agnostics say they do not know if there is a God or not. In the early
*church, the Gnostics claimed that they had secret knowledge.
(Greek 'ginosko' — to know/'gnosis' — knowledge). Thomas
Huxley invented the word 'agnostic' in 1809.

See Atheism.

Alexandrian school

A school of theology which grew up in Alexandria (Egypt) in the
late second century AD.

In the third century Clement and *Origen taught there, seeking to reconcile Greek philosophy with the Scriptures. Origen produced the Hexapla, a volume putting together six translations of the Old Testament, and wrote commentaries in which he emphasised the *allegorical meaning of the Scriptures.

In the fourth century Athanasius of Alexandria insisted (contrary to *Arius) that Jesus Christ is God — he is 'homoousios', the same essence, as God the Father.

See Antiochene School. See also Arianism.

Allegory

A section of Scripture (or other literature) which means more than it seems to say when one first reads it. Gal. 4:21-31 is allegory. Paul says so in v. 24. Every detail of the passage has a spiritual meaning.

John Bunyan's 'Pilgrim's Progress' is a good example of allegory. Every character and circumstance has a spiritual meaning.

See Parables.

A-Millennialism

See Millennium.

Anabaptist (from Greek 'to baptize again')

The Anabaptists 'baptized again' by immersion believers who had been baptized as infants. They arose in Germany and other European countries after the Reformation. Because of certain theological errors and moral practices they had a poor reputation at first, but in the mid-sixteenth century an Anabaptist leader, Menno Simons, led them into more *evangelical beliefs and practices. The present day American Mennonites claim to hold the same theological views as Menno Simons.

See Baptist.

Anglicans

The word 'Anglican' comes from the same root as the word 'English'. Anglicanism refers to the doctrine and church government of the Church of England. An Anglican is a member of the Church of England. In Scotland and America the word 'Episcopalian' denotes the Anglican denomination.

'Episcopalian' comes from the Greek 'episkopos' — one who oversees a congregation. The word is translated 'bishop' in the Authorised Version. The chief figure in the Anglican communion is the Primate (i.e. first man), the Archbishop, with bishops exercising authority over local Anglican congregations in cities and towns (for example, the Bishop of London). A vicar (Latin 'vicarius', a substitute) is the incumbent or occupier of a particular Anglican parish, an area having its own church. The parishioners are the people of that particular area. A curate, who has the 'cure' or care of souls, assists the vicar.

Other Anglican personnel include —
Archdeacon — one who administers authority under a bishop.
Canon — a member of a cathedral staff (a prebendary).
Dean — the head of a cathedral church, immediately under a bishop.
Rural Dean — head of a group of parishes.

The 39 articles are the official doctrinal standard of the Anglican Church. All clergy — i.e. those ordained to serve in the Anglican Church — are required to subscribe to these. The Anglican Church practises baptism of infants, followed by the confirmation of the person in question at a later date (usually during teenage years). By confirmation the candidate is admitted to the Anglican Church, and has the right to partake of the bread and wine at the communion service.

Stemming from the events of the Reformation (Henry VIII's breakaway from the Church of Rome) and the later Elizabethan Settlement, the Anglican Church has always been under the authority of the State. Archbishops and bishops are appointed by the Queen. Another term is 'the Established Church'.

Animism

Animism teaches that spirits live in natural objects such as trees, rivers and stones, and are to be worshipped. The belief exists in some primitive religions which do not believe in one true God. Nineteenth century and early twentieth century *liberalism believed that animism was the religion of the Hebrews before they came to *monotheism.

Annihilationism (Latin 'nihil' — nothing)

Annihilationists who do not believe in God say that all people come to nothing when they die, i.e. they cease to exist. Annihilationists who believe in God say that the unconverted cease to exist at death, but the converted continue to live in a conscious state.

See Conditional Immortality.

Anthropomorphism (Greek 'anthropos' — man, and 'morphe' — form)

To use an anthropomorphism is to speak of God as if he were a man. Anthropomorphic language is a figure of speech used in Scripture to help people to understand God better. For example, God is said to have a hand (Josh. 4:24), a mouth (Isa. 58:14), and to walk (Gen. 3:8).

Antichrist

One who is opposed to Christ. The actual word 'antichrist' only appears in John's epistles. John speaks of many antichrists who have already come, saying that Jesus is not the Christ and so deny both Father and Son (1 John 2:18,22; 4:3).

Although the word 'antichrist' is not in any other Bible book, other New Testament books do speak of an opponent or opponents of Christ, who even say that they are Christ. Christ himself warns of 'false Christs' (Matt. 24:4; Mark 13:22). He speaks in John 5:43 of one who comes in his own name. He also speaks of 'many deceivers' who do not acknowledge that Jesus Christ has come in the flesh, that is, in a human body. The person who says this is 'a deceiver and an antichrist' (2 John:7).

Paul speaks clearly in 2 Thess. 2 of an enemy of Christ. He calls him 'the man of lawlessness' ('man of sin', AV), and 'the lawless one', whose coming will be 'according to the working of Satan' (2 Thess. 2:3,8-9). He claims to be God (v. 4), deceives people (vv. 9-10) and will finally be destroyed by Christ (v. 8). He is called 'the son of perdition' (v. 3, AV), i.e. one who will be finally destroyed. Jesus calls Judas Iscariot 'the one doomed to destruction' (John 17:12).

2 Thess. 2:7 speaks of 'the mystery of lawlessness' (AV), a principle of evil already at work when Paul was writing. This evil principle will become personal in 'the man of lawlessness'.

In Revelation, we read of the dragon (12:7) which stands for Satan. We also read of beasts who are associated with Satan, in that they do his work (11:7; 13:1,11). The dragon and the beast from the sea were worshipped (13:4). The beast from the earth did a great miracle (13:15). These show teaching very similar to Paul's man of lawlessness and John's antichrist. There are many different interpretations as to when all these events in Revelation take place and what the different symbols such as the beasts stand for. However, these all support the fact that Satan works through people and people's organisations to oppose Christ and set up alternative religions and other world views.

Note: The Greek preposition 'anti' in antichrist can mean both 'opposed to' and 'instead of'. The meaning 'instead of' is certainly there when Christ warns of false Christs and of one who comes in his own name (see above). The man of lawlessness claims to be God (2 Thess. 2:4).

Antinomianism (Greek 'anti' — against, and 'nomos'- law)

Some people say that believers have no need to keep the commandments of God because God has *justified them by *faith. This is antinomianism. Such believers are living 'contrary to the law' of God.

Paul opposed this false teaching. He said: 'Shall we continue in sin that *grace may abound? God forbid' (Rom. 6:1; see also 6:15). Jude 4 speaks of those who 'turn the grace of God into a licence for immorality' (NIV).

The words antinomian/ism were probably first used by Martin *Luther.

Antiochene school

The school of theology at Antioch in Syria, which existed in the early centuries of the Christian *church. Its theologians emphasised the plain, literal meaning of the books of the Bible, while the school of *Alexandria emphasised the *allegorical meaning. Antioch also emphasised that Jesus Christ was a man, while the school of Alexandria emphasised that he was God.

Apocalyptic (Greek 'apokalupto' — to reveal)

The noun 'apokalupsis' occurs in Revelation 1. The word is used of Jewish prophetic literature whose main theme is the final triumph of God and good over evil at the end of the age. The literature often includes visions, numbers and animals.

Daniel (Old Testament) and Revelation (New Testament) are apocalyptic books. Other books have apocalyptic passages, e.g. Joel 2:30-31; Mark 13:24-27.

Outside the Bible many such writings were produced between the second century BC and the first century AD. They are often written as if they are the work of a well-known Bible character, e.g. 'The Assumption of Moses'. This device is known as *pseudepigraphy — false writing.

Apocrypha (Greek 'ta apokrupha' — the hidden things)

The Apocrypha is a collection of thirteen books written after the Hebrew Old Testament. These books are included in the *Septuagint as an addition to the Old Testament books. The Roman Catholic Douai Version of the Bible (printed 1609) includes eleven of the apocryphal books scattered among the Old Testament books — i.e. not printed separately.

Many of the apocryphal books are valuable for showing us how Jews in the period between the Old and New Testaments thought about God and the future age, and 1 and 2 Maccabees show us the history of that time.

List of apocryphal books

    1 and 2 Esdras
    Tobit
    Judith
    Sequel to Esther
    The Wisdom of Solomon

Ecclesiasticus (The Wisdom of Jesus, the Son of Sirach)
    Baruch
    The Letter of Jeremiah
    The Additions to Daniel
    The Prayer of Manasses
    1 and 2 Maccabees

Apocryphal Gospels

In addition to the four *canonical Gospels, that is, Matthew, Mark, Luke and John which are in our New Testament *canon, there are several books which call themselves Gospels but which were never included as Scripture by the people who collected together the New Testament books. These false Gospels were not accepted because there was much in them which was not like the four biblical Gospels, showing that they were clearly not inspired by God. Some of them, e.g. the Gospel of Peter, the Gospel of Thomas, claimed to be by biblical writers but they seem to be the work of men who lived later than the men who wrote our four Gospels.

Apologetics (Greek 'apologia' — a defence)

In 2 Tim. 4:16 Paul uses this word: 'At my first defence no one stood by me.'

Apologetics is the defence of the Christian faith. The early apologists (Justin, Tertullian, etc.) defended the faith against the philosophies of their day, or showed how the faith and philosophy could be reconciled.
    Modern apologetics seeks to show on what basis Christians believe in God and how he can be known. It asks and answers such

questions as: 'What is revelation? What is *faith? What are the proofs of God's existence? What are miracles? What is the relationship between religion and science?'.

Apollinarianism

Apollinarius (AD310-390) taught that Jesus Christ was fully God, but not fully human.

Apostasy (Greek 'apostasia' — a fall away from)

The word was originally used of desertion of a post of duty, or of a revolt. In the Bible it refers to a departure from the true faith.

See a Bible Dictionary.

Arianism — Arius

Arius, a presbyter in *Alexandria, taught that Christ was more than man but less than God. The Son was not an eternal being. Athanasius (see Alexandrian School) opposed Arius and Arius was condemned at the Council of Nicaea in AD325.

The 'battle of the diphthongs' still raged, however. Athanasius and his followers insisted that Christ and the Father are 'homoiousios' — of one substance (essence). Those who sympathised with Arius but did not wish to deny Christ's deity altogether, taught that the Son and the Father are homoiousios — of similar substance (essence).

Arminianism

From Arminius, a Dutch theologian (1560-1609). He reacted against the teaching usually associated with John *Calvin on the *sovereignty of God in salvation, though this teaching is only Calvin's *systematic organisation of the teaching of Scripture. Arminius' followers drew up 'The Remonstrance' (a protest) in

1610 in which they set out their views, for example, that God
*elected his people because he saw ahead of time that they would
have *faith; and that Christ died for all people, making salvation
possible for all people. This would mean that it is a person's will, not
God's, which decides if that person shall be saved or not. Arminians
are sometimes called Remonstrants (Protesters).

Ascension

Christ's departing from this world to be at the right hand of God in
heaven until his second coming. Jesus spoke of his ascension in John
6:62 and 20:17 and Luke describes the event in Luke 24:51 and Acts
1:9. The two angels refer to it in Acts 1:11. The epistles refer to the
ascension in Eph. 4:10; 1 Tim. 3:16; Heb. 4:14; 1 Peter 3:22. The
many references to Christ's sitting at the right hand of God (e.g. Col.
3:1; Heb. 1:3) and to his future return to earth imply that the
ascension has taken place.

Asceticism (Greek 'askesis' — exercise, discipline, training)

Ascetics are people who discipline their bodies in order to be more
holy in spirit.

There are examples of asceticism in the Bible. The Old Testament Nazarites (alternative spelling 'Nazirites' [NIV and RAV]
following the Hebrew 'nazir' — to separate, which suggests that this
spelling is the more accurate: Num. 6:2-8) were ascetics. John the
Baptist was an ascetic (Matt. 3:4), as was Jesus to a certain extent —
he was not free to marry or enjoy normal human relationships (Mark
3:31-35).

Fasting is part of biblical asceticism. There is no command to fast
in the New Testament but Jesus clearly expected his disciples to fast
(Matt. 6:16; 9:15).

Unfortunately, asceticism has become used for wrong purposes;
that is, people have thought that they can obtain salvation by living
ascetically, by living with little food and the normal enjoyments of
human life. This idea is particularly to be found in Roman Catholic
theology.

Assurance of salvation

Believers may know with certainty that they are believers, children of God, born again, possessors of eternal life.

The Greek word translated assurance is 'plerophoria' — full conviction. It is found in Col. 2:2; 1 Thess. 1:5; Heb. 6:11; 10:22.

Believers base their assurance on several things:

1. The promises of God. E.g. Jesus' words: 'He who comes to me I will not cast out' (John 6:37).

2. The inward witness of the Spirit of God (Rom. 8:16).

3. The moral evidences of salvation. 'By their fruits you shall know them' (Matt. 7:20).

John's first epistle gives three tests to help the children of God to be assured of their salvation:

1. The test of right belief about Jesus Christ (3:23; 4:2; 5:5,10,13. See also 2 John 7).

2. The test of behaviour (1:5,6; 2:3; 3:6,9).

3. The test of love (4:7,8).

All these tests go together. The people who have a biblical *faith in Christ will keep the commandments of God and will love their fellow Christians.

The fact that believers may have assurance does not mean:

1. that all believers have it; some may lack it, yet still be true believers. It is not good to remain so uncertain.

2. that the assurance of believers is constant. They may have more assurance at one time than at another. Sin, coldness of heart, lack of spiritual food, wrong teaching, can all make people less sure that they belong to the Lord. But the Lord who gave the assurance in the first place is well able to restore it.

Atheism (Greek 'a' — negative, and 'theos' — God)

Denial of the existence of God. A person who does not believe that God exists is an atheist.

See Agnosticism.

Atonement   ~~Malcolm~~ Wesley

The death of Christ on the cross by which he satisfied the demands of the law of God and obtained salvation for his people. Atonement is an inclusive word to describe all that Christ did towards God and towards his people by his death. He *propitiated (covered over) the wrath of God by taking upon himself the punishment of the sin of his people. Christ's atoning work is the basis of his people's *regeneration, forgiveness, reconciliation, reception of the Holy Spirit, *adoption and final salvation.

Christ's death was *vicarious (substitutionary), i.e. he died in the place of sinners (1 Peter 3:18). It was also juridical (from Latin 'jus, juris' — law), i.e. it satisfied the justice of God, fulfilled the law of God (Rom. 10:4). Christ kept the law of God during his earthly life and by his death satisfied the demands made on sinners by the law of God (Rom. 3:26).

Attempts have been made to explain the atonement in other ways than the paragraph above. Some of these theories are summarised below:

1. Those which have God in view

a. The Satisfaction theory of Anselm

Mankind sinned by not giving to God the honour due to him. Christ's death brought honour to God and God rewarded this. Christ did not need this reward, so passed it on to sinners in the form of salvation. (Sometimes known as the Commercial theory).

b. The Governmental theory of Grotius

The death of Christ showed God's wrath against sin, so that God might be seen to be the moral Governor of the world.

c. The Vicarious *Repentance theory of McLeod Campbell

If mankind could have repented enough, they would have atoned for their sin. But they could not, so Christ repented *'vicariously' for them, offering a substitute repentance.

\\ *In the place of* \\

2. *Those which have mankind in view*

a. The Recapitulation theory of Irenaeus

c175 - c195 Bishop of Lyons

Christ recapitulated (gathered up) into himself all the stages of mankind's life and so transforms their moral behaviour.

b. The Moral Influence theory of Peter Abailard

The love of God, as shown in the death of Christ, would have a moral influence on people and cause them to repent.

c. The Example theory of the *Socinians (followers of Socinus)

Christ showed mankind how to be obedient, both by his life and by his death, so that they would follow his example.

d. The Mystical theory (Schleiermacher)

This is very like the Moral Influence theory in that it teaches that the death of Christ brought about a change in mankind. The Mystical theory, however, emphasises the incarnation and says that when Christ became man his divine life entered into human life to raise it and change it.

(This and the Recapitulation theory are forms of a theology which emphasise Bethlehem and not Calvary, the birth and not the death of Christ. It is known as *Incarnation theology and tends to speak of what Christ did for the whole human race by his becoming man, rather than what he did for his people by his death and resurrection).

3. *Those which have Satan in view*

a. Ransom to Satan

By Adam's sin Satan had captured mankind. Christ died to buy mankind back from Satan. This was taught by *Origen. c185 - c254

b. Satan deceived

Origen further taught that Satan was deceived by Christ's death and one of the Cappadocian fathers of the fourth century, continuing Origen's teaching on this point, taught that Satan was deceived as a mouse is deceived by the piece of cheese in a mouse-trap! Such crude illustrations made people unwilling to believe this teaching and it died out.

See a Bible Dictionary.

Attributes of God

An attribute is a characteristic. Some of the attributes of God belong to him alone. He does not communicate them to mankind. So we call these his incommunicable attributes. Other characteristics he does give to people to some extent. We call these his communicable attributes.

Examples of God's incommunicable attributes

1. Eternity. God has no beginning and no ending.

2. Immanence. Latin 'in manere' — to remain in. God is present in his world and yet is not part of it. His presence is his 'immanence', the opposite of his transcendence (see below). Isa. 57:15 speaks of both his transcendence and his immanence.

3. Immutability or unchangeability. God cannot become better, as that would mean he is not perfect. Clearly he cannot become worse.

4. Impassibility. God is unable to suffer.

5. Independence. God depends on no one for his existence or continuance.

6. Infinity. God is not limited in any way.

7. Omnipotence. God is all powerful. He can do everything.

8. Omnipresence. God is present everywhere.

9. Omniscience. God knows everything.

10. Transcendence. God is above his world and removed from it, not a part of it. (Contrast Immanence above).

(Numbers 7,8,9 above are sometimes called 'the three O's').

Examples of God's communicable attributes

1. Intellectual attributes — knowledge, understanding, wisdom, truth.

 All human beings have something of these attributes in themselves, even though they may not realise that they come from God.

2. Moral attributes — goodness, love, mercy, *grace, longsuffering, holiness, *righteousness.
    Again, God gives something of these attributes to mankind. A central point of the gospel is that God gives his own righteousness to believers (Rom. 3:22; Phil. 3:9), and commands his people to be holy, as he is holy (1 Peter 1:16, cf. Lev. 11:44).

Augustinianism

Augustine was Bishop of Hippo in North Africa in the fourth century. He taught the great doctrines of the Scriptures on the *sovereignty of God, the complete inability of mankind to save themselves or to do anything towards their salvation, God's *electing and prevenient *grace and the necessity of *faith in Jesus Christ alone. His biblical theology was the forerunner of that of *Calvin, *Luther and the other Reformers in the sixteenth century.

See Pelagianism.

Authority of Scripture

The authority of Scripture arises from its *inspiration. Scripture is authoritative because it is God's own Word, God's own revelation of himself to mankind. Because it comes from God, Scripture is the standard for all that the *church believes and practises. Roman Catholics believe in the authority of church tradition, but this can have no authority unless it is in accordance with Scripture.

Authorised Version

The English translation of the Scriptures published in 1611. It was authorised by, and dedicated to, King James I and is sometimes called the King James Version.

Backsliding

In the Authorised Version there are seventeen references to backsliding (thirteen in Jeremiah, three in Hosea and one in Proverbs). The Hebrew words translated 'backslide' have the idea of turn, or turn back. To backslide is to turn back from what one has previously believed and loved, i.e. God himself. Backsliding is less final than *apostasy. There is no hope of restoration for the apostate, but in Jer. 3:12,14 the Lord calls on backsliding Israel to return to him and in 3:22 he promises: 'I will heal your backslidings.' (Cf. also Hosea 14:4: 'I will heal their backsliding. I will love them freely').

Baptism (Greek 'baptisma' — baptism)

The act of washing in water, showing publicly that people have entered spiritually into the Christian *church, i.e. God has made them his own people, has brought them to believe in Jesus Christ as their Saviour. Christ was baptized in order to show his union with his people (Matt. 3:13-15) and commanded that people should be baptized when they believed the gospel. Baptism was to be in the name of the Father, the Son and the Holy Ghost (Matt. 28:19), though Acts 19:5 speaks of baptism in the name of the Lord Jesus only.

The manner of baptism

Baptism by immersion in water, i.e. by being put completely into water, was practised from the early days of the church. Acts 8:38 and the symbolism (picture-language) of Rom. 6:3-6 and Col. 2:12 speak of immersion. The 'much water' of John 3:23 may also be a hint that people were put completely under water. This agrees with the meaning of 'baptizo' — I baptize, which meant to plunge, to dip. In secular Greek the word was used of dyeing cloth and even of sinking a ship. It does not mean to pour or sprinkle.

The recipients of baptism

Baptism is a 'picture' of several aspects of the gospel.

1. Washing, cleansing. Titus 3:5; 1 Peter 3:20-22; 1 John 5:6,8.

2. Entering the kingdom of God. John 3:5.

3. Dying to the old life and rising again to newness of life. Rom. 6:3-6.

Infant baptism (*Paedobaptism. Greek 'paidion' — a child)

Those who practise infant baptism see this practice as the New Testament parallel to Old Testament *circumcision, the sign of the *covenant. Jewish boys were circumcised at eight days old to signify that they belonged to the people of God. Therefore, it is said, infants should be baptized to show that they are part of the Christian community. Those children are expected to make their personal response in later years by being confirmed. But most *evangelicals teach that an inward experience of salvation is the New Testament parallel to Old Testament circumcision (Rom. 2:29).

There is no command in the New Testament to baptize infants, nor is there a command not to do so. The New Testament knows no recipient of baptism other than believers. There were household baptisms but we have no means of knowing the age or spiritual state of the younger members. Such baptisms always followed the teaching of gospel truth and therefore it may be presumed that those being baptized were able to understand such *preaching: i.e. they were not infants.

Baptismal regeneration

Some people teach that a person (an infant or an adult) is born into God's family by being baptized in water. Such teachers have clearly not seen the difference between the outward action (baptism) and the inward action (being born again). The Bible teaches that a person is born again inwardly by the work of the Holy Spirit (John 3:5,6,7,8) and that baptism is the outward sign of that inward work (Mark 16:16).

See Regeneration.

Baptist

A Baptist believes that:

1. *Church membership consists of born-again believers only.

2. The church is both invisible and local. All believers in heaven and earth make up the invisible church. The local church is that body of believers who meet together in a particular place and acknowledge Christ. All church members are equal in status though each has different gifts.

3. A local church is governed by the influence of the Holy Spirit through the Scriptures in the hearts of the believers.
    Baptist churches are not in any way ruled by the State, but they welcome association with Baptist churches which believe the same truths.

4. The local church has the two ordinances usually recognised by Christians, baptism and the Lord's supper. Baptist churches are distinctive, however, in that they:

a. prefer the term 'ordinance' to the term *'sacrament' because of the priestly associations of the latter. The word 'ordinance' means that Christ has ordained it (or, commanded it).

b. believe that baptism should be by immersion, and is for believers only.

c. believe that the Lord's supper is a 'means of *grace', i.e. the Holy Spirit is able to use the supper to 'arouse ... feelings of awe and love and prayer' in the believer.

d. add to these two ordinances the ordinance of *preaching, which is also carried out at the command of Christ.

5. The ministry (Greek 'diakonia' — service) 'is as broad as the fellowship of the church'. But in the narrower sense the Baptist minister is one who, it is recognised, has received gifts and authority from God to *preach the Word.

(Quotations in 4c. and 5. are from Baker's Dictionary of Theology, 'Baptist').

6. Believers of all denominations can be united in belief of the truths of the gospel. But Baptists cannot join in an official way with other churches which have different views on the Lord's supper, baptism and church government.

General Baptist — Free will Baptist

A person who belongs to a Baptist church and believes in the baptism of believers by immersion but usually with theology which is more *Arminian than *Calvinistic.

Particular Baptist

A Particular Baptist believes in particular redemption, i.e. that Christ died to save a particular people. See Limited Atonement.

Strict Baptist (Grace Baptist)

Strict Baptist churches normally only invite believers who have been baptized by immersion and who are members of local churches to take the Lord's supper with them, i.e. they have a *restricted communion.

See Anabaptist.

Beatific Vision (Latin 'beatus' — happy)

(cf. The Beatitudes, the 'blesseds', the description of the 'happy' man in Matt. 5:3-11.)

The beatific vision is the sight of God himself. Matt. 5:8 says that those who are pure in heart shall see God. It is possible to 'see him', i.e. to commune with him, even now, spiritually. The final beatific vision will come to believers when they see God in heaven (Jude 24; Rev. 22:4).

Benediction (Latin 'bene-dicere' — to speak well of)

A benediction is a blessing. A minister of God speaks a benediction of God upon the people of God.

The two biblical examples are Num. 6:22-27 (Aaron and his sons are to bless the people of Israel), and 2 Cor. 13:14 (Paul ends his second letter to the Corinthians with these words).

Note that the opposite word is malediction (a curse) from Latin 'male-dicere' — to speak evil of.

Bible (Greek 'biblion' — a book or scroll)

The 'ion' ending in Greek is a diminutive, i.e. a small form. So **biblion** is a small **biblos**, a book. ('Biblos' is the first word in the New Testament — Matt. 1:1). In New Testament Greek the 'ion' ending has largely lost its diminutive meaning.

Both 'biblos' and 'biblion' come from the word 'byblus', a reed, on which people could write. Also known as 'papyrus' from which comes the English word 'paper'.

The words 'biblos' and 'biblion' could refer to any book but the word 'Bible' is only used of **the** book, the Scriptures of the Old and New Testaments.

Biblical Theology

The branch of study which seeks to state the Bible's whole teaching — of both Old and New Testaments — on a given subject, i.e. the nature of God, the life after death, etc. Biblical Theology traces the development of the Bible's teaching on a subject, i.e. sacrifice in the Old Testament to the sacrificial work of Christ in the New Testament. More narrow treatments (e.g. *Pauline theology) fit into this wider framework.

*Systematic Theology, by contrast, is a way of putting the material into a system, under headings, without necessarily having regard to the development of the teaching through Scripture periods.

Bibliolatry (Greek 'biblion' — a book, and 'latreia' — worship)

The worship of a book. (cf. idolatry — the worship of idols; mariolatry — the worship of Mary).

Some people accuse *evangelical Christians of bibliolatry — of worshipping the Bible. But Christians do not worship the Bible. Christians worship the Lord Jesus Christ, of whom the Bible speaks, but they value the Bible highly because it is God's Word to mankind.

Bondage of the will

God gave to Adam freedom and ability to obey God's commands. When Adam disobeyed, he lost the ability to do good, that is, to please God. This inability was passed on to his descendants, the whole human race. Human beings cannot please God because their wills are limited by their sinful natures. This is the bondage of the will. 'Bondage' is the noun, from the verb 'to bind'.

When God puts his Spirit into people to *regenerate them, and gives them new birth, he takes away this bondage to sin and makes them willing and able to please him.

Call — general and effectual

The word is used biblically of God's touching the lives of men and women by his power to draw them into the experience of salvation. Two calls can be distinguished in Bible teaching:

1. A general call. By this is meant the public presentation of the gospel message indiscriminately to any person, who may or may not respond.

2. An effective call. By this is meant an inward conviction of the truth of the gospel message brought about by the Holy Spirit's use of biblical *preaching resulting in the conversion of believers.

The two calls can be distinguished in Jesus' words (Matt. 22:14).

See a Bible Dictionary.

Calvinism / Calvinist

John Calvin was born in France in 1509. He was one of the foremost of the Reformers.

Calvin taught no new doctrines. He simply put into *systematic form (in his book 'The Institutes of the Christian Religion') the whole range of the doctrines of the Scriptures.

A Calvinist believes all that the Bible teaches about God and the human race. Calvinism emphasises the *sovereignty of God and the sinful nature of mankind because the Bible teaches these doctrines.

Hyper-Calvinism is a logical but not a biblical conclusion of Calvinism. Hyper-Calvinism teaches that because God has chosen a people for himself, there is no need to *preach the gospel to the unconverted. But the Bible teaches that God's people must preach the gospel everywhere and Calvin taught this emphatically. He taught that people have the responsibility to believe on Jesus Christ, though God the Holy Spirit must give them the ability to do so.

Canon (Greek 'kanon' — a rule or standard, or that which is measured by a standard)

The canon of Scripture is the sixty-six books of the Bible.

Old Testament Canon

Jews believe that Ezra arranged the canon of the Old Testament in the fifth century BC. In AD100 twenty-four books of the Hebrew Bible were acknowledged as Scripture, corresponding to thirty-nine of the *Septuagint, the Greek translation. (The books of Samuel, Kings, Chronicles and Ezra/Nehemiah were counted as one book each, and the twelve minor prophets formed one book).

New Testament Canon

The books of the New Testament were in use, that is, they were being read in public worship, but the process of deciding which should be included as Scripture and which excluded took a long time and the final form of the New Testament canon was not decided until AD397 at the Council of Carthage.

See Canonicity.

Canonicity (Greek 'kanon' — rule or standard)

The men who decided on the canon had to apply various rules or standards. The main rule was apostolicity, i.e. if a book was known to be written by an apostle — Paul's letters — or one closely associated with an apostle — e.g. Luke and Acts — or if its contents were clearly like that of the *preaching of the apostles, it was included in the canon. This is why the *Apocryphal Gospels were excluded; they did not have the marks of apostolic authenticity.

Note: Martin *Luther in the sixteenth century refused to acknowledge James' epistle and called it 'ein recht stroherner Brief' ('a right straw-y epistle!'). If read rightly, of course, it does not contradict Paul's letters, as Luther thought it did. Both Paul and James say that people who are *justified by *faith must show their faith by their good works.

Canon law (Greek 'kanon' — a rule or standard)

The rules or laws by which the *church is governed (a term used particularly in the Anglican and Roman Catholic Churches).

Note: A 'canon' is also the title of an official in the Anglican Church. He is connected with a cathedral. In the Middle Ages the clergy (the personnel of the church) lived under a certain rule of life. This is where the name of the official comes from.

Captivity epistles

The letters which Paul wrote while in prison in Rome — the letters to the Philippians, Colossians, Ephesians and Philemon.

Catechism

A published set of questions and answers for instruction in the Christian faith (e.g. the Presbyterian Larger and Shorter Catechisms).

Catechize (Greek verb 'katechein' — to instruct thoroughly)

To catechize is to instruct in the Christian faith by means of question and answer; the student learns to repeat the answers when asked the questions.

Catechist

A person who conducts catechetical instruction by means of question and answer.

Catechumen

A convert who is being instructed in the Christian faith by the question and answer method.

Catena (Latin 'catena' — a chain)

A series of Old Testament quotations in the New Testament (e.g. Rom. 3:10-18). Also used of quotations taken from early post-biblical writers on a biblical book or subject, so long as those quotations are numerous enough to form a series or chain. (e.g. Ignatius, Irenaeus, Justin Martyr, Tertullian on *church order and discipline).

Catholic (Greek 'katholikos', from two words meaning — according to the whole, universal)

The catholic *church is the whole worldwide church, the body of believers of all nations. Strictly speaking, 'Roman Catholic' refers to a church which began in Rome but has spread through the whole world.

Catholic epistles

The letters written to all believers everywhere, not to one particular *church, i.e. James; 1 and 2 Peter; 1,2,3 John; Jude.

Ceremonial Law

Hebrew 'torah', Greek 'nomos' (= law).

A comprehensive term which includes all the commandments of God in Scripture.

The *moral law is to guide the personal behaviour and belief of God's people in all ages.

The ceremonial law of the Old Testament includes all the commandments concerning the sacrifices and other outward rituals which the Old Testament believer had to keep. These rituals were a picture of Christ the true priest and true sacrifice. He himself said that he came to 'fulfil the law' (Matt. 5:17). The theme of the letter to the Hebrews is that Christ's work has put an end to the ceremonial law.

See Civil Law.

Charismatic (Greek 'charisma', plural 'charismata' — spiritual gifts)

The charismata are given by the 'charis' (*grace) of God. Rom. 5:15; 6:23 say that salvation is a charisma. 1 Cor. 7:7 says that the married man has the 'charisma' of being married, and the unmarried man has the 'charisma' of being unmarried. All Christians are therefore 'charismatic' simply because they are Christians, before we even begin to speak about more specific spiritual gifts. 1 Cor. 12 is about the charismata. It mentions a variety of such gifts given by God to believers for the purpose of building up the *church. All believers have one gift or more. See also 1 Peter 4:10.

In view of the wide use of the word 'charisma' in the New Testament and the fact that all believers are charismatic, it is unfortunate that the modern so-called charismatic movement limits the 'charismata' to those mentioned in 1 Cor. 12 and particularly to healing, tongues and prophecy. Scripture teaches that there are many more gifts than these.

Chiasmus (Greek 'chiasmus' — a criss-cross arrangement from the Greek letter 'chi')

Hebrew writing sometimes arranged its material in a pattern where several thoughts were suggested in an order, and then another aspect of those same thoughts were presented in inverse order, e.g. Matt. 13:13-17:

Therefore I speak to them in parables,
1   because seeing **they see not** and hearing **they hear not, nor understand**.
  2   And it is fulfilled to them the prophecy of Isaiah which says,
    3   'Hearing **you shall hear** and shall **not understand**,
      4   and seeing you **shall see** and shall **not perceive**.
        5   For this people's **heart** is become dull
          6   and the **ears** are dull of hearing
            7   and their **eyes** they have closed,
            7   lest they should perceive with the **eyes**
          6   and hear with the **ear**
        5   and understand with the **heart**, and should turn again and I should heal them.'
      4   But blessed are **your eyes**, for they see,
    3   and your **ears**, for they **hear**.
  2   For truly **I say unto you** that many **prophets** and righteous men
1   desired to see what **you see**, and **did not see**, and to hear what **you hear**, and **did not hear**.

Chiliasm

See Millennium.

Christology

The study of the *Person and Work of Christ.

Church

The English word is derived from the Greek adjective 'kuriakos' — (Greek 'Kurios' = lord) a word used first of the house of the Lord and then of the Lord's people.

Church militant (i.e. fighting)

A term used of all the Christians everywhere in the world now.

Church glorious

A term used of all the Christians after death who are in heaven now.

See a Bible Dictionary.

Church councils

Formal meetings of representatives of Christian churches brought together to determine the consensus of Christian opinion on some doctrinal subject. Some of the early great councils have been:

Table of early church councils

Place	Date	Subject
Jerusalem (Acts 15)		*Judaism
Nicea I	AD325	*Arianism
Constantinople I	AD381	*Apollinarianism
Ephesus	AD431	*Nestorianism
Chalcedon	AD451	*Eutychianism
Constantinople II	AD553	*Three Chapters
Constantinople III	AD680	*Monothelitism
Nicea II	AD787	*Iconolatry

After this date and until the modern *ecumenical movement began, great councils have all been within the Roman Catholic Church only.

Circumcision (Latin 'circum-cido' — to cut around;)

The removal of the male foreskin. This was practised among the nations, but in Israel was the sign of the *covenant with Abraham (Gen. 17:11).

'The circumcision' and 'the uncircumcision' are used in Gal. 2:7-12 (AV, NIV margin) meaning Jews and Gentiles respectively.

Circumcision was a sign of the *righteousness that comes by *faith (Rom. 4:9-12). So a person who has that righteousness by faith has no need to be circumcised (Gal. 5:6). Now that Christ has come, 'the circumcision' means all true believers, Jews and Gentiles, that is, those who worship God in the Spirit and rejoice in Jesus Christ (Phil. 3:3).

See a Bible Dictionary.

Civil Law

Those commandments of God in Scripture which guide the life of the believer as a citizen.

In the Old Testament, Deut. 5-30 showed Israel how they were to live in the promised land as the people of God. Now that the people of God are no longer of one nation, they do not keep the commandments relating to the Jewish nation.

In the New Testament, Rom. 13:1-10 and 1 Peter 2:11-21 give instructions to believers as citizens of their country.

See Ceremonial Law.

Clinical Baptism (Greek 'kline' — a bed; cf. English 'clinic' — a hospital)

To baptize a person who is ill and thought to be dying, i.e. to baptize at home, is to practise clinical baptism.

Clinical Theology

A part of the subject of pastoral theology. It seeks to study how the various parts of a person — spiritual, physical and mental — all fit together and fit into biblical statements on the nature of mankind.

See Pastoral Theology.

Codex

A codex consisted of sheets of vellum or papyrus and so was the forerunner of the modern book. It replaced the ancient scroll. Codex Sinaiticus, Codex Alexandrinus, manuscripts which lie behind translations of the New Testament, were written in this codex form.

Common grace

The favour which God gives to all people, including those he does not intend to save. He 'makes his sun to rise on the evil and on the good, and sends rain on the just and on the unjust' (Matt. 5:45). Acts 17:25,26; 28-29a also speak of God's *grace to all people. Because of common grace, there is a certain goodness in human beings though not, of course, a goodness which saves them (Matt. 5:46-47; 7:9-11). Unconverted people can enjoy the good things which God has created and can use the talents he gives them in art, in music, in writing, in inventing, etc. 2 Thess. 2:6,7 says that God holds back evil until a certain time when it will break loose (v.8). The restraining power is part of God's common grace.

See Grace — Saving Grace.

Communion (Greek noun 'koinonia' — that which people have in common, i.e. that which they share; the adjective is 'koinos' — common, shared. The verb 'koinonein' — to share; noun 'koinonos' — one who shares, a partner.)
  The New Testament speaks of a communion between believers and God (1 Cor. 1:9, 'koinonia' — translated 'fellowship', AV,

NIV) and between believers and each other in the *church, the body of Christ (1 Cor. 10:16; 2 Cor. 8:4 — 'fellowship' in AV in second reference). Because of such communion, believers must not have fellowship with devils by partaking in idolatry (1 Cor. 10:20-21).

The word communion has become a term used to describe the Lord's supper; this is the meaning of communion in 1 Cor. 10:16. The word emphasises the oneness between believers as they share in the same bread and wine, the symbol of the body and blood of Christ.

Comparative religion

The study of the different religions of the world — Buddhism, Islam, Confucianism, Hinduism, Shintoism, *Judaism, Christianity — by comparing and contrasting them. The study does have value, but Christianity must never be put on a level with the other religions. Only by holding fast to the fact that Jesus Christ is the Son of God and that he is the only way to God is there a safe and valid basis from which to study other religions.

Conditional immortality

Some people do not believe that the unconverted will suffer eternal punishment. They teach that immortality (being unable to die — contrast, mortality, ability to die) is a gift given by God only to people on condition that they are trusting in Jesus Christ; i.e. it is given only to believers. They teach that unbelievers will suffer *annihilation, i.e. they will cease to exist. Conditional immortality contradicts the many scriptures which teach that unbelievers will suffer eternal punishment.

Confessions of Faith

From the time of the Reformation, Protestant *churches have set out their beliefs in a *systematic way. These statements are known as the confessions of the church. The main ones are the Confession of Augsburg (1530), the Helvetic Confession (1536), the Heidelberg

Confession (1563), the Canons of the Synod of Dort (1618), the Westminster Confession (1642) which is the work of the Westminster Assembly and is the statement of faith of the Presbyterian Church, the Baptist Confession of Faith (1689). See a Bible Dictionary.

See also Creed.

Conservative

A person who wishes to conserve (keep, or retain) the belief in the Bible as the revealed Word of God without mistake (see Inerrancy). This is in contrast to the *liberal, who believes that the Bible is only a book produced by human beings and therefore containing mistakes.

The phrase 'conservative *evangelical' describes the person who believes in the evangel (the gospel message, the good news of Jesus Christ) and who is determined to preserve that belief.

Constitution of Man

Does a person consist of two parts (body and soul) or of three parts (body, soul and spirit)?

Dichotomy (Greek 'dicha' — in two, and 'temno' — I cut)

The suggestion that a person consists of two parts, the material (body) and the immaterial (soul), and makes no further distinction within the immaterial part. 'Spirit' is regarded as a spiritual activity of the renewed soul.

Trichotomy (Greek 'tricha' — in three, and 'temno' — I cut)

This says that a person consists of three parts, body, soul and spirit. Two Scripture passages seem to support this: 'Your whole spirit and soul and body be preserved' (1 Thess. 5:23, but note the word 'whole', in two different forms, in the verse); 'The dividing asunder of soul and spirit' (Heb. 4:12). The problem with this view is that the Christian is thus one who possesses more parts than the non-Christian, which is difficult to understand. Adam was made only body and soul.

For the most part the words 'spirit' and 'soul' are used interchangeably, cf. Mary's words: 'My soul magnifies the Lord and my spirit has rejoiced in God my Saviour' (Luke 1:46,47). The Hebrews taught that the body and soul were a unity (Gen. 2:7).

The Greeks taught that the body was simply the casket for the soul. They used the phrase 'soma sema' — the body a prison. They thought that at death the body perished and the soul survived. It is no accident that it was to the Greeks that Paul wrote 1 Cor. 15 emphasising the resurrection of the body, not merely the survival of the soul. In modern theology this emphasis is more important than the academic discussion outlined here.

Consubstantiation (Latin 'cum' — with, 'sub' — under, 'sto, stare' — to stand)

*Luther taught that the body and blood of Jesus Christ are present in the bread and wine of the Lord's supper (the body and blood 'stand with [each other] under the literal elements, the bread and wine').

See Transubstantiation.

Conversion (Latin 'convertere' — to turn)

The Hebrew word 'sub' and the Greek word 'epistrepho', both translated 'to convert', have this meaning of to turn, to change, i.e. to turn from sin to God.

Conversion is the act of turning, after *regeneration. A convert is a person who converts or is converted.

Conviction of sin

The action which the Holy Spirit performs in people to show them that they are sinners before God and need a Sin-bearer, the Lord Jesus Christ.

The Greek word 'elegcho' — to reprove, rebuke — occurs fifty times in the *Septuagint and seventeen times in the New Testament. Some examples are John 3:20; 1 Cor. 14:24; Eph. 5:11; Titus 1:9; Rev. 3:19.

John 16:7-11 speaks of the Holy Spirit's work in the world. He will reprove (AV) the world of sin, and of *righteousness and of judgment. (RAV and NIV here put 'convict').

The story of Lydia is a beautiful example of the convicting work of the Holy Spirit, even though the actual word 'elegcho' does not occur. Acts 16:14 says that the Lord 'opened her heart' to listen to Paul's *preaching.

Covenant Theology

Covenant theology sees the covenant idea occurring throughout Scripture, i.e. the covenant of works and the covenant of *grace. It is important to understand that this does not mean that the old covenant (the Old Testament) is a covenant of works and the new covenant (the New Testament) is a covenant of grace.

God made his covenant of works, it is suggested, with Adam. 'You must not eat from the tree of the knowledge of good and evil, for when you eat of it you will surely die' (Gen. 2:17). Adam would die if he disobeyed. God implies that he will live, i.e. enjoy God's presence, if he obeys. Adam disobeyed and died, i.e. no longer enjoyed God, and finally died physically. His action brought spiritual death (separation from God) and physical death into the human race (Rom. 5:12).

From that time, it is argued, God dealt with people on a basis of grace, the covenant of grace. As soon as sin entered the world, he promised a coming Saviour from sin (Gen. 3:15), sometimes called the 'protevangelium' — the first announcement of the gospel.

Covenants were made with Noah, Abraham, Israel and David, and Jeremiah foretells the new covenant. The fullest of the covenants is that in Exodus chapters 19-24, the covenant which the Lord made with Israel through Moses, including the ten commandments. In form it is very like covenants of that time in the surrounding nations. It names the author of the covenant (20:1,2a), shows the past relationships of the two parties (20:2b) and lays down the author's commandments which the recipients of the covenant are to obey (20:3-17), together with blessings which will follow obedience and curses which will follow disobedience.

Jer. 31:31-34 is an important passage about the coming new covenant. Heb. 8:8-12 quotes this and the whole epistle declares that Christ has brought in this 'better' covenant (8:6). The main point of the new covenant is that it is inward (its laws are written in people's hearts) and the covenant is no longer linked with outward ritual.

Those who practise infant *baptism suggest that the children of believers should be baptized because they, as well as their parents, are in the covenant of grace and belong to the people of God.

See Federal.

See a Bible Dictionary.

Creationism

See Origin of soul.

Creed (Latin 'credo' — I believe)

A creed is a statement of what believers believe, based on Scripture. There appear to be early creeds in the New Testament. For example: when Philip baptized the Ethiopian eunuch, who said: 'I believe that Jesus Christ is the Son of God (Acts 8:37, AV). See also Rom. 10:9; 1 Cor. 12:3 — 'Jesus Christ is Lord'; the baptismal formula of Matt. 28:19 (the threefold name of the *Trinity); and the baptismal formula of Acts 19:5 (the name of the Lord Jesus only).

Creeds were used in the instruction of converts and as a test of *orthodoxy against unorthodox teaching.

Well-known creeds are: The Apostles' Creed, the Nicene Creed (both known and used by the fourth century) and the Athanasian Creed (possibly fifth century).

See Confessions of Faith.

Crux / Crux interpretum (Latin)

A particularly difficult passage of Scripture on which people hold different opinions. E.g. 1 Peter 3:19.

The word crux means cross. Just as the cross was the most important event in history, so a crux is an important passage. Cf. also the English phrase 'the crux of the matter' and the adjective 'crucial', meaning central, what is all-important.

Cult (Latin, 'cultus')

The practices of worship carried out by a particular religion. The word is sometimes used to describe a deviation from historic Christianity.

See Sect.

Cultural mandate (Latin 'mandare' — to command.
 Past participle 'mandatum' — that which is commanded)

The cultural mandate is those commands which God gave to mankind to govern their life in society on this earth. The mandate is given in its basic form in Genesis but is expanded throughout the ethical sections of Scripture, e.g:

Environment

Before the fall, human beings were told to subdue the earth and have dominion over living creatures. They were to cultivate the Garden of Eden (Gen. 1:28; 2:15).

Descendants

They were to be fruitful, to multiply and replenish the earth (Gen. 1:28).

Man-woman relationship

The woman was created to be a partner suitable for the man (Gen. 2:18). As a result of the fall the man was to rule over the woman (Gen. 3:16). 1 Cor. 11:3, 8-10 refers back to Genesis.

Agricultural and cultural pursuits

Gen. 4:19-22 speaks of the entry of these into the world, though not with any specific command. Jabal was the father of all who dwell in tents and have cattle, and his brother Jubal was the father of all who handle the harp and organ.

Cuneiform (Latin 'cuneus' — a wedge)

This began as writing in pictures (pictographic script) and developed into a wedge shaped script made with a pointed instrument on clay tablets. Writing of this type was common in Mesopotamia in the Old Testament period. The Ras Shamra texts are written in cuneiform script.

Cursive (Latin 'currere' — to run)

The connected script in which biblical manuscripts were copied from about the ninth century AD.

See Uncial.

Decalogue (Greek 'deka' — ten, and 'logos' — word)

The decalogue is the name given to the ten commandments which God gave to Israel through Moses at Mount Sinai (Exod. 20:1-17).
    The first four commandments show how people should act towards God and the last six how they should act towards other people. Jesus summed up these two divisions in Matt. 22:36-40 and called them 'two commandments'. It is customary to speak of 'the two tables of the law', meaning the two divisions, but the word

'tables' refers to the two tablets of stone on which God wrote the commandments (Deut. 4:13 et al).

The word decalogue is not in Scripture but the phrase 'ten commandments' appears in Exod. 34:28; Deut. 10:4 et al.

Decisionism

This is the theory that a person becomes a Christian simply by making a decision. Becoming a Christian, it is said, is no different from making any other decision — the decision comes from a person's own mind. Against this, the Bible teaches that no one becomes a Christian merely through a personal decision. Believers are born again 'not of ... the will of the flesh, nor of the will of man, but of God' (John 1:13). God must first choose them and send his Holy Spirit to give them spiritual understanding before they can put their *faith in Christ. (Cf. Lydia 'whose heart the Lord opened' — Acts 16:14).

Deism (Latin 'deus' — God)

Certain people in the seventeenth and eighteenth centuries taught that there is a personal creator God but that this God has not revealed himself to people nor intervened in their history. Having created the world, he left it to continue according to fixed natural laws, rather like a clock which continues according to its own workings and finally stops. As a result of this teaching, deists denied the *incarnation and the possibility of miracles.

Demythologisation

See Myth.

Depravity

The popular use of the word must be distinguished from the theological use.

In the popular use of the word, some people — a minority — are depraved, i.e. morally perverted, full of vices and violence.

In the theological use, all people are depraved, that is, all people are sinful in the sight of God. They have inherited their sinful natures from Adam. In Scripture language, they are 'dead in trespasses and sins' (Eph. 2:1). They cannot bring themselves out of this state of spiritual death, nor can they do anything to win the favour of God.

The phrase 'total depravity' does not mean that there is no good in people, nor does it mean that every person is given over to every vice, or even that unconverted people do not have a conscience to tell them what is right and wrong. Total depravity means that inherited sin has affected every part of human nature — the outward (body) and the inward (mind and will, thoughts and affections).

Diaspora (Greek; English word — dispersion)

This term can denote either Jews scattered in the non-Jewish world (as in John 7:35; 1 Peter 1:1), or the places in which they reside (James 1:1).

Dichotomy

See Constitution of Man.

Dispensation (Greek 'oikonomia', from two words meaning — house, and to manage).

The Greek noun 'oikonomos' means a steward, e.g. 1 Cor. 4:1.

The word is used of the gospel which God commits to Paul, as a master commits his house, estate and affairs to his steward (1 Cor. 9:17; Eph. 3:2; Col. 1:25). It is also used of God's so ordering history that his purposes in Christ would be fulfilled at exactly the right time (Eph. 1:10).

In theology, the word dispensation is used of God's different administration of his two *covenants, the old and the new.

Under the old covenant, God made use of a temple, earthly priests and a sacrificial system as 'figures of the true' (Heb. 9:24), i.e. pictures of what was to come. When Christ came, God took away 'the first that he might establish the second' (Heb. 10:9).

Under the new covenant, there is one high priest, Christ himself. The old ceremonial order has been abolished by his sacrifice. There is a new dispensation, a new way of administering the *grace of God to believers.

Dispensationalism

This is a suggestion that there are several different dispensations of time in Scripture, ranging from the dispensation of human innocence in the Garden of Eden to the dispensation when the kingdom of God will finally come. This view point is used in the notes of the Schofield Reference Bible. But it should be noted that dispensation never means a period of time; this theory misuses the word dispensation.

See a Bible Dictionary.

Dispersion

See Diaspora.

Doctrine (Latin 'docere' — to teach; cf. English 'doctor')

The word occurs in the English versions of the Bible (Isa. 28:19 — AV, margin; John 7:16 — AV, to give one example each from the Old and New Testaments). It means the teachings of Scripture. It can refer to the teaching in general, i.e. the whole of the Christian faith (as in 1 Tim. 4:16), or it can refer to a particular division of Christian teaching, e.g. the doctrine of God, the doctrine of mankind and sin, i.e. what the Scriptures of both Testaments teach on these subjects.

It is not possible, or desirable, to separate true Christian devotion or experience from doctrine. A true experience of God will agree with the biblical teaching concerning God.

Documentary theory

Nineteenth century German scholars, Graf and Wellhausen, denied that Moses wrote the *Pentateuch (Genesis to Deuteronomy). They claimed to discern in these books four sources or documents which a redactor (an editor who combines material from a number of sources into one literary form) had combined into the first five books of the Old Testament.

These four supposed sources were said to be:

1. J document — those sections of the *Pentateuch which call God by his name Jahweh *(Yahweh), translated as 'LORD' in English Bibles.

2. E document — those sections which call God by his name Elohim, translated as 'God' in English Bibles.

3. D document — the book of Deuteronomy.

4. P document — those sections, particularly in Exodus and Leviticus, which deal with priestly matters. These sections were said to have been added after the return from exile in Babylon.

The theory is sometimes known as the Graf-Wellhausen theory after the names of its founders. Many *evangelical scholars reject the theory and it is much less rigidly held now, even among non-*evangelical scholars. Nevertheless it is still to be found, if in a modified form.

Dogma / Dogmatic (Greek 'dokeo' — to think, seem, seem good)

The word 'dogma' is used in Scripture of a decree issued by an earthly authority (e.g. Dan. 2:13; 6:8; Luke 2:1) and of the commandments of God (Eph. 2:15; Col. 2:14). It has come to be used of a belief of a particular section of the Christian *church on a subject, e.g. the Roman Catholic dogma of papal *infallibility.

The adjective 'dogmatic' is often used to describe Christian teaching and Dogmatic Theology is synonymous with *Systematic Theology. In popular usage, 'dogmatic' has a negative meaning. 'He is very dogmatic' means that he holds his opinions very strongly and hardly acknowledges that another opinion can exist.

Douai Version

Douai is a town in France. At the Roman Catholic College in Douai, the Bible was translated into English in 1609. The translation was based on the Latin *Vulgate. This Douai version was the accepted Roman Catholic version until the more modern translations (Knox 1949 and the Jerusalem Bible 1966).

Doublet

A 'double saying' or 'double story'. Sometimes a Bible saying or story appears on two separate occasions. Some people claim that the one is simply a duplicate account of the other, with differences in detail. The feeding of the four thousand in Mark 8 is said to be a doublet of the more familiar feeding of the five thousand in Mark 6. *Conservative scholars would see these as two different incidents. Jesus referred to them as such (Mark 8:19,20).

Doubt (verb or noun)

To doubt is to disbelieve, or to be slow to believe, a fact.
In the religious or Christian context, there are levels of doubt.

1. The intellectual doubt of unbelievers. They do not believe the Scriptures.

2. The practical doubt of unbelievers. They may believe that the Scriptures are true, but see no need to apply them to themselves.

3. Believers may from time to time doubt the promises of God's Word as applied to themselves. This is a state of mind from which God delivers them as they read the Scriptures.

4. Believers may from time to time doubt their own salvation. This again is a state of mind from which the Holy Spirit can deliver them by restoring *assurance to them.

Dualism (Greek 'duo' — two)

The word can be used in various contexts. For example:

in psychology dualism refers to a belief in mind and body as two separate entities.

in philosophy dualism refers to a belief in mind and matter as two separate entities.

in theology dualism refers to a belief in God and Satan, or good and evil, as two co-equal beings or principles respectively. Biblical Christianity rejects any dualism here. Satan, a created being, and the evil brought into the world by Satan, cannot be co-equal with God and good.

See Monism.

Ecclesiology (Greek 'ekklesia' — assembly)

The study of the *church — its nature, its behaviour, its government, etc.

Eclectic (Greek 'ek-legein' — to choose from)

When used of translations of the New Testament, the word means that the translation has been made from a combination of more than one source of early Greek manuscripts.

Ecumenical (Greek 'oikoumene' — the inhabited world)

The English word is sometimes spelt oecumenical. The word 'oikoumene' occurs fifteen times in the New Testament. (E.g. Matt. 24:14; Acts 17:31. See also Luke 2:1; Acts 11:28 et al for the narrower sense of 'Roman world').

The early *church began the use of this word. Ecumenical church councils represented the whole church of that period. The Roman Catholic Church describes its councils as ecumenical (but they only represent the whole Roman Catholic Church).

In the twentieth century, the ecumenical movement arose, a movement to join together churches of all denominations. The World Council of Churches was formed in 1948. At the time of writing (1988), the ecumenical movement is seeking to bring the Anglican Church into much closer union with the Roman Catholic Church. The Anglican/Roman Catholic International Commission (ARCIC) is the group of representatives from each Church seeking to bring about this union.

Effectual calling

By the Holy Spirit's activity in them, God calls particular sinners to put their *faith in Christ as their Sin-bearer, and calls them in such a way that those sinners believe in Christ. The 'call' has its 'effect'; it is 'effectual calling'. The sinners have heard the call of God in their hearts, and respond.

The Scripture says: 'Many are called, but few are chosen' (Matt. 22:14). This shows that there is an external call which many people hear as they listen to the gospel being *preached. But they do not respond inwardly to its call. On the other hand, the 'few who are chosen' are the ones who are inwardly called and are saved.

Election

The act of choosing.

The nation of Israel was elect (Isa. 45:4). The Messiah was elect (Isa. 42:1). Christian believers are people whom God has chosen in Christ so that they may be holy (set apart for him). This election was made before the foundation of the world (Eph. 1:4; 2 Thess. 2:13).

See Foreknowledge.

See a Bible Dictionary.

Eschatology (Greek 'eschatos' — last)

Eschatology is the study of the last things. Personal eschatology concerns the last things of the individual person — death and destiny, as a believer or an unbeliever. General eschatology includes the study of the second coming, the end of the age, the general resurrection, the judgment day, the new heavens and the new earth.

'Realised' eschatology is a phrase first used by C.H. Dodd in 1935. He meant that the kingdom of God had entered the history of mankind now, with the coming of Christ, i.e. eschatology is realised now, has come to pass now.

Jesus said: 'The kingdom of God is among you' (Luke 17:21), so there is no difficulty in believing that his kingdom is here now. The danger is to take 'realised eschatology' to mean that there will not be a final 'eschaton', i.e. a public display of the kingdom in its fulfilment.

Eternity

See Attributes of God.

Eutychianism

Eutyches (died AD454) taught that there was only a divine *Person in the Lord Jesus Christ.

Evangelical (Greek 'euangelion' (noun) — good news)

Evangelical Christians believe that the Scriptures from Genesis to Revelation are God's revealed Word to mankind and therefore show us what we must believe and practise. Because of this belief in Scripture, evangelicals believe that Jesus Christ, the Son of God, died a substitutionary death for his people and rose again for their *justification. They also believe all the other doctrines of the Christian faith. It is this view of Scripture which distinguishes evangelicals from *liberals.

The word evangelical can be a noun or an adjective. A person can be an evangelical; a *church can be an evangelical church.

The adjective 'evangelistic' describes the activity of people or a church, and corresponds to the verb 'to evangelise' and the noun 'evangelism'. An evangelistic meeting is a meeting where the gospel is *preached.

Evolution (Latin 'evolutio' — unrolling of a scroll)

The theory that animal and human life has developed from earlier, primitive forms. The theory fails to show the beginning of life itself.

The Bible (Gen. 1-2 et al) teaches that God is the uncreated Creator of all life, and that humanity is the crown of that creation, made in the *image of God (Gen. 1:26-27).

The theory of Theistic evolution teaches that God created living creatures by an evolutionary process over a long period of time.

Excommunication

The practice of excluding a member from the fellowship of the *church as an act of discipline. Old Testament passages include Exod. 30:33,38; Lev. 13:46; 17:4.

An important New Testament passage is 1 Cor. 5:1-8. Also in 1 Tim. 1:20 Paul speaks of 'delivering a person to Satan'. In 2 Cor. 2:5-11 Paul asks the church to be lenient in church discipline.

Some aspect of excommunication is found in the situation described in Matt. 18:15-17. The practice became widespread after New Testament times.

Exegesis (Greek 'exegeomai' — to lead out, draw out)

Exegesis is explaining and making clear the meaning of a passage of Scripture. Exact exegesis demands some knowledge of the biblical languages (Hebrew and Greek), and knowledge of facts concerning that particular section of Scripture — its position in Scripture, its place in the whole of Bible teaching, its 'genre' (type, i.e. whether it is poetry, parable, narrative, doctrine), and any relevant history or geography.

Spoken or written exposition of the passage by the preacher is based on accurate exegesis beforehand, whether that exegesis has been done direct from the Scripture by the preacher or is found in a commentary.

Existential

The word can have a popular-theological, or a technical-theological use.

If I say that *faith is existential, I mean that it must have its effect on my existence — my life and thinking. It must be a personal, vital *faith, a relationship with God. This is the popular-theological sense, and the biblical sense. This existential *faith must be based on Scripture. Subjective hymns about spiritual experiences reflect this aspect.

In recent years, with the introduction of *neo-orthodoxy, the word existential has acquired a more technical meaning and has come to refer to a rejection of authority. Existence, life, subjective experience, immediate encounter with the supernatural — these are the important things, and they can be experienced, says the existentialist, apart from a belief in the objective truths of Scripture. Kierkegaard's phrase 'leap in the dark' sums up existentialism — experience, unrelated to knowledge.

Ex nihilo (Latin — out of nothing)

A phrase used about the creation. God created the world 'ex nihilo', out of nothing. That is, he worked with no pre-existing material.

Ex opere operato

See Opus Operatum.

Experiential / experimental (From Latin — to try out)

Experiential is the adjective from the noun 'experience'. Experimental is an adjective from the verb 'to experiment', in the sense of 'to try for oneself and find to be true'. The words are synonyms, i.e. they have the same meaning. They describe a knowledge of God, of Christ, of the promises of Scripture, of spiritual truth, which is not only head knowledge but is based on personal experience.

Note that the words 'experimental/experiment' are not used here in the sense of 'to try something out to see if it works'. In the realm of Christian devotion, experimental means 'I try (God) in my own experience and find him to be true'.

Faith

Theologians distinguish the following elements in faith:

1. 'Notitia' — knowledge of facts. (Latin, 'notitia' — an idea, knowledge; cf. English word 'notion').

2. 'Assensus' — acknowledgement that the facts are true. (Latin, 'assensus' — that appearances are true; cf. English word 'assent').

3. 'Fiducia' — personal trust in and commitment to the fact that those facts are true. (Latin, 'fiducia' — ground of confidence).

So: I have notitia of the facts about Jesus Christ. (I may not believe them).

I give assensus that the facts are true. (I acknowledge that they are true, but the facts do not save me).

I exercise fiducia that the facts are true. (I rest on the facts. I commit myself to the *Person of Jesus Christ).

Faith, the

When used with the definite article 'the', the word faith refers to the historic doctrines of Christianity.

Fatalism

The belief that everything that happens has been previously determined without any particular purpose and cannot be avoided. Fatalism has no place for God, and so is very different from the

Christian belief in a wise God who 'works all things after the counsel of his own will' (Eph. 1:11). The phrase 'Whatever will be, will be' describes fatalism.

Federal (Latin 'foedus' — *covenant)

Federal theology teaches that there was a covenant of works between God and Adam. Adam broke this covenant. He was not a private individual, but was in federal relationship with the human race which was to follow him. If Adam had kept the covenant of works, he and his descendants would have lived in unbroken fellowship with God. His disobedience to the covenant of works meant that not only he, but all his posterity, became separated from God. The last Adam, Christ, came to give to God the obedience which God required and to restore to fellowship with God all who are 'in Christ' as once they were 'in Adam'.

Important passages on Federal theology are Rom. 5:12-21; 1 Cor. 15:22.

Festschrift (German — feast writing)

On the occasion of the birthday, retirement or other notable occasion in the life of a distinguished theologian, his colleagues present him with essays written by themselves on subjects similar to those on which he himself has written. This collection is known as his 'Festschrift'.

Filioque (Latin — and from the Son)

The Nicene Creed states that the Holy Spirit proceeded 'from the Father'. In the sixth century the western *church added 'filioque' (and from the Son), based on John 15:26. The eastern church has never inserted the phrase.

Final perseverance

All true believers will finally arrive in heaven. Once saved, they cannot be lost.

Final perseverance is consistent with the other great doctrines of salvation. God *elects his people, *calls them, *justifies them and finally *glorifies them (Rom. 8:30). Because he preserves them by his *grace, they persevere to the end. He cannot fail to finish what he has begun to do in them (Phil. 1:6).

The perseverance of the saints is the last element in the mnemonic TULIP (see Limited Atonement) which sums up biblical teaching on salvation. Perseverance is the biblical outcome of *unconditional election.

See Preservation of the Saints.

Foreknowledge

God's ability to know events before they happen. He knows events beforehand because he has *predestined them.

It is sometimes wrongly claimed that God's *election of his people merely means his foreknowledge of them. It is suggested that God chooses those whom he has foreseen will believe on the Lord Jesus Christ. Scripture, however, uses the verb 'to know' to mean 'to enter into a relationship with' (Gen. 4:1; Amos 3:2; Luke 1:34 — all AV). So 'to foreknow' means 'to enter beforehand into a relationship with'. God entered beforehand into a relationship of *grace with his people, and 'as many as were *ordained to *eternal life believed' (Acts 13:48).

Form Criticism

This is a modern method of biblical study which examines Scripture (especially the Gospels) to find the forms which, it is suggested, the material had before it was written down. This oral material is then classified. The following is a common classification.

1. Narratives

stories in which a particular circumstance leads to a pronouncement.
E.g. the healing of the paralytic in Mark 2:1-12 leads to Jesus'
saying: 'The Son of Man has power ... to forgive sins'.

miracle stories, whether in the realm of nature (stilling the storm),
of healing, or of raising the dead.

stories about Jesus (the *baptism, the transfiguration, the resurrection appearances). These are sometimes called '*myths and legends'.

2. Sayings — of wisdom, of prophecy, or apocalyptic.

Some of the terms connected with Form Criticism are:

Gemeinde-theologie, German for 'community theology'. The
community was the early *church after the resurrection. It is
suggested that the community remembered certain Old Testament
prophecies of Jesus — e.g. Ps. 110:1 — and that they put them into
Jesus' own mouth (Mark 12:36).
Sitz im Leben, German for 'life-setting'. The Gospel narratives in
their oral form, as (it is suggested) they may have passed from
person to person.

paradigm, a name given to the Gospel narratives because the early
preachers used them as illustrations.
   Whatever may be the value of Form Criticism, it cannot be
correct if it casts doubt on the fact that the original Scriptures were
finally written under the *inspiration of God.

Free Church

The word 'free' here means 'independent of any control by the
state'. The Free Church is free to appoint its own personnel and to
conduct its own affairs. The Anglican Church, on the other hand, or
any national church, is ultimately responsible to bishops, archbishops and the state.

Free offer (Latin 'offero' — to present, bring forward)

The free offer of the gospel. This is a view which suggests that God gives a genuine opportunity of salvation to everyone, or, at least, to everyone hearing the gospel message. The term 'offer' relating to salvation does not, however, occur in Scripture.

It is sometimes suggested that salvation cannot honestly be offered to everyone because God has *elected his own people and only the elect respond. Scripture, however, clearly commands that the gospel must be *preached to every creature (Mark 16:15) and also clearly says that 'Whosoever shall call on the name of the Lord shall be saved' (Rom. 10:13); and that if people do not believe and so are lost, the responsibility is their own.

Free will

See Arminius, Decisionism, General Redemption and Pelagianism.

Fundamentalism

In the 1920s some American Christians defended in writing the fundamentals (the foundation truths) of the Christian faith. The term fundamentalist came to be synonymous with *conservative *evangelical, and fundamentalism synonymous with a conservative view of Scripture. The word is not so much used now in British theology.

Gemeinde-theologie

See Form Criticism.

General Baptist

See Baptist.

General redemption

The view that Jesus Christ paid the price for the salvation of every person in the world, though not every person will be saved. It is the will of a person which decides if he or she will be saved, or not. The view is not according to the teaching of Scripture.

See Limited Atonement.

See also Particular Redemption.

General revelation

See Revelation.

Geschichte (German — history)

There is another German word also — 'Historie'.

Historie is history proper, an objective record of past events. Geschichte is more than that. It looks more at the meaning of past events than at the events themselves. Indeed, often those who distinguish the two words would say that the recorded events in question are not historical; they did not 'happen like that'.

*Evangelicals would put Gen. 1-3, the narrative parts of the Gospels, and other historical parts of Scripture, into the category of Historie. Others would put them into the category of Geschichte. For example, Bultmann would say that it is unimportant, even doubtful, whether Jesus rose bodily from the dead; the meaning of the story is all that is important. For the *evangelical believer, however, the historical events of Bible history are important.

Glorify / glorification

Glorification is the final state of believers in their resurrection bodies in heaven, when they will be without sin and all earthly limitations, and will see God face to face.

Glossolalia (Greek 'glossa' — a tongue, and 'laleo' — to speak)

Speaking in tongues; the miracle that took place in Acts 2:4.

See a Bible Dictionary.

Gnosticism (Greek 'gnosis' — knowledge)

Gnosticism was a dangerous heresy which attacked the early
*church as early as the first century, the apostolic period. Several
passages of Scripture are written with gnosticism in view.

Gnostics claimed that they had secret knowledge which was only
given to spiritual people, the 'pneumatic' (Greek 'pneuma' —
spirit), not to the general mass of people. It is impossible to reduce
gnosticism to one system of teaching. It was syncretistic, that is, it
included elements from various philosophies and religions.

The following are some of its main teachings, particularly as they
are relevant to the New Testament:

1. There is a supreme being who is not the God of the Scriptures.
From this being descended a series of beings or 'aeons' (Greek).
One of these was the Demiurge (Greek, craftsman), i.e. the creator
God of the Old Testament. Further down the hierarchy (the descend-
ing line) came Christ.

In Colossians Paul stresses the full deity of Christ. He says that
in him dwells 'all the fulness of the Godhead bodily' (2:9). And also
'It pleased the Father that in him should all the fulness dwell' (1:19).
'Fulness' translates the Greek word 'pleroma' and means that the
whole of God's nature is in Christ. Paul speaks of Christ's divine
nature, creating power, pre-existence and power to sustain the
created order (1:15-17).

2. Some Gnostics said that the Christ acted in the man Jesus. This
denied a real *incarnation (see point 3). Other Gnostics taught that
Jesus Christ never had a true human body and so did not truly suffer.
He only **seemed** to have a true human nature. These became known
as the Docetists (Greek 'dokeo' — to seem).

3. Gnostics taught that tangible matter is evil, so there could never have been a true incarnation of God in human form. 1 John 2:22 affirms that Jesus is the Christ, and 4:2,3 that he came 'in the flesh'. 1 John 1:1-3 insists that John and others heard, saw and handled the Word in flesh.

4. This belief in the evil of matter led to two schools of thought in the realm of morals. Some Gnostics were licentious. (They said that if matter is evil and only the spiritual is important, it did not matter what they did with their bodies). Others were *ascetic. (They said that if matter is evil, they must handle it as little as possible). Paul wrote against this in Col. 2:20-23.

The Christian apologists Irenaeus and Tertullian wrote to refute Gnosticism.

Grace — saving grace

God's favour to his people in saving them through Christ. Other terms relating to grace are:

Free grace

The term emphasises that salvation comes because of God's grace alone and from nothing in believers. An important verse is: 'By grace are you saved through *faith; and that not of yourselves: it is the gift of God' (Eph. 2:8). (The word 'it' does not refer to faith, but to the whole fact of being-saved-through-faith-by-grace).

Prevenient grace (Latin 'praevenire' — to come before)

Grace which goes before. God takes the initiative in salvation. He *elects his people and sends his Spirit to draw them to Christ. His grace is prevenient. The believer's act of faith is only a response to God's grace.

Irresistible grace (Invincible grace)

The people whom God has chosen to save cannot finally resist the grace of God, though they may resist it for a time. The wonderful thing is that they do not resist it when it comes to conversion. God makes them willing (Ps. 110:3).

Doctrines of grace

Those doctrines (teachings of Scripture) which emphasise that God has chosen a people for himself from all *eternity, that he sends his Spirit to convict them of sin, to *regenerate them, to create faith in them, to *call them effectually to Christ, to *justify them, to *sanctify them, to be their God and to bring them to heaven.

See Limited Atonement — TULIP.

Hagiographa

See Writings.

Harmony of the Gospels

Various people have tried to put together the four Gospel narratives into one consecutive narrative known as a Harmony (a musical word for a blending or joining together).

In the second century a Syrian — Tatian — compiled a Harmony called the Diatessaron (Greek — 'through four').

Hebraism

A point of Hebrew grammar or style which appears in the style of the Greek language in the New Testament. The term Semitism is used with the same meaning. E.g. several sentences connected with 'kai' (Greek — and) reflect Hebrew sentences connected with 'waw' (Hebrew — and).

Heilsgeschichte (German — salvation history)

Some theologians teach that the Bible is a history of God's plan to save people. It is 'salvation history', with the emphasis on the word history. Those who use the term say that God's revelation of himself is only in his actions in history, actions which purpose to save people, and not in doctrinal statements or propositions concerning the nature of God. If, however, we believe that all the Scriptures are God's revelation of himself, we believe that biblical propositions are as much a part of that revelation as the acts of God. Indeed, the propositions explain the acts. How could we understand the record of the crucifixion without the statements of the epistles to explain that act?

Hellenism

Alexander the Great (fourth century BC) wished to make the countries which he conquered adopt the Greek language and way of life. The Greek word 'Hellen' means Greek. So this new culture became known as 'Hellenism'. In the *providence of God, the Old Testament was translated into Greek (the *Septuagint) thanks to Hellenism. The Jews in Palestine were influenced by Hellenism, and there is a specific reference to Hellenists in Acts 6:1.

Henotheism (Greek 'henos' — of one, and 'theos' — god)

This word must not be taken to refer to *monotheism, the worship of one God. A henotheist is one who worships one God but claims that other gods also exist. 'Monolatry' (Greek 'monos' — only, and 'latreia' — worship) is used almost synonymously.

Heresy (Greek 'haeresis' — a choice)

A belief or an opinion which a person chooses to hold and which is contrary to biblical teaching.

A heretic is one who holds such teaching and a heresiarch is one who founds or originates a heresy.

See a Bible Dictionary for biblical usages of the word.

Hermeneutics (Greek 'hermeneuo' — to interpret)

The study of the principles of interpreting the Scriptures. It is important, for example, to know if a passage is history, poetry, or doctrine; if it is spoken, who said it, to whom, in what circumstances. The study of the individual words and grammar is most important. The historico-grammatical approach to hermeneutics means interpreting a passage according to its historical and grammatical form. For example, Paul addresses his words 'Be filled with the Spirit' (Eph. 5:18) to believers. The verb is in the command form (imperative mood), in the passive form (passive voice), and in the plural. So Paul is saying that all believers must continually be under the control of the Holy Spirit.

Accurate hermeneutics lie behind accurate *exegesis.

Heterodox

See Orthodoxy.

Hexapla

See Alexandrian School.

Historical Theology

Closely linked to Church History, Historical Theology studies how a particular doctrine (e.g. the *Person of Christ, the Holy Spirit, or *eschatology) has been understood at a particular period of Church History.
 The study is also known as History of Doctrine.

History of Religion School (German — Religions geschichtliche Schule)

Some theologians teach that Christianity is not a religion in a class by itself, but is simply part of the whole continuous history of religion. If this is so, then Christianity has borrowed elements from religions which preceded it and heathen religions which were in existence at the same time. In the very nature of things it is true, of course, that Christianity developed from *Judaism. The Old Testament was a preparation for the New. But *evangelicals deny that Christianity is part of an evolving process of religions or that it borrowed from heathenism.

Homiletics(Greek 'homileo' — to converse)

The study of the principles of conversing; that is, of *preaching.

Humanism (Latin 'homo' — man)

The philosophy which sees mankind, not God, as the centre of history and of life. (Adjective — humanistic).

The word has a bad sense to Christians because it is used to deny God. But it must not be confused with words of a similar derivation, such as:

a. human, a neutral word, describing man as man: for example, the human race, a human being.

b. the humanities — those subjects of study which concern human beings, or have been produced by human beings: for example, literature, art, music.

c. humane — compassionate; for example, humane methods of killing animals.

Human responsibility

People are responsible, as God's created and rational beings, to obey God. Before the fall (Gen. 3) they were able and willing to do this. But their freedom to do so was *mutable (changeable); i.e. they were able to choose to live obediently or not. At the fall they chose not to obey God.

From the time of the fall, all Adam's descendants have had neither ability nor desire to live according to God's commandments. Only God can give them the ability and the desire. But their responsibility to obey him remains the same.

Hyper-Calvinism

See Calvinism.

Hypostatic union (Greek 'hypostasis' — a standing under)

The union of the divine and human natures in Christ is a hypostatic union. In theology 'hypostasis' can refer to any one of the three distinct *Persons in the one undivided Godhead. The definition of the Godhead put forth at the Council of Chalcedon (AD451) was 'one essence in three hypostases'.

In reference to Christ, hypostatic union means the one unified *Person of Christ, i.e. both divine and human natures in one *Person.

Cyril, bishop of *Alexandria, defended the hypostatic union against Nestorius, bishop of Constantinople, who taught that Christ was Jesus the man indwelt by God the Word. Christ was, he said, a dual personality. He denied that Mary was 'theo-tokos' (Greek — the bearer of God). Nestorius was deposed at the Council of Ephesus (AD431).

Iconoclasm, iconoclast (Greek 'eikon' - image 'klaein' - to break)

Iconoclasm is the breaking of images and an iconoclast is one who shows his objection to the use of images in worship by smashing them.

Iconolatry

The use of icons (a picture usually painted on wood of the Lord or of some saint) as objects to be venerated in worship. The practice

was condemned in AD726 but re-established in AD787 and continues today in the Greek and Eastern *Orthodox churches.

Image of God (Latin 'Imago Dei')

Mankind was made in the image of God (Gen. 1:26,27). V. 26 uses
the phrase 'after our likeness'. This is an example of Hebrew
*parallelism, that is, it means the same as 'in our image'. Some
theologians have tried to distinguish between the two. They say that
the likeness (mankind's ability to commune with God) has been lost
through Adam's sin, but the image (mankind's power to reason)
remains, though defaced.

Christ is the image of God (Col. 1:15; Heb. 1:3); that is, he
exactly reflects God's character, and part of his work is to restore the
image of God in his people. Eph. 4:24 speaks of *righteousness and
true holiness and Col. 3:10 speaks of knowledge.

Immanence

See Attributes of God.

Immutability

See Attributes of God.

Impassibility

See Attributes of God.

Imputation (Greek 'logizomai' — to put to the account of)

A commercial word, from the world of banking. (The related
word is 'ellogeo' — to impute, Rom. 5:13 (AV), and Philemon 18
where Paul asks Philemon to put Onesimus' debts to his account).

An important passage for the imputation of Adam's sin to the human race is Rom. 5:12-21, though the actual word impute only occurs once (v. 13). The fact of imputation is present in v. 12 — 'all sinned'. The tense here is aorist (Greek — the tense that describes a momentary action in the past), signifying that all people sinned in Adam when he sinned. His sin was their sin.

The fact that the sin of mankind was imputed to Christ is clear from such passages as Isa. 53:4-6; 2 Cor. 5:21; Gal. 3:13; 1 Peter 2:24, though the actual word impute is not used. (Note in 2 Cor. 5:21 that the relative pronoun 'who' refers back to 'him', not, of course, to 'us'. In the Greek there is a relative pronoun here — the construction is 'the-one-not-having-known-sin-for us he made sin, that we might become ...')

An important passage for God's *justifying his people by *faith is Rom. 3:21-5:21. He does this by imputing his own *righteousness to believing sinners (Rom. 4:3,5,6,9-11,22-24). See Gal. 3:6; James 2:23.

On the opposite truth — God's not imputing sin to believers — see Ps. 32:2; Rom. 4:8; 2 Cor. 5:19.

Incarnation (Latin 'in' — in, 'cars, carnis' — flesh)

The coming to earth of the Son of God in a human body. John 1:14 says: 'The Word became flesh'; 1 John 4:2 and 2 John 7 speak of this coming 'in the flesh'. See also Rom. 8:3; 1 Tim. 3:16 et al.

The word is sometimes used to refer to all the earthly life of Jesus. E.g. 'During his incarnation' = while he was on earth.

Incarnation theology stresses Christ's taking our human nature as more significant than his substitutionary death. In Scripture, the former is the necessary preparation for the latter.

Independence

See Attributes of God.

Indifferent things

See Adiaphora.

Indulgence (Latin 'indulgentia' — kindness)

The Roman Catholic Church claims to grant indulgence to its members for certain sins, so that they need not do penance.

In the Middle Ages the practice had become so abused that it was claimed that a soul could be set free from purgatory if money were paid to the Church which was, of course, enriched thereby! This was the practice which moved Martin *Luther to begin his campaign which led to the Reformation.

Inerrancy (Latin negative 'in', with 'errare' — to make a mistake; English word 'err')

The impossibility of making a mistake.

To say that the Bible is inerrant is to say that the inspired original contained no mistakes, whether of science, history, geography, description or doctrine.

Infallibility (Latin negative 'in', with 'fallere' — to deceive)

The impossibility of deception.

To say that the Bible is infallible is to say that the inspired original was absolutely reliable and that it could not deceive; it is to be wholly trusted in what it says of God, Christ, mankind, salvation and, indeed, of every doctrine.

Both the *inerrancy and infallibility of the Scriptures spring from its original *inspiration by God.

Infinity

See Attributes of God.

Infralapsarianism

See Sublapsarianism.

Inspiration of Scripture

The phrase 'given by inspiration of God' (2 Tim. 3:16, AV) translates one compound Greek word 'theopneustos' — breathed by God.

In Scripture the breath of God is often a figure of speech for his creating power (Job 33:4; Ps. 33:6).

Plenary inspiration (Latin 'plenus' — full)
By this we mean that the whole of Scripture has its source in God; it is 'breathed out' by God.

Verbal inspiration (Latin 'verbum' — a word)

The words of Scripture are 'breathed out' by God.

A belief in inspiration does not commit us to believing that God merely dictated the Scriptures to the writers. He took up and used their personalities and circumstances. Indeed, he created those men with their personalities and circumstances in order to use them in this task of writing Scripture as he wanted it written. God used different means (Heb. 1:1): he spoke through dreams, visions, direct encounters, and superintended such writings as court archives (e.g. in Samuel, Kings, Chronicles) to produce the Scriptures. The word 'theopneustos' does not confine us to any theory of inspiration.

Inter-Testament period

The period of history between the close of the Old Testament and the beginning of the New. No prophetic voice was heard between Malachi and John the Baptist. Some knowledge of the history of the period is important as a background to the New Testament, e.g. the rise and fall of ruling powers which brought Rome to power and the emergence of such groups as the Pharisees and Sadducees.

Irresistible grace

See Grace.

Jerusalem Bible

The Roman Catholic School of Biblical Studies in Jerusalem produced La Bible de Jérusalem in 1956. It is a scholarly work containing notes on Roman Catholic studies. It was published in English in 1966.

Johannine

Adjective, meaning 'of John'; e.g. Johannine theology, Johannine literature (cf. *Pauline, *Petrine).

Judaisers

In Esth. 8:17 some Gentiles became Jews as a result of the decree which allowed the Jews to take revenge on their enemies (8:13). The *Septuagint uses the verb 'to judaise' in v. 17. In Gal. 2:14 Paul rebukes Peter for trying to compel the Christian Gentiles to keep some Jewish customs in order to be saved as did the Jewish party of Judaisers who followed Paul about on his journeys.

Paul's gospel of the *grace of Jesus Christ was completely opposed to the practices of the Judaisers. Such practices suggested that something needed to be added to the work of Christ. The Council of Jerusalem (Acts 15) dealt conclusively with the subject.

Judaism

The word comes from Judah, the southern kingdom of the nation of Israel. (Israel proper was the northern kingdom). The word 'Jew' is also connected.

Loosely, Judaism refers to everything Jewish, but is more precisely used of Jewish theology, worship and life beginning after the return from exile.

Justify / justification

To justify a person is to declare that person to be *righteous. It is a forensic word, that is, a word connected with law-courts. A judge justifies a person, declaring that person to be in the right.

God justifies believers on the basis of what Jesus Christ has done for his people. He has perfectly kept the law of God and has borne the punishment of sin. God now counts righteous the people who put their *faith in Christ's life and death. 'He is the justifier of him who believes in Jesus' (Rom. 3:26). Christ's righteousness is *imputed to believers (Rom. 4:1-5:1).

Kenosis (Greek 'kenoo' — to empty)

Phil. 2:7 says that Christ, on coming to earth, 'emptied himself'. (AV and RAV, 'made himself of no reputation'; NIV, 'made himself nothing').

The context explains this self-emptying. He did not cling on to equality with God (v. 6) by refusing to become *incarnate. He took the outward form of a servant, in the likeness of men (v. 7). He was fashioned as a man (v. 8), and humbled himself, being obedient enough even to die on a cross (v. 8).

John 17:5 further explains the self-emptying. He laid aside his glory when he came to earth, i.e. he came as a man.

We must never say that Christ, in becoming human, ceased to be God, or laid aside his deity (his nature as God).

Kerygma (Greek 'kerugma' — that which is *preached, from 'kerusso' — to herald or preach)

'The kerygma' is the word used of the apostles' preaching about Jesus Christ, his life, death, resurrection and coming again.

Koine (Short for the Greek words 'koine dialektos' — common language)

When Alexander the Great aimed at 'Hellenising' (or making Greek) the nations he conquered, Hellenistic Greek became the language of those nations. This is the koine, the common Greek, as opposed to the pure classical Greek of Greece. The *Septuagint, the Greek translation of the Hebrew Old Testament, and later the New Testament, were both written in koine Greek.

Last rites

The performance of certain ceremonies by a Roman Catholic priest as a last religious act before the death of a person.

Laity (Greek 'laos' — people)

The laity is strictly the Lord's people, but unfortunately the word has come to refer to those who are not ordained to *office in the Anglican and Roman Catholic Churches. A lay preacher is one who *preaches, though he has not been ordained by a bishop of these Churches for that work.

Legalism (Latin 'lex, legis' — law)

The gospel upholds the law of God (Rom. 3:31) by showing that the *righteous Lawgiver must punish sin and has punished the sins of all believers in the death of his Son.

Legalism has a bad sense also. To be legalistic is to seek to win the favour of God by law-keeping as, for example, the Pharisees did. For the Christians who have been saved by the *grace of God, to be legalistic is to seek to make progress in the Christian life merely by observing legal requirements. Col.2:16-23 is an important passage about this. Paul specifies eating, drinking, festivals (2:16). See also Gal. 4:10 and Paul's teaching on *circumcision in Gal. 5:1-15. We can be free from legalism by walking in the Spirit, being led by the Spirit, living in the Spirit (Gal. 5:16,18,25). The Spirit will produce his own fruit in us (vv. 22-23) which is in accordance with the *moral law of God.

Liberalism (Latin 'liber' — free)

Theologically, liberalism means freedom from the necessity of believing the Bible to be God's revelation to mankind. When once people are 'free' from this necessity, they are 'free' to deny all the central doctrines of the Christian faith — the moral demands of God, the sinful nature of Man, the deity of Christ, the substitutionary death of Christ, the resurrection, the dwelling of the Holy Spirit in believers.

Liberalism grew up in Germany in the nineteenth century and spread to England. The theory of evolution helped liberalism because if mankind has evolved physically, they are evolving morally also. All that is needed is to improve their outward circumstances in order to help their moral 'climb'. In this way the 'social gospel' came into being. The first world war (1914-1918) did much to destroy this optimistic view of mankind.

Liberation theology

A theology which claims to set people free, but certainly does not speak of the freedom of which Christ and Paul spoke (John 8:36; Gal. 5:1).

The theme of the World Council of Churches Conference in Bangkok in 1973 was 'Salvation Today'. The conference defined salvation as 'realising one's full human potential'. In third world countries the sociological-economic-political order hinders this 'personal wholeness' and people must, therefore, be 'liberated' from this hindrance. The task of theology is seen by liberation theologians as bringing economic justice and political freedom to oppressed people.

How does this come about? Liberation theology appears to teach that God plans to save all people. All are already 'in Christ', but Christ is not in all people. People, Christian or not, must 'open themselves up' to God and to other people, because they encounter God in other people. By doing this they are 'converted' and join the struggle by which people are set free from the political, economic and sociological factors which oppress them.

Liberation theologians claim to have Scripture warrant for their teachings. For example, they quote the exodus from Egypt as a wonderful example of liberation from oppression. It was, but it was solely the act of God, and Scripture writers see it as a picture of the greater spiritual 'liberation' from sin and death, to be brought about by the Lord Jesus Christ (John 8:36). Only as more people are thus spiritually liberated will society lastingly be affected.

In its emphasis on the oppressed peoples, liberation theology is like communism. In its use of biblical language, the movement is like Christianity. Liberation theology has been described as communism with a Christian face. Liberation theology does have some value in recognising and seeking to solve some of the earthly troubles of mankind, but it does not address itself to their deepest need, the need of having their sins forgiven.

Limbo (Latin 'limbus' — border)

Roman Catholics teach that certain departed souls go to a place called 'limbo', which is not heaven and not hell.

They distinguish the 'limbus patrum' (the limbus of the fathers) to which the Old Testament saints went, and the 'limbus infantum' (the limbus of infants) to which unbaptized children go.

The form 'limbo' is used after the preposition 'in'. For example, 'in limbo' means 'in the border' (of hell).

Limited Atonement   Calvin

Christ died to make salvation certain for his *elect people, and God *calls and *justifies those whom he has chosen in Christ. Their salvation depends on God's will, not theirs, though they do exercise *faith in the Lord Jesus Christ.

This is contrary to the teaching which says that Christ died to make salvation possible for everyone (*Arminianism), and it is the will of each person, not of God, which decides if that person will be saved.

Because the phrase 'limited atonement' is rather negative, emphasising that Christ's atoning death is limited in its design and effect, many people prefer to use the phrase 'particular redemption', with its more positive emphasis that those on whom Christ has set his particular love will most certainly be redeemed.

Note: Limited atonement is the third element of the mnemonic word Tulip which conveniently sums up the biblical teaching on the state of mankind and the plan of salvation.

T otal depravity
U nconditional election
L imited atonement
I rresistible grace
P erseverance of the saints

See articles on all these terms in this dictionary.

Liturgy

The noun with its adjective, liturgical, usually refers to a service of worship which has set forms, e.g. the Church of England Prayer Book Service.

The word comes from two Greek words meaning 'the work of the people'. It was originally a secular word, used of public service to the state. Then it came to have the religious usage of 'service to the gods', and lastly acquired its Christian meaning.

Liturgiology is the study of liturgies.

Note: Greek 'leitourgia' can mean either worship or service. So our worship of God is not only our verbal praises, but we worship him through our service for him.

Locus classicus (Latin — classical place)

A passage of Scripture which is a particular example of a subject. E.g. 1 Cor. 15 is a 'locus classicus' on the resurrection. Often translated into English as 'a classical passage'.

Lord's Supper

See Communion.

Lutheranism

Martin Luther was born in 1483 in Germany. As a monk in the Roman Catholic Church, he read, 'The just shall live by *faith' (Rom. 1:17), and these words became the foundation truth of the Reformation, in contrast to the Roman Catholic teaching that one becomes just by doing good works.

Lutheranism is summed up in three ways:

1. 'sola (Latin 'solus' — only) scriptura': Scripture alone.

Scripture alone is the source and authority for Christian belief and practice.

2. 'sola gratia': by *grace alone.

The grace of God alone is the source of salvation. There is no way in which anyone can earn salvation.

3. 'sola fide': through *faith alone.

Faith alone is the instrument by which a person comes to God through Jesus Christ.

On the Lord's supper, Luther taught a doctrine of *consubstantiation.

LXX

The Roman figures for 70, the symbol for the *Septuagint.

Masoretic text

The authors who first wrote the Hebrew Old Testament wrote it with consonants only. The readers had to put in their own vowels.
    Certain scribes who became known as the Masoretes inserted the vowels in the early years of the Christian era. The Hebrew Scriptures

which we now use are the Masoretic text, the text with vowels. The word 'masora' means tradition, so the Masoretes were people who preserved a traditional pronunciation.

The symbol MT stands for Masoretic text.

Mennonite

See Anabaptist.

Millennium (Latin 'mille' — a thousand)

The word millennium comes from the references to a thousand years in Rev. 20:1-10. Millennialism is the teaching concerning the millennium. Several views are held on this subject:

Pre-millennialism teaches that Christ will return before the millennium and set up his kingdom of peace and *righteousness on earth for a thousand years.

Post-millennialism teaches that Christ will return after the millennium. The millennium will be a golden age when the world will be becoming gradually better through the *preaching of the gospel.

A-millennialism. The word with its negative letter 'A-' seems to say that there is no millennium. A-millennialism does not say this. It says that the millennium is not a literal thousand years period.

A-millennialism denies pre-millennialism because the last judgment and the *eternal state follow immediately on the second coming of Christ (Matt. 24:30-25:46; 2 Thess. 1:6-10).

A-millennialism denies post-millennialism because the Bible does not teach that the world will become better before the return of Christ (Luke 18:8).

The A-millennialist teaches that the thousand years of Rev. 20:1-10 are a symbol, a picture, just as the other numbers in Revelation are a symbol. The number one thousand represents completeness, i.e. the **whole** period between the first and second comings of Christ. So:

a. Satan bound for one thousand years means that Satan is bound in such a way that he cannot harm the people of God.

b. The saints reigning for one thousand years means that they reign with Christ now. They are already sitting with him 'in heavenly places' (Eph. 2:6).

The term 'chiliasm' is sometimes used instead of millennialism. It comes from the Greek 'chilias' — thousand.

Modernism

An erroneous view of the nature and reliability of Scripture, so-called because the idea is only a comparatively recent development. It is a reaction to older, *conservative teaching on Scripture.

In one sense, of course, modernism is not modern. It is as old as mankind's sinful desire to contradict the words of God.

See Liberalism.

Monism (Greek 'monos' — alone, only)

An inclusive term for systems of thought (philosophies) which teach that there is one reality underlying all that exists. All that exists is simply a manifestation of that one principle.

Christianity is monistic in that it teaches that God is the origin of all things, but not that all things are the manifestation of God. That latter teaching is *pantheism.

The Scriptures teach that God is *transcendent above and separated from his creation.

See Dualism.

Monophysitism

See Eutychianism.

Monotheism (Greek 'monos' — only, and 'theos' — God)

The belief in and worship of only one God. *Judaism, Islam and Christianity are monotheistic.

Contrast *polytheism and *henotheism.

Monothelitism

The heresy that the Lord Jesus Christ had only one will, though having two natures. It was an attempt to reconcile *monophysite and *orthodox views of the *Person of the Lord Jesus Christ.

Moral Law

The ten commandments (Exod. 20) and all other commandments of God in Old and New Testaments which tell people how they should live. The ceremonial law has passed away with Christ, but the moral law is still in force (Matt. 5). Christ has fulfilled the demands of the law for his people. It can no longer condemn them. Nevertheless, they have the responsibility to keep the moral law, and the power to do so through the Holy Spirit (Rom. 8:4).

See Ceremonial Law.

See also Civil Law.

Moral Theology

The study of how people should act in the sight of God. The term is used more frequently in Roman Catholic studies. Protestants more often speak of Christian Ethics.

Muratorian fragment/Muratorian canon

An Italian, Muratori, discovered this list of New Testament books in the eighteenth century. It seems to date from the second century AD and includes all but five of our New Testament books.

Mutable

See Attributes of God and also Immutability.

See also Human Responsibility.

Mystery religions

This phrase (sometimes simply 'the mysteries') refers to various religions which flourished early in the Christian era. Their beliefs and methods of worship were a mystery to all but the participants. They offered a certain salvation (deliverance from evil and immortality) but they had no foundation in Scripture or in the one true God.

Mysticism

The Oxford Dictionary defines a mystic as 'one who .. believes in spiritual apprehension of truths beyond the understanding'. By this definition every true believer is a mystic, so long as those truths are the truths of Scripture, and so long as they believe that the Holy Spirit gives them that spiritual understanding (Eph. 1:18).

Unfortunately, however, mysticism usually ignores Scripture. Another definition in the Oxford Dictionary is 'one who seeks by contemplation and self-surrender to obtain union with or absorption into the deity'. This is the primary aspect of non-biblical mysticism.

Many false religions (e.g. Hinduism, Buddhism) are mystic religions. There have been — and are — Christian mystics, such as Eckhart, St. John of the Cross, Madame Guyon, Evelyn Underhill. There is much truth and comfort in their writings, but mysticism is to be regarded with caution as a deviation from *evangelical Christianity.

Mystic union

This phrase is used of the union between Christ and his people, described in Scripture under the figure of vine and branches, husband and wife, head and body. The word mystic here means 'not to be understood by rational means, but only as the Holy Spirit brings about the union and makes it real to the believer'.

In view of what has been said about *mysticism, the use of the word mystic is unfortunate.

Myth

1. Popular usage — a story which is known to be fiction. The word occurs with this meaning in 1 Tim. 1:4; 4:7; Titus 1:14; 2 Peter 1:16.

2. Theological usage. Bultmann taught that the New Testament is full of myths and legends surrounding a core of truth. These myths, to him, include heaven and hell, Christ's pre-existence and virgin birth, his resurrection, ascension and future return. Bultmann insists on demythologisation, i.e. removing these so-called myths from the New Testament. What is left is the *kerygma, i.e. the core of Christian truth which must be *preached.

Many people claim that the stories of the creation and fall in Gen. 1-3 are myths, i.e. they did not actually happen as described — there was no literal garden, literal tree, literal serpent. They say these are simply pictorial ways of saying that sin entered the world.

Natural

Natural revelation

See Revelation.

Natural religion

Any religion which claims that people can find God by themselves, without the need for God's revelation of himself.

Natural theology

This claims that it is possible to make statements about the existence and nature of God based on human reason only, without the need for God's revelation of himself in Scripture. The so-called 'philosophical proofs' of God (Aquinas' 'Five Ways') are natural theology.

Natural ethics

Because of God's common grace, there is some good in all people. They are able to be kind, compassionate, to perform works of benefit to humanity, etc. Natural ethics develops this ability into a system, without regard to God, his nature and his commands; i.e. natural ethics is concerned with the good that the 'natural' person can do, while Christian ethics is concerned with the good that only the *regenerate person can do.

Neo- (Greek 'neos' — new)

When put before another word, this prefix speaks of a new, a revised, form of that particular school of thought, often with differences from the old form.

E.g. Neo-classicism

A revival of classical literature.

Neo-orthodoxy

A revived *orthodoxy which in some ways is different from the old orthodoxy. The term is used to describe the teachings of Barth and Brunner in the twentieth century. Neo-orthodoxy emphasises that God has revealed himself, but says that this revelation is not identical with the Scriptures. The Scriptures 'become' the Word of God to a person only as God speaks through the Scriptures to that person. In contrast, the *orthodox teaching is that the Scriptures are, objectively, the Word, the revelation of God, whether or not they speak to a person subjectively.

Neo-evangelicalism

A new form of *evangelicalism which does not believe in the absolute *inerrancy and *infallibility of the Bible, and therefore ought not to claim the title 'evangelical'.

Nestorianism

Nestorius (died AD451) taught that there were two separate *Persons, one human and one divine, in the Lord Jesus Christ.

Non-conformist

One who does not conform to, i.e. agree with, certain teachings.

In theology, the word describes a Protestant who does not conform to the Anglican *Church. An older word, used in the eighteenth century, was 'Dissenter'. That is, a person who does not assent (agree) but dissents.

The prefix is Latin 'non' — not.

Numinous (Latin 'numen' — will of the gods)

A twentieth century German theologian called Otto wrote a book, 'The Idea of the Holy' in which this word occurs. It refers to the feeling of dread, awe and fascination which a person feels in the presence of the supernatural.

Nunc Dimittis (Latin — now dismiss)

From the first words of Simeon's prayer in Luke 2:29-32.

The English version beginning 'Lord, now lettest thou thy servant depart in peace' is one of the canticles (hymns) which are sung in the Anglican service.

Offices

Of Christ

Theologians speak of Christ's work as prophet (to speak for God), priest (to offer to God) and king (to govern) as his three offices. All his work falls under one or other of those headings.

Ecclesiastical offices

A word used in Anglican and Roman Catholic Churches for the positions and functions of its official personnel; e.g. the office of archbishop, bishop, vicar, etc.

Liturgical offices

A form of worship or prayer authorised by the Anglican or Roman Catholic Church; e.g. morning and evening offices — morning and evening prayer.

Ceremonial offices

A duty performed in connection with a *liturgical form of service; e.g. to perform the last offices — to perform the *last rites for the dying.

Omnipotence

See Attributes of God.

Omnipresence

See Attributes of God.

Omniscience

See Attributes of God.

Opus operatum (Latin — a work performed)

When used in the form 'ex opere operato' (Latin — by means of a work done), this phrase teaches that a sacrament (*baptism, for example) has an effect in and of itself; i.e. baptism as an act *regenerates a person. The person who is baptized is said to be regenerate 'by virtue of the work performed'. The phrase is used in Roman Catholic theology to refer to baptism, the eucharist, and confession.

This teaching contradicts Scripture which says that God's *grace comes to a person inwardly, not through any outward ceremony.

Oral tradition

See Tradition.

Ordain

The word is often used nowadays to refer to a ceremony by which believers are set apart for some public ministry.

Different Greek verbs are translated by the word 'ordain' in the English Bible with the meaning of command, decree, set apart, order beforehand (e.g. Acts 13:48), but, in fact, the word is not used in the New Testament to speak of a person's entry into the Christian ministry.

The seven men set apart in Acts 6 began their ministry after the apostles had prayed and laid their hands on them (v. 6). Laying on of hands is also mentioned at Timothy's beginning his ministry (1 Tim. 4:14; 2 Tim. 1:6).

Ordinance

The word is used to translate three Hebrew words in the sense of 'law' and a variety of Greek words with the meaning of 'what is ordained, instituted, declared right' (e.g. Luke 1:6, 'dikaioma' — that which is right; Rom. 13:2, 'diatege' — arrangement; Col. 2:14, 'dogma' — edict; 2 Thess. 2:15, 'paradosis' — tradition; 1 Peter 2:13, 'ktisis' — institution).

The word ordinance is sometimes used as a synonym for the Lord's supper, or, *communion (as something commanded by the Lord).

Ordo Salutis (Latin — order of salvation)

The order of events by which God saves a person. Rom. 8:30 gives a basic framework — God *predestinates, *calls, *justifies, *glorifies.

Calling consists of his granting *regeneration, *repentance and saving *faith.

*Sanctification (a life lived in the power of the Holy Spirit) lies between justification and glorification.

Origen

An early Christian theologian (AD185-254) of *Alexandria. He wrote many commentaries and other theological works, most of which have been lost. He produced the *Hexapla. He taught that Scripture can have three meanings — literal, moral and *allegorical — and he preferred the latter. Some of his teaching on the *Persons of the Trinity also differed from *orthodox views.

Origin of soul

There have been various theories about the origin of the soul in a person:

1. Creationism

The opinion that God creates each individual soul and unites it with its body at conception.

2. Traducianism (Latin — 'trans-ducere' — to lead across)

The opinion that the soul of a person, as well as the body, is obtained from the parents.

Original sin

The Bible does not use the phrase original sin, but it teaches the fact of it very clearly. All people are born into the world with a sinful nature, and the origin of that sin is Adam's disobedience at the time of the fall (Gen. 3). Sin entered into the world by one man (Rom. 5:12). It is impossible to understand the *incarnation and death of Christ or the doctrines of *grace without some understanding of original sin.

Orthodoxy (Greek 'orthos' — straight, and 'doxa' — opinion)

Literally, straight teaching.

To be orthodox is to accept biblical teaching. To be heterodox (Greek 'heteros' — different) means not to accept biblical teaching.

The term orthodox is also used of certain national *churches; e.g. the Russian, the Greek, Orthodox Church. But by biblical standards, these churches are not truly orthodox.

Paedobaptism (Greek 'paidion' — a child)

Infant baptism.

See Baptism.

Palimpsest (Greek 'palin' — again, and 'psao' — I rub)

A sheet of vellum or papyrus from which the original writing has been rubbed out and which is then used for a new writing. A number of copies of Bible manuscripts are palimpsests.

Pantheism (Greek 'pan' — all, and 'theos' — god)

The belief that 'all is god', that god is so *immanent in his creation that he cannot be separated from it. Pantheism and *deism are opposites.

Christian theology teaches the immanence of God, but teaches that God the creator is separate from and *sovereign over his creation. He is not identified with it.

It is good to have some understanding of pantheism if one is to understand eastern religions, particularly Hinduism.

Parables (Greek 'parabole' from two Greek words 'para' — beside, and 'ballo' — I put)

A parable is a story with a meaning 'put beside' it, i.e. a story with which the reader or hearer compares some other truth. In the *LXX the word 'parabole' translates the Hebrew 'mashal' — an important saying — as in Prov. 1:1; 10:1. It is linked with the riddles of Psalm 49:4 and Ezek. 17:2. It can be a longer saying, such as Num. 24:20-24. Nathan's story to David in 2 Sam. 12:1-4 is a story with a meaning, though the actual word 'parable' is not used.

The Jewish rabbis often taught in parables, so Jesus was using a method of teaching familiar to his hearers. He drew his parables from nature, from daily life, from contemporary events. They may consist of short sayings (Mark 7:17), of a story with a clear moral (Matt. 20:1-16; 21:33-44), or of an *allegory — the story of the sower in Matt. 13:3-9, which is called a parable yet is given an *allegorical meaning in vv. 19-23.

In Matt. 13:10 the disciples asked Jesus why he taught in parables, and he replied that it was granted to them to know the mysteries of the kingdom of heaven. They would be given the ability to understand the hidden meanings of the parables. But a further purpose of his teaching by parables was to conceal spiritual truth from those who did not want to know it. They would hear and understand the story but not understand the deeper meaning. Jesus was quoting Isa. 6:9-10.

Paradox (Greek 'para' — beside, and 'doxa' — opinion)

Literally, an opinion side by side with another opinion.

A paradox is a teaching with two sides to it, which seem to contradict each other, yet which are both true. For example, the person who trusts in Christ 'will never thirst' (John 4:14), i.e. the believer will never again desire anyone but God. Yet the believer 'thirsts' for God (Ps. 63:1), i.e. the believer longs for more of God.

Paradigm

See Form Criticism.

Parallelism

A common feature in Hebrew poetry. Three examples:

a. Synonymous parallelism

The second line (of a couplet) restates what has been expressed in the first:

i.e.   Deliver me from my enemies, O God
Protect me from those who rise up against me.
(Ps. 59:1)

b. Synthetic parallelism

The second line adds to or completes the first:

i.e.   O that I had the wings of a dove!
I would fly away and be at rest.
(Ps. 55:6)

c. Antithetical parallelism

The second line contrasts to the first:

i.e.   The Lord watches over the way of the *righteous,
But the way of the wicked will perish.
(Ps.1:6)

There are other variations, including parallel triplets.

Paranomasia (Greek 'para' — beside, and 'onoma' — name)

Two names or words placed side by side, i.e. a pun, or play on words. Matt. 16:18 is a good example. Jesus says to Peter 'You are Peter (Greek 'petros') and on this rock (Greek 'petra') I will build my *church.'

Micah 1:10-15 has a list of names of towns. The instructions connected with each town are a pun on that name. For example: v. 10 — Gath is from the same word as the Hebrew for 'to tell', so 'Tell it not in Gath' could be paraphrased 'Tell it not in Tell-town'.

v. 10 — Aphrah means dust, so, 'in the house of Aphrah roll thyself in the dust' could be paraphrased 'Roll in the dust for shame'.

Particular Baptist

See Baptist.

Particular redemption

See Limited Atonement.

Paschal (Hebrew 'pasakh' — to pass over; The verb gives rise to the noun 'pesakh' — the passover (feast).

An adjective meaning suffering. The Hebrew was translated into Greek as 'pascho' — to suffer. Passover was the time when the sacrificial lamb suffered. English adopted the word in the adjective 'paschal', suffering. The Paschal Controversy was concerned with the date of Easter (the time of suffering). The Paschal Lamb refers either to the Jewish literal lamb, or to Christ.

Passion (Latin 'passio' — suffering, from Greek 'pascho' — to suffer)

The passion of Christ is the suffering of Christ.

As used in music, e.g. St. Matthew's Passion means Christ's suffering as portrayed in Matthew's Gospel and set to music.

See Paschal.

Passive obedience of Christ (Greek 'pascho' — to suffer)

Christ's passive obedience is his suffering and his death by which he paid the penalty for the sins of his people. He was passive (yielding) under this suffering, in that he allowed evil people to lay these sufferings upon him. The real cause was God who laid upon Christ the punishment of his people's sins (Acts 2:23).

We must distinguish the *active and the passive obedience of Christ, but the two are not wholly separate. He was active even in his passive sufferings: 'No man takes it (my life) from me, but I lay it down of myself. I have the power to lay it down, and I have power to take it again' (John 10:18). He suffered, passively, temptation and opposition during his thirty-three years of life when he was actively obeying the law of God.

Pastoral (Latin 'pastor' — shepherd)

Pastoral epistles

The letters of Paul to Timothy and Titus instructing them how to act as shepherds to their people.

Pastoral theology

The study of the work of a pastor in all its aspects. Also known as pastoralia.

Patriarchs (Greek 'pater' — father, and 'archo' — to rule)

The biblical patriarchs were Abraham, Isaac and Jacob, the fathers of the nation of Israel, together with the twelve sons of Jacob. Acts 2:29 refers to David as a patriarch.

In the time of the early Christian *church, the bishops of *Alexandria, Antioch, Constantinople, Jerusalem and Rome were known as patriarchs.

Patristics/patristic period

Certain leading men in the early *church (after the apostles) became known as the Fathers; e.g. Athanasius, Jerome.

The study of the writings of these men is known as patristics and their period (from the second to about the sixth century AD) as the patristic period.

Pauline/Paulinism

Pauline is an adjective meaning 'by Paul, of Paul'. The epistles (letters) of Paul are the Pauline epistles; the theology of Paul is Pauline theology. Paulinism is a noun meaning Paul's teaching and theology.

See Petrine.

Pelagianism

Pelagius was a British monk who lived in Rome in the early 5th century AD. He taught that people are born without *original sin, without a bias towards evil. They can choose to do good, just as they can choose to do evil. Augustine taught from Scripture that God by his *grace must save people and make them holy, but Pelagius denied that God's grace was necessary. People have the power in themselves to follow the example of Christ.

Pelagius was condemned at the Council of Ephesus in AD431.

Semi-pelagianism did teach the necessity of the grace of God to save people, but said that they could decide whether or not they would be saved. *Arminianism has its roots in Pelagianism and semi-Pelagianism of the fifth and sixth centuries AD.

See Augustinianism.

Penal (Latin 'poena' — pain. English derived noun — penalty)

The penal view of the death of Christ is that he died to take on himself the pain, the punishment, of sin; i.e. he died a *vicarious, substitutionary death.

Pentateuch (Greek 'pentateuchos'- five-volumed)

The first five books of the Old Testament. The books are known in Hebrew as 'the law', the first of the three divisions of the Old Testament (law, prophets, writings).

See Torah.

See also Documentary Theory.

Pentecostal

The adjective takes its name from Pentecost (Acts 2) when the Holy Spirit was poured out on the *church. It is applied now to a particular denomination whose churches emphasise the baptism in the Holy Spirit as a separate experience from conversion. Most Pentecostal churches also teach that the gift of speaking in tongues is an evidence of being baptized in the Spirit. The word Pentecostal is often used to describe the alleged experience itself, as in 'the Pentecostal experience', 'the Pentecostal blessing'.

Pentecostalism as a denomination originated at the beginning of the twentieth century. It is now to be found all over the world, with rapidly growing congregations, particularly in South America.

Pericope (From two Greek words meaning 'to cut around')

A pericope is a short section or paragraph of the Gospels which is obviously a unit in itself. E.g. the section John 8:1-11 — the woman guilty of adultery — is known as a pericope.

Perseverance

See Final Perseverance.

Person

When we speak of three Persons in the divine *Trinity, we must not think of persons with bodies like human people. Physical character-istics are not essential to being a person. A person's true 'personal-ity' is made up of the mind, heart and affections, apart from the body. So the Persons of the Trinity have characteristics of love, wrath, goodness, compassion, power, etc. The second Person took a human body because of mankind's sin, but he existed before that as a Person.

The terms first, second, third Person of the Trinity are for our convenience only, speaking of the distinctive acts of each Person. We must not think in terms of superior or inferior rank.

Personification

Only a person can speak. When a non-living, or abstract, thing is described as speaking, singing or using other personal forms of communication, that device is called 'personification'.

E.g. 'The mountains .. shall break forth .. into singing' (Isa. 55:12). This speaks of joy. And wisdom speaks of herself as a person in Prov. 8.

Perspicuity of Scripture (Latin 'perspicuus' — transparent; 'per' — through, and 'specto' — to look at)

The 'see-through-able-ness', i.e. the clarity, of Scripture. All that we need for salvation is taught somewhere in Scripture and can be found by that person who really wants to find God. Some passages of Scripture are difficult for believers to understand and there is certainly much that is obscure to the unbeliever. But enough is clear to make a person 'wise to salvation' (2 Tim. 3:15).

See Sufficiency of Scripture.

Petrine

The adjective from 'Peter'. The Petrine epistles are Peter's epistles. Petrine theology — Peter's theology.

(Cf. Pauline, Johannine).

Pietism

Pietism was a definite historical movement in seventeenth century Germany. It was a reaction to dead *orthodoxy and emphasised holiness of life (piety).

The word pietist(ic) describes a type of Christianity which emphasises individual, subjective Christian experience and sees little need for Christians to be involved in the wider life of the *church or in social action in the world.

Pneumatology (Greek 'pneuma' — spirit, wind)

The study of the *Person and work of the Holy Spirit.

Polytheism (Greek 'polus' — much [plural, many], and 'theos' — god)

Belief in more than one god. (Contrast *monotheism)

Post-Millennialism

See Millennium.

Preach

There are three Greek words usually translated 'preach' in the English Bible — 'euangelizesthai', 'katangellein' and 'kerussein'. These words are used in the Greek New Testament to mean 'telling the gospel to people who have not heard it before'.

Predestination

The biblical teaching that God has planned beforehand, foreordained, everything that is to happen in his world. He is not, however, the author of sin, nor are people merely machines.

The Westminster Confession says: 'God from all eternity did by the most wise and holy counsel of his own will, freely and unchangeably ordain whatsoever comes to pass: yet so as thereby neither is God the author of sin, nor is violence offered to the will of the creatures, nor is the liberty or contingency of second causes taken away, but rather established.'

See Dan. 4:35; Acts 2:23; Eph. 1:11.

See Election.

Pre-existence of Christ

The Scriptures teach that Christ is eternal with the Father and the Holy Spirit. The Son is one of the three members of the Godhead. His life did not begin with the *incarnation.

Old Testament evidence:

1. His eternal nature. Isa. 9:6; Micah 5:2.

2. His Sonship. Ps. 2:6-12; Isa. 9:6.

3. His oneness with God. Ps. 110:1; Dan. 7:13; Zech. 13:7.

4. His presence at creation. Prov. 8:22-31.

New Testament evidence:

1. He is the eternal Word, i.e. revelation of God. John 1:1.

2. He was active at creation. John 1:3; Col. 1:16; Heb. 1:2.

3. He perfectly expresses God. John 1:18; Heb. 1:3.

4. God addresses him as God, and quotes Old Testament Scriptures which are used of God. Heb. 1:5-12.

5. He was the Rock in the wilderness. 1 Cor. 10:4.

6. He was before Abraham. John 8:58.

In the fourth century AD the *Arian controversy split the *church. *Arius of Alexandria taught that Christ was not eternal, though he was the first and greatest created person. Col. 1:15 was one of his main evidences. (Col. 1:15 refers to the pre-eminence of Christ, in a society which attached much importance to the first son in a family). Athanasius of *Alexandria defended the deity of Christ against Arius.

Pre-millennialism

See Millennium.

Preservation of the Saints

Scripture teaches that true believers persevere to the end because God preserves them to the end. This follows from the fact that God chose his people from all eternity and so will keep them and finally *glorify them. A clear Scripture is 1 Peter 1:5 — believers are 'kept by the power of God through *faith unto salvation ready to be revealed in the last time'.

See Final Perseverance.

Presbyterians

The Greek word 'presbyteros' is translated 'elder' in the New Testament. A comparison of Acts 20:17 with v. 28 shows that the elders of v. 17 are called 'episkopoi' (overseers) in v. 28, to shepherd or pastor the church. Titus 1:5+7 shows a similar identification of elder and bishop.

The Presbyterian Church is governed by elders all of equal rank, i.e. it does not recognise a bishop. The Moderator presides over a presbytery, a group of presbyters, i.e. a synod (council) or General Assembly. He is primus inter pares, the first among equals.

Under John Knox (1513-72) the Presbyterian form of church government was introduced into Scotland.

The Westminster Confession of 1648 is the official doctrinal standard of the Presbyterian Church. Like the Anglicans, Presbyterians practise infant baptism.

Priesthood of all believers

The New Testament does not teach that there is an ecclesiastical *office of priest. Christ has fulfilled the Old Testament priesthood and is the only priest.

The New Testament does, however, teach that all believers are priests in a lesser sense (1 Peter 2:5,9; Rev. 1:5,6). They have access to God as have priests (Eph. 2:18; 3:12), they offer the sacrifices of praise and of good works (Heb. 13:15,16). Figuratively, their prayers are associated with an altar and with incense, emblems of Old Testament worship (Rev. 8:3,4).

Pronouncement stories

See Form Criticism.

Propitiation

See Atonement.

Providence (Latin 'providere' — to see before)

The providence of God is his care over his creation.

God orders all events in history for his own glory (Eph. 1:9-12), gives and sustains all life (Ps. 104; Matt. 6:26-29; Acts 17:25-28), and works all events in the lives of his people to their good (Romans 8:28). His providence witnesses to his existence and power (Acts 14:17), even to the ungodly (Rom. 1:18-23). By his providence God will bring history to its conclusion at Christ's return (1 Cor. 15:24).

Pseudepigraphy (Greek 'pseudos' — a lie, and 'graphe' — writing)

Non-biblical writers would sometimes give a biblical name to their work (e.g. the Assumption of Moses, the Gospel of Thomas). This literary device was presumably not intended to deceive the readers, but was to make them think the writing was important.

Purgatory

According to the Roman Catholic Church, purgatory is the place to which *baptized people go who still have a greater or lesser amount of sin needing to be 'purged' (cleansed away). The relatives and friends of the person whose soul is in purgatory can help to shorten the time that soul spends there by paying for masses to be said for him or her.

The biblical teaching that Christ saves completely all who trust in him by *faith contradicts this doctrine.

Puritan

One who wishes to keep the *church pure. The name was a nickname given by their enemies to those who, in the reign of Elizabeth I (AD1558-1603), were not satisfied that the reformation of the church had gone far enough.

At this early stage the Puritans did not separate from the Anglican Church, but in the seventeenth century denominations independent of that Church grew up and the word Puritan was given both to members of those denominations and to members of the Anglican Church who believed in the *sovereignty of God in salvation and practised purity in daily life.

The Puritan movement produced several theologians of a high calibre (e.g. John Owen, Richard Baxter, Richard Sibbes). The Presbyterian Westminster Confession (1648) is a product of Puritan theology.

Q (The first letter of the German word 'Quelle' — source)

Some experts in the Synoptic Gospels (Matthew, Mark and Luke) note that there is much material in Matthew and Luke which is not in Mark. They suggest that Matthew and Luke have taken this material from a source which Mark did not use. The scholars give the symbol 'Q' to this source, which consists mostly of the sayings of Jesus.

Quickening

'Quick' is an old English adjective meaning alive. To quicken is the verb meaning to make alive (Eph. 2:1,5). The English phrase 'the quick and the dead' means the living and the dead people.

Quietism

Quietists believe in being passive (quiet) before God. Quietism is a state in which people do not exercise their wills, not even to do good works. Any extreme mystical or pietistic teaching leads to an emphasis on quietism, but in the seventeenth century the word was particularly used of the teachings of Molinos, Madame Guyon and Fénelon.

Qumran

In 1947 several scrolls of Jewish writings were found in the desert near the Dead Sea. They became known as the Dead Sea scrolls. The place where they were found was called Qumran. Monastery buildings were excavated nearby and the men who lived there and produced the scrolls were given the name 'the Qumran Community'. Some of these scrolls contain copies of Old Testament books dating from the first or second centuries BC, the text of which is remarkably similar to what we have today translated in our Bibles.

Received Text (Latin — Textus Receptus: symbol, TR)

The Greek text on which the Authorised Version translation is based. There are thousands of Greek manuscripts of the Scriptures in existence, but most agree with each other to a great extent. None of them is earlier than the fifth century AD but their readings are often supported by earlier works (translations into ancient languages, or quotations in the writings of the early church fathers). This large body of manuscripts lay behind the text used for centuries by Greek-speaking *churches and is known as the Received Text of the New Testament. From the sixteenth century it was the chief printed text.

The TR is sometimes known as the Byzantine text, as it originated in Byzantium, site of the Emperor Constantine's Constantinople.

Redactor/redaction

See Documentary Theory.

Reformed

From the verb 'to re-form'. A reformed *church is one which has reformed its beliefs and practices according to Scripture. The Reformation of the sixteenth century was an historical movement when believers broke away from the Roman Catholic Church and made Scripture the standard for their beliefs and practices.

To be reformed includes: belief in the Scriptures as the *inerrant Word of God; belief that God is *sovereign in his world; that he has *elected his people to salvation and will effectually *call them in his time, through the *preaching of the true gospel; that all worship must be in accordance with Scripture; and that the lives of believers as individuals, family members, members of the state and members of the Christian *church, must be increasingly conformed to the standard of God's Word.

Regeneration (Latin 're-generare' — again to bring forth)

New birth. The action by which God gives spiritual life to a person who becomes 'a new creation' (2 Cor. 5:17). Jesus told Nicodemus, 'You must be born again' (John 3:7), i.e. born from above, born by a supernatural act of God. Only those who are regenerate receive Christ, are children of God, and believe on his name (John 1:12,13).

See a Bible Dictionary.

Regulative principle (Latin 'regula' — a rule, a pattern)

The regulative principle regulates true worship. It states that true worship consists in doing only what God has commanded in Scripture and limited by his revealed will.

The circumstances (i.e. time, details of place, etc.) of worship are governed by common sense, but the actual content of worship must be in accordance with the principles of Scripture.

See Adiaphora

Religionsgeschichtliche Schule

See History of Religion School.

Renewal

Renewal as a technical term, often with a capital R in English, refers to the attempts of the charismatic movement to 'renew' the *churches of the main denominations by an emphasis on tongues, healing and prophecy. The movement has been prominent in the United Kingdom since the 1960s.

Renewal ought not to be confused with *Restoration which sees the denominations as incapable of revival. *Restorationism seeks to 'restore' the kingdom of God, i.e. to set up one 'restored' church in place of the present-day denominations.

See Spiritual Gifts.

Repentance

In the Old Testament, the Hebrew word 'naham' is used more of God apparently changing his dealings with people and nations than of human beings changing their behaviour.

In the New Testament, the Greek word 'metanoia' is used of individuals 'turning back' from wrong behaviour. It denotes an inward change of thinking and conviction, arising from a sorrow for offences against God and resulting in endeavours to live in holiness.

See a Bible Dictionary.

Reprobation (Latin 're' [negative], 'probare' — to approve)

Just as God has determined to save some people, so he has determined to pass some people by and punish them eternally for their sins. The latter is reprobation. Both actions are for the glory and vindication of God.

Reprobation is the logical counterpart of *election, but it is also biblical. Rom. 9:22,23 is a clear Scripture, 'vessels of wrath fitted to destruction'. See also Jude 4.

Augustine and Calvin and most reformed theologians have taught this doctrine.

Restorationism

See Renewal.

Restricted communion

See also Baptist - Strict

The Scriptures show that the taking of communion is restricted to certain people. All believers may partake of the bread and wine at the Lord's supper (Matt. 26:27), but unbelievers, and indeed any believer who after self-examination is found to be eating and drinking 'unworthily' (1 Cor. 11:27,29) may not partake.

In Scotland Presbyterian *churches practise 'fencing the table', i.e. making sure as far as possible that only believers who are partaking worthily eat the bread and drink the wine.

The word 'unworthily' must be understood in the whole context of 1 Cor. The letter has said much about the sins in the church at Corinth. Paul says in 1 Cor. 11:29 that a person who eats the bread and drinks the wine while still practising those sins 'eats and drinks unworthily'. The fact that Paul adds 'not discerning the Lord's body' — i.e. not understanding that the church is the body of Christ, seems to indicate that disunity in the church (see 1 Cor. chapters 1-4) is the sin he has chiefly in mind.

Revelation

God has given us a revelation of himself. Without this revelation, human beings would know nothing of God's existence or his nature.

This revelation has two aspects:

1. General or natural revelation — God's revelation of himself in creation and through the human conscience.

2. Special revelation — God's revelation of himself in the Scriptures and particularly in Christ.

General or natural revelation.

This is all around us in the trees, flowers, sun, moon, stars, etc. Scripture has some very clear passages on it. For instance:
Ps. 19: 'The heavens declare the glory of God'.
Acts 14:17: Rains and fruitful seasons are a witness to God.
Rom. 1:19-20: The invisible things of God, his eternal power and divinity, are seen through the things he has made.
General or natural revelation is to be found also in human consciousness. The Gentiles did not have God's law revealed to them as the Jews did, yet they had the law written in their hearts (Rom. 2:14-15). People can come to a certain knowledge of God through natural revelation (Rom. 1:19-21). Indeed, they know enough of him to make them 'without excuse' for their rejection of him (v. 20). Yet they cannot know of his holiness, his hatred of sin, and his provision for salvation without the further revelation of the Scriptures.

Special revelation

Deut. 29:29 tells us that there are some things which God keeps as his secret; there are other things which he has revealed for our benefit. Even Adam when first created needed special instructions from God (Gen. 2:16-17).

Ps. 119 speaks repeatedly of the law of God as God's Word. John 17:17 says: 'Your Word is truth.' Just as human words reveal what human beings are, so God's Word reveals what God is.

Most important of all, God revealed himself to mankind through the *incarnate Word, Christ himself. 1 John 1:1: 'In the beginning was the Word .. he has declared him' (v. 18). And Heb. 1:1 tells us that the climax of God's revelation is his Son.

*Liberal theology inevitably denies revelation. *Neo-orthodoxy believes that God has revealed himself, but does not equate the revelation with Scripture. Karl Barth, in his anxiety to recover revelation from liberal denials of it, taught that there is no general or natural revelation.

Revival (Latin 're' — again, 'vivere' — to live)

To revive is to make alive again, so it is the people of God who have already been made alive spiritually, who experience a renewing of spiritual life, whether individually or as a larger community.

At certain periods when the people of God in a *church, a district or a country have been spiritually dead, God has come to them again in the power of his Holy Spirit — usually in answer to prayer — and has given them new life, new desire for himself and his Word, and has added to the church converts in greater or lesser numbers.

Revival is an act of God and it is quite wrong to speak of organising, or holding, a revival. This confuses revival with evangelism.

See Quickening.

Righteousness

The Hebrew word translated 'righteous' originally meant 'straight'. The corresponding Greek word in Greek usage referred to anything in accordance with the law. In the Old Testament the God of Israel is shown to be righteous because he acts rightly in all his works and judgments.

Righteousness as applied to human beings can be thought of in several ways:

1. Original righteousness. Adam and Eve were created upright and morally good.

2. Christ's righteousness. Since the events recorded in Gen. 3 Christ is the only human being who has perfectly fulfilled God's law.

3. *Imputed righteousness. Because Christ is also God his righteousness is of infinite value and can be credited to those who believe in him (see Justification).

4. Restored righteousness. Having been born again, the believer becomes increasingly righteous in actual behaviour (see Sanctification).

See a Bible Dictionary.

Sacerdotal (Latin 'sacerdos' — priest, 'sacerdotium' — priesthood)

An adjective describing something which has to do with priests, e.g. a sacerdotal form of worship is worship in which only an *ordained priest can perform certain ceremonies.

Sacrament (Latin 'sacer' — sacred)

'Sacraments are holy signs and seals of the covenant of *grace' (Westminster Confession XXVII).

The Lord Jesus Christ commanded his *church to keep two sacraments — *baptism and the Lord's supper, or *communion.

The sacraments are signs. A sign points not to itself but to something else. So believers' baptism points to the fact that the believers have been buried and raised with Christ. The bread and the wine of the Lord's supper point to the body and blood of Christ, and believers' taking the bread and wine points to their trusting in Christ.

The sacraments are also seals. A seal confirms and declares something to be true. A seal on a document declares that the document is the document of the person it concerns. The two sacraments confirm that God's grace in salvation has come to the believers.

A sacrament has been defined as 'the outward sign of an inward experience'.

Roman Catholics have seven sacraments — *Baptism, the Lord's supper, Confirmation, Penance, Extreme Unction, Orders and Marriage. Scripture does not give the last five of these as sacraments.

*Baptism and the Lord's supper do not bring grace to a person. So they can only be meaningful to believers; they are not valid sacraments if practised by an unbeliever.

See Opus Operatum.

Sanctify/sanctification

The basic meaning is 'to set apart'. God is set apart (Ezek. 36:23); Christ sets himself apart for his work (John 17:19). In the Old Testament, people, places and inanimate objects were set apart for God's use (Exod. 28:41; 30:29; Lev. 27:14-22; Job 1:5).

Christ prays that the Father will sanctify his people.

Sanctification is that progressive work of God's Holy Spirit in believers by which he makes the believers increasingly holy (set apart for God). This is the work of making them conform 'to the image of his Son' (Rom. 8:29). The work is never completed in this life, but will be complete in heaven.

The epistle to the Hebrews uses the word for an experience almost synonymous with *justification (Heb. 10:10; 13:12). It speaks of Christ's initial setting apart of believers to God and his service, but of course implies their continual growth in holiness.

See a Bible Dictionary.

Second coming of Christ

The actual English phrase is not in Scripture, though the New Testament clearly teaches that the Lord Jesus Christ will return to the earth.

Several Greek words are used to describe Christ's return.

1. 'Parousia' — presence, with an arrival preceding.
Phil. 1:26 et al.

2. 'Epiphaneia' — a public appearing. 2 Tim. 4:1.

3. 'Apocalypsis' — an unveiling. 2 Thess. 1:7.

John uses the verb 'phaneroo' — to manifest (same root word as in 'epiphaneia'): 'when he shall be manifested' (1 John 2:28). Heb. 9:28 has the simple verb 'horao' — to see: 'he shall be seen'.

Christ will come to gather his saints, dead and living, to himself (1 Thess. 4:13-18), to judge unbelievers (2 Thess. 2:8-10) and to set up a reign of *righteousness (2 Peter 3:10-13).

Sect (Latin 'secta' — a faction or following)

Any group of people who follow some different teaching or practice from the main beliefs of Christian believers. The members of such a body do not usually call themselves a sect; the word is used about them by others who do not belong to that group.

The word sect, usually referring to a small group, is not to be confused with the word denomination, which refers to a large, recognised group within mainline Christianity.

Seeking sinners

The phrase describes people whom the Holy Spirit has shown that they are sinners before God and that they cannot find a way to God by themselves. The Spirit has further shown them that God has provided a way of salvation and the sinners are seeking God, i.e. praying to God to reveal himself to them and to grant them *faith to believe in Christ.

See Sensible sinners.

Semi-Pelagianism

See Pelagianism.

Semitism

See Hebraism.

Sensible sinners

The word 'sensible' is here used in its old English meaning of 'knowing, being conscious of', not in the modern sense of 'intelligent'. Sensible sinners are those who know they are sinners before God. The Holy Spirit has shown them that fact, so that they know it in their hearts and not just in their heads.

Septuagint

The translation into Greek of the Hebrew Old Testament. This was made in *Alexandria (Egypt) in the third century BC. The New Testament writers quoted from this version.

There is a tradition that says that seventy Jewish scholars did this work. So the symbol for the Septuagint is LXX — Roman figures for 70. An alternative tradition that the work took seventy days can very probably be rejected.

See Hellenism.

Simony

Buying or selling official positions in a *church organisation. The word comes from the story of Simon Magus in Acts 8:18,19.

Sitz im Leben

See Form Criticism.

Social gospel

See Liberalism.

Socinian

The theology of Maria Sozini (AD1525-1562) and Paolo Sozini (AD1529-1604), uncle and nephew, who denied the doctrine of the *Trinity. Nowadays this teaching is represented by Unitarianism.

Soteriology (Greek 'soter' — Saviour; 'soteria' — salvation; and verb 'sozo' — to save)

Soteriology is the study of the doctrine of salvation.
At its widest meaning it deals with all that God has done in Christ

for the salvation of mankind; i.e. it includes the doctrines of mankind, sin, and the *Person and work of Christ. At its narrowest meaning, it deals with all that God does to apply salvation to his people; i.e. it includes the doctrines of the Person and work of the Holy Spirit, *ecclesiology and *eschatology.

Soul sleep

Some people teach that when people die, they sleep until the resurrection; i.e. they are not conscious.

The Bible calls death a sleep (Matt. 27:52; John 11:11; Acts 13:36; 1 Thess. 4:13,14), but the figure of speech seems to speak merely of the death of the body. The fact that Paul says that to be with Christ is far better (Phil. 1:23) implies that believers are in a conscious state of existence in heaven.

Sovereignty of God

The words 'sovereign' and 'sovereignty' do not occur in the English Bible (Authorised Version), but the doctrine is present throughout Scripture.

God is the source of all that exists. He does not depend on anyone or anything else for his existence or his *attributes, and he is absolutely in control of all that happens in heaven or on earth, in creation, *providence and redemption.

Special revelation

See Revelation.

Spiritual desertion

Believers often feel that God has deserted them. They seem to have little desire for God or for prayer, and they see few answers to prayer.

The Bible says that God does not desert his people, but there are times when he takes away the conscious sense of his presence, either because of some unconfessed sin in them or in order to make them seek him and trust him even when they do not feel him near.

Spiritual gifts

The most important New Testament passage for spiritual gifts is 1 Cor. 12-14.

There has been much debate in recent years as to whether the gifts of tongues, prophecy and healing are for every age of the *church, or not, and if, therefore, they can be expected in church life today.

Cessationism

This school of thought says that the 'foundation gifts' (the signs of an apostle) ceased with the apostles.

Restorationism

This school of thought says that the unbelief and sin of the church has prevented the whole range of gifts from being exercised, except at intervals, throughout church history. They have been restored in the twentieth century, probably as an indication that the end of the age is very near. *Restorationists further teach that apostles and prophets have been restored to the church in the latter half of the twentieth century.

See Renewal.

Strict Baptist (Sometimes known as Grace Baptist)

See Baptist.

Sublapsarianism (Noun. Latin 'sub' — under, 'lapsus' — fall)

Sublapsarianism teaches that God's decree to permit the fall preceded his decree to *elect his people; i.e. the latter decree was under (subordinated to) the former decree.

Infralapsarianism (Latin 'infra' — later than) Similar to sublapsarianism.

Sufficiency of Scripture

The Scriptures are sufficient for all spiritual needs. Scripture contains all that people need to know concerning God, sin, Christ, the way of salvation and destiny. Rev. 22:18,19 warns against adding anything to or taking anything from Scripture.

See Perspicuity of Scripture.

Supererogation, works of

In Roman Catholic theology, any good deed which is not strictly obligatory to be done.

Supralapsarianism (Latin 'supra' — earlier, 'lapsus' — fall)

Supralapsarianism teaches that God's decree to elect some people and reprobate the rest preceded his decree to permit the fall, indeed even to create the world.

Synergism (Greek 'sun' — with, 'ergon' — work)

Synergism means 'working together'. It refers to any view of salvation which sees God and people as co-operating. The Bible teaches that God and people do not co-operate in the work of initiating salvation. See Eph. 2:8,9. In the work of *sanctification, however, there is some synergism when believers obey the Scriptures and co-operate with the Holy Spirit's work in their lives.

Synoptic (Greek 'sun-optikos' — seen together)

An adjective applied to the three Gospels, Matthew, Mark and Luke, because these describe the Lord Jesus Christ in a similar way. They 'see him together', whereas John's Gospel sees him in a different, though complementary way.

Systematic Theology

See Biblical Theology.

Talmud (From Hebrew 'lamad' — to learn)

A Jewish commentary on Old Testament Scriptures. It was compiled over several centuries to as late as the sixth century AD.

It includes:

the Mishnah (Hebrew 'shana' — to repeat), a word for the oral traditions which developed around the law.

the Halakah (Hebrew 'halak' — to walk), biblical principles of ethical conduct applied to specific situations.

the Haggada (Hebrew 'higgid' — to declare, from 'nagad' — to be prominent), proverbs, parables, etc.

The Halakah and the Haggada are together known as the Gemara (Aramaic 'gemar' — to study completely).

The Talmud is important background material for the New Testament.

Targum

A general word for a translation but technically it is specifically used of a translation of the Hebrew Scriptures into Aramaic. Each different section was known as a Targum — for example, the Targum on the *Pentateuch. Comment and interpretation of the text was included with the translation.

Targums were originally oral and spontaneous (see Neh. 8:7) but were written down as time went on.

Textual criticism/textual studies

The word criticism is here used with its simple meaning of judging.

Textual criticism aims to discover as far as possible the original text, or words, of a passage of Scripture. Its method is to compare manuscript with manuscript, to note the differences in a particular passage, and to assess which of the variant readings is nearest to the original.

Textus Receptus

See Received Text.

Theism (Greek 'theos' — god)

The word can be used loosely of belief in God, and so could include *deism, *pantheism and even *polytheism.

It is used more strictly of belief in one creator God (the God of Judaism and Christianity), and, further, of a God who is in constant contact with his world. This excludes *deism. Theism is often used in compound words such as *henotheism, *monotheism and *polytheism.

Theocracy (Greek 'theos' — god, and 'kratein' — to rule)

The rule of God. A nation ruled over by God, as was Israel. (Compare demo-cracy, rule by the people). Josephus the Jewish historian of the first century AD was apparently the first to use the word.

Theodicy (Greek 'theos' — god, and 'dike' — justice)

When philosophers or theologians attempt to show that God is just even though there is so much evil in the world, their work is a theodicy (a justification) of the ways of God. The word was first used by Leibnitz in the eighteenth century.

Theology (Greek 'theos' — god, and 'logos' — word)

In its narrow sense, the word means the study of God. In its wider sense, it includes all the subjects which make up a course of theological study.

Theophany (Greek 'theos' — god, and 'phaino' — to appear)

God appeared from time to time in the Old Testament period in the form of a man or an angel. (E.g. Gen. 16:7-13; Josh. 5:13-15). Such appearances are known as theophanies (God-appearances). They were very possibly appearances of Christ before his coming to earth as a man.

Three Chapters

Three writings which contained the teachings of *Nestorius and which attempted to reconcile *monophysite views with *orthodox doctrine.

Torah (Hebrew for 'teaching', usually translated 'law')

This word is used widely, sometimes of the *Pentateuch, sometimes of oral instruction as in Exod. 18:15, sometimes of the Decalogue (the ten commandments), sometimes of all the law given to Moses, sometimes of all God's requirements.

Total depravity

See Depravity.

Tradition (Latin 'trans' — across, and 'do, datum' — to give)

Something which is passed down. Oral tradition refers to the handing over of certain narratives and teachings (for example, of

Jesus) until such time as they were written down. Jesus, however, promised that the Holy Spirit would bring to the memories of the apostolic writers all that they needed to write (John 14:26), so we need not fear that the biblical tradition (what has been handed over) is in any way untrue.

Traducianism

See Origin of soul.

Transcendence

See Attributes of God.

Transubstantiation

The Roman Catholic Church teaches that the bread and wine of the Lord's supper actually becomes the body and blood of Christ. This is transubstantiation.

Roman Catholics distinguish between the substance (the reality) of the elements (the bread and the wine) and the accidents (the outward appearance). They teach that the latter do not change — the bread and wine still look like bread and wine — but the former, the substance, is changed 'across' ('trans' is Latin for across) into the body and blood of Christ. This is not taught in the Scripture.

See Consubstantiation.

Trichotomy

See Constitution of Man.

Tridentine

The Council of Trent (1545-1563) set out Roman Catholic teaching as opposed to Reformation teaching. 'Tridentine' is the adjective describing those teachings.

Trinity

The word speaks of one God in three *Persons, Father, Son and Holy Spirit. The doctrine is hinted at in the Old Testament (the Spirit was active at creation and someone distinct from both the Lord God and his Spirit speaks in Isa. [e.g. 48:16; 61:1]).

Although the word 'Trinity' does not appear in the New Testament, the fact of three Persons in one Godhead is clearly seen. The Father plans salvation, the Son carries it out, and the Spirit applies it to human hearts. (See also the baptism of Jesus [Matt. 3:16,17] and 2 Cor. 13:14).

There is never any hint in Scripture of tri-theism (the existence of three separate gods). The three Persons of the Trinity are not separate (there is only one God), but they are distinct from each other. All three Persons are equally God and fully God. The Father is God (Eph. 1:2), the Son is God (John 1:1; 20:28), the Spirit is God (1 Cor. 2:10-14). Yet there is only one God (James 2:19).

We cannot understand the Trinity by natural reason, any more than we can understand other doctrines. But we believe the doctrine because we see three Persons in Scripture and know three in our experience (John 14:17,21,23).

See Person.

Typology

The study of the types of the Old Testament and their fulfilment in the New Testament, the anti-types. For example, Jesus in Matt. 12:40 sees the story of Jonah as picturing the resurrection of Christ, and in John 3:14 he compares his own crucifixion to Moses lifting up the serpent in the wilderness. These Old Testament incidents and many others are types (models, pictures) of New Testament truths.

Uncial (Latin 'uncia' — an inch)

An adjective describing manuscripts written in capital letters, i.e. tall letters, not in cursive (running, or small, letters).

See Cursive.

Unconditional election

When God elected his people in Christ (Eph. 1:4; 1 Thess. 1:4) he chose them unconditionally, that is, there was no special quality in them which decided his choice; the choice was God's free, wise choice.

Some who misunderstand *foreknowledge (Rom. 8:29) say that God knew beforehand that his people would believe and elected them because of that foreseen *faith. In Scripture, however, to 'know' someone means to enter into a relationship with that person (Genesis 4:1; Luke 1:34), so to foreknow means to enter into a relationship beforehand. So God entered into a relationship with his elect people in Christ with nothing in them to move him to do so. Deut. 7:7,8: 'The Lord loved you and chose you ... because he loved you' (paraphrase).

Unconditional election is the second element in the mnemonic TULIP which sums up the biblical teaching on salvation.

See Limited Atonement.

Unitarianism

See Socinian.

Universalism

The teaching that everyone will finally be saved, including, some would add, the devil himself. This is contrary to biblical teaching.

Urmarcus (German 'Ur' — origin, and 'Marcus' — Mark)

Experts in the Synoptic Gospels (see Synoptic), Matthew, Mark and Luke, say that the writer of Mark's Gospel had an earlier, original document which he used as a source for his material. This is called the Urmarcus, the original Mark.

Vaticinium ex eventu (Latin — prophecy out of the event)

The phrase is used in its Latin form to mean a prophecy which looks like a genuine prophecy, i.e. looks as if written before it was fulfilled but which was really written **after** the event of which it speaks. Those who believe that there are such prophecies quote Christ's predictions of his coming death and resurrection and say that the early *church produced such predictions after the event, and added them into his teaching after his death. Some *liberals suggest that Daniel's prophecies of the four kingdoms were written long after the four kingdoms had come and gone.

Vica media (Latin — middle way)

Anglo-Catholics of the nineteenth century said that Anglicanism (the beliefs and practices of the Church of England) were a via media (a middle way, a compromise) between Roman Catholicism and non-conformity.

Vicarious (Latin 'vicarius' — a substitute)

Adjective applied to the death of Christ for his people. That death was a substitute for his people's death. He took upon himself the punishment they deserved.

Vulgate

In the early fourth century AD Jerome translated the Bible into Latin, the language of the people. The Latin for people is 'vulgus', so the translation became known as the Vulgate.

Weltanschauung (German 'Welt' — world, and 'anschauen' — to look at. Noun 'Anschauung' — a view, a sight)

The word is used in its German form to mean a world-view, how one sees the world, one's philosophy of life. One's belief or non-belief in God lies at the very basis of such a philosophy. The Christian on the one hand, and the *humanist on the other, have a completely different world-view from each other.

Western text

The *Received Text of the New Testament came from the Greek or Eastern *churches. The Western text came from the Latin or Western churches. It is these manuscripts which Westcott and Hort worked with and which lie behind the Revised Version of the New Testament.

Whitsunday

This day celebrates Pentecost, when the Holy Spirit was poured out on the *church (Acts 2). It falls seven weeks after Easter because the Spirit was given seven weeks after the crucifixion and resurrection of Christ.

The prefix 'Whit' means white and no doubt refers to the white clothes worn by the believers who were *baptized on this day.

Wisdom Literature (Hebrew 'hokma' — wisdom)

The books of Job, Proverbs and Ecclesiastes form the Wisdom Literature. The Song of Solomon and also some psalms are some-times included in this category. The actual word 'hokma' occurs 150 times in the Old Testament, and over half of these occurrences are in the Wisdom Literature.

The key phrase of the Wisdom Literature is 'The fear of the Lord is the beginning of wisdom' (Prov. 9:10). The truly wise person is not the clever person but the one who lives in the fear of God and obeys him. This is the message of the Wisdom Literature.

Job

Wisdom is to submit oneself to God in times of suffering.

Proverbs

Wisdom is to live in the fear of God in everyday life, in conversation, conduct of family and business and even in caring for animals.

Ecclesiastes

Wisdom is to remember our creator (Eccles. 12:1) in all the vanity of earthly life, however rich, brilliant and pleasure-giving it may be.

The Old Testament Apocrypha also contains Wisdom books — the Wisdom of Solomon, Ecclesiasticus and Baruch.

Worldliness

To understand the word worldliness, it is necessary to understand the Bible usage of the word 'world' (kosmos). The word can mean heaven-and-earth together (Acts 17:24), the created world visible to mankind (Rom. 1:20), the world of people (John 3:16), the world of ungodly people as controlled by Satan (1 John 5:19). God, of course, is still *sovereign even over the world under Satan's control.

The world as governed by Satan has standards, ideas, practices which are completely contrary to God's Word. It is **that** world that the believer is told not to love. 'Do not love the world' (1 John 2:15-17). James 4:4 speaks similarly.

Worldliness, then, is love of and allegiance to those things which are on the side of Satan and not of God. It is all too possible for a believer to have a worldly spirit, through neglect of God and his Word, even though he may not indulge in certain specific actions which are often condemned as worldly.

Writings, the

The third division of the Hebrew Scriptures. (The first division is the law [*Pentateuch] and the second division is the prophets [Joshua to Malachi]).

The Writings consist of:

a. 3 poetical books — Job, Psalms, Proverbs.

b. 5 rolls or scrolls (which are read at the annual feasts of the Jews) — Song of Solomon, Ruth, Lamentations, Ecclesiastes, Esther.

c. 3 books of history/prophecy — Chronicles, Ezra, Nehemiah, Daniel.

In the Hebrew Bible the Writings are the Kethubim (those things which are written), and in the *Septuagint they are the Hagiographa — holy writing (Greek 'hagios' — holy, and 'graphe' — writing).

Yahweh (Hebrew — LORD)

The Jews revered God's name so much that they would not even pronounce it. When they found the consonants Yhwh in Scripture, they said the word Adonai (my Lord). Gradually the vowels a-o-ai (of Adonai) came to be read with the consonants Yhwh and this led to the English form Jehovah. The form Yahweh is the usual spelling in modern books.

The Hebrew consonants are related to those of the Hebrew verb 'to be' and in Exod. 3:14 God calls himself the 'I am'. The phrase refers not only to his eternal existence, but to the fact that he is always acting for his people, whether in the exodus or in their future history.

Also available in this series:

A Dictionary of Bible Symbols

A Dictionary of Bible Knowledge

The Railway Age
in Bedfordshire

F. G. Cockman

This revised edition published September 1994
by
The Book Castle
12 Church Street
Dunstable
Bedfordshire LU5 4RU

First published as Volume 53, 1974
by
The Bedfordshire Historical Record Society

© F. G. Cockman and B.H.R.S., 1974, 1994

ISBN 1 871199 22 0

Printed by the Alden Press, Oxford.

Cover: The famous, former London and North Eastern Railway, Pacific type locomotive 'Flying Scotsman' on one of her infrequent visits to Midland Metals, seen here on 11th September 1965 just south of Bedford, in charge of a special train run for the Gainsborough Model Railway Society.

The watercolour painting, specially commissioned in 1994 from Edwin Lambert, is based on a Bedfordshire Times photograph.

CONTENTS

APPENDICES

Key to Railways proposed but not built 1844–1910

——————— 1844–1846

– – – – – – – – 1852–1864

—·——·——·— 1865–1910

Railways proposed but not built 1844–1910

Key to Map of Lines Constructed

1846–1872

Map of lines constructed 1846–1872

ILLUSTRATIONS (between pages 70 and 71)

PLANS

Plans and illustrations. The two plans were drawn by the County Council Planning Department. The illustrations are reproduced by kind permission of Mr F Banfield (14); Bedford Museum (1); Bedfordshire County Record Office (4, 6, 15, 20, 21, 23–26, 28); British Rail (5); Mr J W Brown (11); Mr H G Clements (16); Mr F G Cockman (8); Bedfordshire Photographic Services (17); Mr E W Curtis (19); Holland Press (13); Luton Museum (2, 3, 7, 10, 12); Totternhoe Lime and Stone Co. Ltd. (27); Mr A G Underwood (9); Mr J Wainwright (22).

INTRODUCTION

Anyone studying the social history of this country cannot fail to be amazed at the change which took place during the 19th century in modes of travel. This change was remarkable not only for the great increase in speed, but also for its suddenness. As travel became easier and cheaper, it became more common. One cause was the adaptation of steam to locomotion which began early in the century. Although pioneers like Blenkinsop, Hackworth and Hedley had done much useful work, it is George Stephenson who assists us in remembering the date, by naming one of his engines 'Blucher'. Another cause was the formation of Corporate Societies or Joint Stock Companies who could command sufficient capital to undertake the building of the new railroads. In this country the old established systems of transport by road and canal quickly fell victims to the steam operated railway because it matched the canal for dependability and beat the road for speed. The following chapters will endeavour to show how the railways attained a high standard of public service after the many initial mistakes which are all too easily condemned by hindsight. The country came to rely on its trains, and, while the railways prospered, the public was never let down. In fact the nation, when once it had abandoned its peripatetic habits and had taken to the flanged wheel on steel rail, became travel conscious and so stepped easily into the petrol age when it arrived.

This book deals with the impact made by railways on Victorian society in Bedfordshire. A suitable date for the commencement is the year 1846 when the Bedford Railway was opened – the county's first line, and I have chosen 1890 or thereabouts for the closing date of the narrative. By 1890 the railways were just beginning to respond to the outstanding 'Regulation of Railways Act, 1889', probably the most important act since Gladstone's of 1844. The 1889 Act brought our railways up to a pitch of safety, comfort and efficiency which could not be matched anywhere else in the world.

In chapter 7 I have mentioned briefly the Bedfordshire lines that were planned, but not proceeded with. These are dealt with in much more detail in my typescript account 'Bedfordshire Railways planned but not built' which can be consulted at the County Record Office. When I was writing this Miss Bell, the County Archivist, suggested that I should tackle the question of the social effects on the county of the coming of the railways. I have drawn heavily on the documents in the County Record Office, and here I can pay tribute to the willing help of the County Record Office staff. I have also had massive help from the Public Record Office, where again the staff are ever ready to assist. The writing of this work has been a great enjoyment, and I hope that some readers will both enjoy reading it, and find the contents instructive.

Bedford 1969   F. G. COCKMAN

SOURCES

It has not been thought necessary to give a separate reference for every individual document quoted in the text. Most documents are among those deposited at the Bedfordshire County Record Office, the main source being the Woburn estate correspondence deposited by the Trustees of the Bedford Settled Estate (R 3). Other documents are the diary of Catherine Young (later Maclear) chapters 1 and 2 (AD 1719); letters to the Clerk of the Peace chapters 1 and 7 (Q.S.R.); the Great Northern Railway's valuer's correspondence chapter 3 (RR 3 and RR 8); Dr Jacob Mountain's letters chapter 5 (X 67/581–7); Bute estate correspondence chapter 5 (G/DDA); Bedfordshire Quarter Sessions Minutes chapters 9, 10 and 14 (Q.S.M.); Bedford General Infirmary Minutes chapter 9 (HO: B/M); Coroner's Register chapter 9 and appendix (CO 11); letter concerning the Leighton Buzzard Enclosure Award Text chapter 10 (BO 1868); the Williamson diaries chapter 10 (M 3/5) and the Brooks diaries in the same chapter (LL 17/281); the Luton petition chapter 13 (Q.G.E.); the Wythes investment book chapter 14 (X 98/7).

The Wade-Gery letters quoted in chapters 10 and 11 are in the possession of Mrs W. R. Wade-Gery; the Midland Railway Board's minutes and company correspondence in chapter 4 are now at the Public Record Office.

Newspaper reports generally come from either the *Bedfordshire Times and Independent* or the *Bedfordshire Mercury*, but of other newspapers the *Railway Times* and *Herapath's Railway Journal* have been most used.

As regards printed secondary sources, I have relied most heavily on *British Railway History* by C. Hamilton Ellis and *The Railway Mania* by H. Grote Lewin.

NOTE

The 1994 edition incorporates amendments and minor corrections to the original text, also a further eight pages of photographs.

CHAPTER 1

BEFORE THE RAILWAYS

If we agree with Pope that the proper study of mankind is man, then we cannot fail to be curious about the methods employed by man to travel. Progress in methods of travel not only saved effort but helped to increase wealth, as Lord Bacon saw when he said 'Truly there are three things which make a nation great and prosperous – fertile soil, busy workshops and easy conveyance for men and commodities from one place to another'. Before the railway era transport in Great Britain depended either on water, which meant canals or rivers, or on land, which implied packhorses or wheeled traffic on inferior roads. Roads preceded the canals, but it will be more convenient to deal with canals first.

Rivers have always provided a cheap form of transport, but can be affected by floods or, conversely, can dry up. It was to obtain something more dependable that Francis, 3rd Duke of Bridgewater began, in the 18th century, to construct that system of canals which bears his name. He obtained a private Act of Parliament and secured the services of a capable engineer – James Brindley. Commencing at Worsley, near Manchester, the canals proved a success, and the system spread over the country. Brindley showed his ability by taking the Bridgewater canal over the Barton aqueduct – a forerunner of the great railway structures which we see today. On the rivers, barges and wherries had to depend on the wind for power, and it was a great step forward when towpaths were laid down alongside the canals permitting the more reliable horse power to be used. It is not surprising, therefore, to read that the canal mileage increased from 1,500 to 5,000 between 1760 and 1830. If we believe that history repeats itself, we shall not be too amazed to learn that there was a 'Canal Mania' in 1794 when twenty new canal schemes costing £3 million received Parliamentary sanction. The construction of these inland waterways required armies of workmen and for the first time we read of the 'navigators' as the men were called. The name was soon shortened to 'navvies' and they numbered in their ranks many Irish and continental workers. It must have given the British public little consolation in 1846 to know that it had all happened before, and when we read of the happenings in 1794 and after, the familiar phrases occur – 'beef and beer', 'poaching of game', 'attacks on prisons' and other disturbances of the peace. The canal promoters, like the railwaymen who followed, had to contend with shortage of labour, expensive legislation and excessive compensation for landowners.

The canals soon began to affect the life of the country. They had a great appeal to manufacturers of fragile goods because of the smooth transit – for example in the Potteries. Nearer home, the Duke of Bedford made great use of the Grand Junction canal at Leighton Buzzard. But the great prosperity of the canals was obtained at the expense of other means of transport. The owners of packhorses suffered a severe loss, and the canal companies paid enormous dividends – far larger than the greatest declared by the railways. The inland waterways made their great contribution to the prosperity of the country when they had only the waggon as a competitor. They had one great weakness – their leisurely pace. This was at best the walking speed of the horse, but it suffered when there were many locks to negotiate. When another means of communication arose, it was a case of the survival of the fastest. The canal boats' fate was shared by the stage and mail coaches.

Travel overland by coach was so expensive that only the wealthier classes could indulge in it, and it was also slow. A schoolmaster named Pennant went from Chester to London in 1739 by stagecoach and took six days to reach the capital. The Edinburgh coach took nine days on the journey to London, carrying six passengers inside and nine outside. The fare of £7 (single journey) must have been far exceeded by the cost of putting up each night at an inn. An alternative for a poor man was to go by stage waggon with wheels 14 in wide sending up dust clouds in dry weather; or if you were rich you could hire a postchaise, which would whisk you to Edinburgh in 36 hours at a cost of £70.

At the turn of the century, Telford with his new gravel roads and Macadam who laid down the modern metalled surface, had so improved stage coach travel that a great industry sprang up. Early in the 19th century it was estimated that there were 3,300 stagecoaches in existence, with an army of 30,000 drivers, guards, ostlers and horse keepers at the various stages, driving and tending the 150,000 horses required to maintain the services. The cost per mile in England was 4d or 5d – a large sum at that time – but the coaching service was fulfilling a public need and it was a safe way to travel. Despite the improvement in the road surfaces and the changing of horses every 12 miles or so, the speed of the stage coach was low – about 9 m.p.h. average. The low speed kept down casualties and on the average only three passengers a year were killed on the road. The coaches and the canal narrow boats were complementary rather than competitive. The former carried passengers and parcels; the latter took manufactured goods to the ports and carried coal from the north. Agricultural produce also went by canal.

In 1832, fourteen years before Bedford saw its first railway, Catherine Young wrote in her diary that she had left Haverfordwest by the night mail coach and had arrived in Oxford at 11.30 p.m. next day. She left Oxford at 7 a.m. on the morning following, and arrived in Bedford at 3 p.m. Her route had been via Carmarthen, Brecon, Monmouth and Gloucester. A letter which she sent on 28th July 1832 required a stamp of 1s. In 1833 Mrs Young left Bedford for London at 8.30 in the morning by the 'Times' coach 'and arrived in Bernard Street before dinner'. When in 1834 she left London by the Kettering coach, arriving in Bedford at 3 p.m., she says 'Very tired'. The journey from Cambridge to Bedford was also slow, as we see from a letter from J. D. Fitch to Theed Pearse, Clerk of the Peace, in 1843 – 'Our coaches to Bedford from Cambridge leave at 7.30 a.m., and arrive at 10.30. Will you say whether I shall be in time for the commencement of the Appeal Business?'

Public opinion is clearly shown by a statement from the wool merchants of Yorkshire in 1844, who in support of the Leeds & Bradford Railway said 'It costs as much to bring wool by waggon from Leeds to Bradford, 10 miles, as from Hull to Leeds, 58 miles by rail'. Bedford had been served by a large number of daily coaches going to all points of the compass. When the London and Birmingham Railway was opened in 1838 many coaches were taken off. One of the last to survive was the Bedford 'Times' coach, but it survived only a week after the Bedford Railway had commenced its operations on 17th November 1846.

Needing faster, cheaper and more reliable transport, the country had taken to the railways. The great railway age had arrived.

CHAPTER 2

THE FIRST THREE LINES: LONDON & BIRMINGHAM;
BEDFORD; DUNSTABLE

The Liverpool & Manchester Railway, opened 1830, showed the way England was to go. The Stockton & Darlington Railway had indeed been in operation for five years, but it was still chiefly a mineral line, and now it was the turn of the big cities. Manchester needed faster transport to bring in the cotton and to take out the manufactured goods. Liverpool was a port with an increasing capacity for shipping; a railway connecting the two was an obvious necessity. The interests of the big cities could be served by (to quote L. T. C. Rolt) 'Self-propelled vehicles of great weight covering long distances at high speed on rail-prescribed courses'. The business-houses of London wished to be connected with the ports of Bristol and Southampton and with the manufacturing centre of Birmingham. Thus by 1833, the two Rennies and Robert Stephenson had surveyed rival routes between London and Birmingham and were waiting the decision of the Board of Directors. The Board cautiously engaged another engineer of repute, J. U. Rastrick (who later built the London & Brighton Railway) to give his opinion on the two proposed routes, and he eulogised Stephenson's by saying 'Let nothing deter you from executing the work in the most substantial manner and on the most scientific principles so that it may serve as a model for all future railways and become the wonder and admiration of Posterity'.

Later in the same year Robert Stephenson staked out the route, and before the first train ran, five years later, he was to walk the distance between London and Birmingham fourteen times. The first turf was cut near Chalk Farm in 1834 and the railway is of particular interest to Bedfordshire because it came so close (its station just across the border in Linslade was called Leighton Buzzard) and the branches it threw off from Bletchley in 1846 and Leighton Buzzard in 1848 were the first lines to serve this county.

It cost the company £500,000 just to get their bill through Parliament and to buy off opposition, and work all along the line started in 1835, employing 20,000 men. Such a vast number of navvies made a great impact on the peaceful countryside, and one of the worst affected villages was Kilsby where the great tunnel was made. In the end the villagers rose against the 'invaders' to cure the worst abuses. Another battle was fought at Wolverton where Stephenson wished to bridge the Grand Junction canal. The bridge was built at Christmas when the canal men were enjoying themselves elsewhere, but the structure was torn down on discovery. However, the railwaymen triumphed when the Court of Chancery granted an injunction against the canal owners. When this part of the line was under construction Robert Stephenson used to stay at the *Cock Inn*, Stony Stratford.

Landowners were in a peculiar position; they might oppose railways from fear of despoliation of the amenities of their estates, or they might invest heavily in the company and welcome the line. Furthermore, there was always the possibility of making some profit by selling materials to the contractors, as we see from this letter to E. Crocker, the Duke of Bedford's Steward at Woburn, from W. G. Adam, the Agent-in-Chief in London, dated 27th November 1835:

'The Duke asked me today whether I had heard of the great demand for timber which the Birmingham Railway had created – that he understood they bought all sorts at a very liberal price and desired me to write to you to say that he thought you should take Ireland through the Woods etc, and see whether this demand could not be made the means of clearing the woods and selling what might not go off readily in other ways.

'I said that we had had some communication about the Railway – but that I did not understand that it was to such an extent. It appears that the Duke speaks from Lord Holland's information and he from Swaffield. And if I understand correctly Swaffield had been dealing. At all events the Duke seemed to think that this was an opportunity. Will you therefore make further enquiry so as to be able to satisfy his Grace and examine the wood carefully with Ireland to see whether you can make any sales particularly of inferior articles.'

The London & Birmingham attracted the attention of the artist J. C. Bourne, who spent day after day watching the engineers at work and sketching their achievements. His pictures were at the Museum of Transport at Clapham. By 1838 the railway was almost ready for opening – except for the dread Kilsby tunnel which had ruined contractors through its hidden quantities of sand and water. Until this great tunnel was completed, trains ran from Euston to Denbigh Hall, just north of Bletchley, where passengers alighted and travelled to Rugby by horse-drawn coach. Here they re-entered a train and proceeded to Birmingham. Robert Stephenson took over the tunnel works, and by 17th September the line was opened throughout from London to Birmingham (Curzon Street). The Leon family, who owned Bletchley Park, have recorded all this in a plaque in the railway bridge which crosses Watling Street near Bletchley. The site of Denbigh Hall was commemorated by an inn on the road and by a signal box on the railway. Both have now gone.

The great works at Kilsby and Roade had increased the cost of the line from the estimated £2,400,000 to £5,500,000, and although this was a burden to the shareholders, the greatest price was paid by Robert Stephenson, whose health was undermined by five years' mental and physical strain.

From September 1838 then, the inhabitants of south-west Bedfordshire could count themselves fortunate as having access to one of the great trunk routes of the country, and Leighton Buzzard station was well patronised from the first. The townsmen of Bedford however were less content as they had to make their own way to the station known as Bletchley and Fenny Stratford, sixteen miles distant. To add to their discomfiture, neighbouring county towns were already enjoying the new mode of travel, for the Northern & Eastern Railway had reached Hertford in 1843 by means of a branch line from Broxbourne, and the same company (now leased to the Eastern Counties Railway) began to serve Cambridge as from July 1845.

It was only to be expected, therefore, that local tradesmen were anxious to form a company to construct a railway to serve Bedford by a branch from the nearest main line. They therefore looked to the London & Birmingham, as a branch line to Bletchley would be only 16 miles in length. As the railway was to run through the estates of the Duke of Bedford he was actively involved. Thus the Bedford Railway Company was formed in 1845 with Theed Pearse junior as Secretary, the capital being £125,000.

This letter from T. Bennett (the Duke of Bedford's Steward at Woburn) to C. Haedy (the Duke's Agent-in-Chief in London) dated 22nd July 1840, shows that the idea was already in the air five years earlier. Elger was a Bedford builder.

'I met with Mr. Elger today at Bedford, and had some conversation with him as to this being a good time for selling Building Ground in Bedford or not . . . Mr. Elger says that should the Railway go on, it is impossible to say what alteration may take place in the value of property in the Town; and upon the whole . . . he thinks that persons who can hold their property should not bring it into Market just at this time.

'There was a meeting held yesterday about the Railway, and the project was most favourably entertained by the Meeting. Mr. Whitbread advocates it most strenuously, and will offer every support he can to it, and so also do many other proprietors on or about the Line. I think that if the Manchester people make up their minds that a second line of rail is required, they will carry it, and if Bedford does not take advantage of the Line, some other Town probably will.

'Northampton at this time is a deplorable instance of refusing to have a great Line passing through or near a Town. They are just as much shut out from the great thoroughfare as Woburn is – with this difference, that Northampton might have had it and did not see the advantage, and now they would give anything to get it when they cannot.'

The reference to Northampton is interesting. The London & Birmingham line missed Northampton, and this was due to the energetic tactics of the Duke of Grafton and Sir William Wake. It was this damaging form of obstruction that Bennett was anxious to avoid. Four years later, the wave of speculation known as the Railway Mania was just beginning and several schemes affected Bedfordshire. Bennett refers to some of these in his letter to Haedy dated 12th May 1844:

'Bedford was quite alive yesterday about Railways – it appears the Birmingham people are determined on a branch from Bletchley (near Fenny Stratford) to Bedford, the Terminus about the Infirmary, [for which] the late Mr. Gotobed's field or one of the Duke's will probably be chosen. The line then proceeds through Kempston, Wootton, Marston, Lidlington, tunnel through Brogborough Hill, come out about Holcut, over the lower part of Aspley to Wavendon and Sympson and Bletchley.

'The Northern line are also surveying from Bedford, Terminus to be near the House of Industry, to cross at Goldington to Cople Meadows past Willington Manor House and Church in a direct line to meet the Rail at Girtford. Then the Direct London & Manchester people are again in the field by St. Albans, Luton, Bedford etc. This line touches upon the Duke's Estate at Maulden, St. Leonards, at the end of Oakley on the Clapham side, then again at Souldrop – so if they all go on we shall have Railways as common as Turnpike roads.'

The letter refers to three railways. The first is the Bedford railway which in the event did not tunnel under Brogborough but went further south; the Great Northern did not in the end build their Bedford branch, and the Direct London & Manchester was never constructed.

The decision of the Board of the Bedford Railway to choose a route south of that originally planned is recorded in a letter from Bennett to Haedy on 8th August 1844:

'The line for the Bedford-Bletchley Rail is now set out to Brogborough Hill from Bedford to the Duke's Lidlington Estate. It is most objectionable, and one which I think should be most strenuously opposed by his Grace, for I cannot see any advantage any other part of the property will get to compensate for the way in which Lidlington Great farm will be cut up. Instead of taking a direct line from Bedford they go south to the race meadow and keep on that (the southern) side of the vale, considerably to the south of Marston church, and in Lidlington village nearly touch upon Mr. Thomas' rick yard. By this line I presume they get more easily through Brogborough Hill, but they pass through much more valuable land almost all the way. I suspect this circuitous line is in some measure to get away from Mr. Littledale who has built a large house [at Kempston] and Mr. Stewart who is building now, but this latter ought not to weigh with them because Mr. S. had not commenced building when the line was projected. Whatever their object may be, I think some means should be taken to ascertain if the present line is what they intend to apply to Parliament for.'

The real reason was, of course, that it was much cheaper to take the line through a deep cutting to the south than to bore a tunnel through the hill to the north. That the owners of land stood to gain by the coming of the railway is borne out by another letter from Bennett to Haedy written on 6th December 1844, which deals also with a proposed Ely to Bedford Railway.

'Mr. Pearse said this would make a wonderful change in the value of the riverside property at Bedford, but even the Bletchley line will do this, and that the Bedford merchants to spite the navigation are promoting the Bletchley line most strenuously without forseeing the effect.

'Evidently this allusion was, that the terminus being at St. Leonards, the Depot for Coals and Merchandise coming from the Birmingham line, will naturally be formed there, and that will become the business part of the town for what is now done at the Riverside. It is true they are to have a main way from the terminus to the River, but it will not answer to put the Coals in boats to carry down a few hundred yards and then to carry them on their wharfs. The labour of this will beat them, so will carting from the Rail to their wharf. If the Ely line goes on, then all carriage both from the east and west must centre there so that the St. Leonards property has the prospect of being immensely improved in value. Mr. Gotobed's field will be required for these purposes also.'

Although the Ely line was not constructed, St Leonards (the present St John's station) became a business centre as forecast by Bennett. He refers again to the Bletchley line when writing to Haedy on 24th January 1845:

> 'I understand the Ely & Bedford people have abandoned their projected line to Bedford, and intend only to try and get one to Huntingdon . . . and before the Bletchley Line is too far advanced, it strikes me that the Duke should ask them . . . to give some proper assurance that they will give us a station either in the parish of Ridgmont, Crawley or Aspley . . .'

Meanwhile the Duchess of Bedford had performed the ceremony of cutting the first sod, approximately at the half-way point, Husborne Crawley. The customary silver spade was used and a wheelbarrow made from oak grown on the Bedford estate. Writing to Haedy from Park Farm Office on 12th November 1845 Bennett once more shows his interest in land values:

> 'I think that they are so anxious to get possession, [that] the landowners may rather dictate their own terms as to payment than submit to the dictation of the Company. All public bodies are disposed to carry things with a high hand, and the only way is to keep them out of possession until we are satisfied.'

The following letter from Bennett to Haedy dated 21st November 1845 is interesting because of the local people mentioned, for example, Mr Swaffield, the founder of the well-known firm of estate agents in Ampthill. Bennett also refers to the branch to the river and to the extension of the Bedford railway to Cambridge, surveyed by Robert Stephenson in 1845, and rejected in Standing Orders in 1846.

> 'I have received the notice to take part of the Misses Gotobed's field for the Railway and I shall be happy to render Mr. Cuming every assistance in forwarding the interests of the ladies.

> 'Mr. Cuming has appointed to come to me on 25th; he has been much engaged on some other lines. Mr. Swaffield has been employed by several parties on the Line and as he was raw at the Trade he came to me for advice, which I was glad to give him, and amongst other things I read over to him Mr. Wing's letter on the subject. This gave him greater confidence to engage with an experienced hand like Mr. Sanders. In return for the hints he had from me, he has given me the result of his dealings and I find that Mr. Sanders has for the Company acted liberally, and I think takes very sound and proper views, though in some cases when imposition is intended (Colonel Leclercq to wit), he has been very firm and decided and has directed the Company's Agents to hand over the amount claimed to the Accountant General in order to have the sum assessed by a jury.

'I apprehend as soon as Mr. Cuming has been here, there will be no difficulty as to the farming land, but in the conversation I have had with Mr. Sanders he appeared thereon struck at the prices I told him were made of building ground at Bedford, and I requested him to ask Mr. Pearse what *his* experience was in such matters.

'The station will still be at St. Leonards. In giving the Notice, Mr. Pearse informed me that the application for the site of the station would remain unmade at present, because until they know whether they get the "Extension to Cambridge" Act they do not know how much station room they require. They therefore at present stop the main line abruptly at St. Leonards, and the line crossing the New Road and going through Misses Gotobed's field is the branch to the River only and is not to be *the* terminus – or what may probably be the Central Station for the "Second Derby".

'With respect to the price to be asked for Misses Gotobed's and the Duke's adjoining Land all of which I consider most desirable for building and for sites for business, I think we may expect to get after the rate of Twelve Hundred pounds an Acre, and my reason is that for the St. Paul's Land we obtained that Sum, and we know that many Lots were resold at an advance of 50 per cent, and some of the low priced back ground is, I believe, worth nearly double what it sold for. Then the late Mr. Palmer's field averaged about 6d. per foot which is £1089 per Acre. There was only one frontage and a great depth. It is true that 2 Lots only fetched 3¾d. per foot, but that was because it was well known Mr. Tacy Wing wished to have it and purchasers did not bid against him. The adjoining lots sold for 6½d. and 8d. per foot. Now Misses Gotobed's field has two frontages, and if we take two frontages each 100 feet deep at shilling per foot and the back ground at sixpence or even fourpence it will come to about the price I say.'

By February 1846 negotiations were well advanced and the purchase price of the ground had been agreed. Thomas Bennett negotiated the sale on behalf of the Duke, and eventually agreed on £1,000 an acre. The Duke of Bedford received £4,756 11s, and his tenants £243 9s, making £5,000 in all.

The construction of the railway proceeded during the winter of 1845 and the spring and summer of 1846. This work could not develop without money and calls on the shareholders were made from time to time, as shown by this notice in the *Bedfordshire Times* for 27th December 1845:

'Bedford and London & Birmingham Railway
2nd call of £5 per share

Notice is hereby given that the Directors have this day made a second call of £5 per share on every share in this undertaking and have ordered and appointed that the same be paid on or before 24th day of January next to Thomas Barnard Esq., Banker at his bank, St. Paul's, Bedford, or to Messrs. Glyn Hallifax Mills & Co., bankers, at their banking house, Lombard Street, London.

Interest at the rate of £5% per annum will be charged upon the amount of calls remaining unpaid from the said 24th day of January next, to the time of actual payment.

Dated this 23rd day of December 1845
by Order of the Directors
Theed Pearse Jnr. Secretary'

The terrain between Bedford and Lidlington is flat, but between Lidlington and Ridgmont stations the line had to climb Brogborough hill, and this involved a gradient of 1 in 105 – a serious encounter for the weak engines of the period. Thereafter the gradients are easy, but an added obstacle to railway operating was, and is, the number of level crossing gates to be worked, fifteen in sixteen miles. The architecture of the station masters' houses and the cottages for the crossing keepers was of a pleasing half-timbered design. A less satisfactory feature was the saving of money by building very low platforms which, at Millbrook, Lidlington and Ridgmont are still something of a hazard for older people.

By October 1846 the line was ready for inspection, but heavy rains caused earthworks to slip so that the opening day was postponed until 17th November 1846. The Victorians celebrated the opening of their railways with gusto, and these are described in chapter 8.

The new route to London from Bedford attracted the custom it deserved. It was 2½ hours by train, 3rd class 5s 3d, compared with 4½ hours by coach, fare £1 1s.

Catherine Young, whose experiences of coach travel are given in chapter 1, was now the wife of the Reverend George Maclear, the Chaplain to Bedford Prison. Her diary tells us a good deal about ordinary life in Bedford, and we see the difference the railway made.

'Tuesday 17th November 1846 – the railroad opened

Thursday 19th November – Walked to the station

Friday 18th December – George went to Bletchley to meet Isabel and brought her home.'

By 1848 the stations in Bradshaw were Bedford, Marston, Lidlington, Ridgmont, Woburn, Fenny Stratford and Bletchley. No additional stations were built, but in 1905 there was a burst of activity among railway companies along their branch lines in an effort to combat the new menace of road competition. The idea was to open halts and to have 'motor trains' serving all stations and halts frequently. These were opened as follows: Kempston & Elstow; Kempston Hardwick; Wootton Broadmead; Wootton Pillinge; Husborne Crawley; Aspley Guise; Bow Brickhill. As these halts were at ground level, special coaches were built fitted with steps which swivelled round at the halts to allow passengers to mount. With the steps in this position the brake was fully applied and could not be released until the steps had folded back close to the side of the coach.

During the 1939–45 war the Kempston & Elstow, Wootton Broadmead and Husborne Crawley halts were closed and never re-opened. Wootton Pillinge was renamed Stewartby in 1935.

Two years after the inauguration of the Bedford Railway the county witnessed another opening. The London & North Western Railway (successors to the London & Birmingham in 1846) were naturally anxious to develop their system as much as possible. They already were connected with Aylesbury (1839), Northampton (1845) and Bedford (1846); they had also proposed a branch from Wolverton to Newport Pagnell (1845) although this was postponed for twenty-two years. The Dunstable railway running from Leighton Buzzard to Dunstable would enable them to tap the traffic in south Bedfordshire, and the branch was opened on 1st June 1848.

The Dunstable Railway left Leighton Buzzard in a southerly direction with a sharp curve to the east, all on a fairly steep gradient. This made very hard work for locomotives hauling trains of wagons loaded with chalk from the direction of Stanbridge. However there was worse to come for trains going to Dunstable, as the town lies in the Chilterns, and had to be approached by a formidable gradient of 1 in 40 (in parts) which was also a test of engine efficiency. An intermediate station, called Stanbridgeford, was opened between Leighton and Dunstable and became fully operational in 1860. Although the platforms were of wood and the station was nearly two miles from Stanbridge on one side and Totternhoe on the other it occasionally became very busy. This was when Volunteer Regiments had a field day. Otherwise it was always very quiet.

The line to Dunstable was a pretty and a useful branch. Freight traffic, particularly chalk, was always good, but passenger traffic fluctuated. In the days of 'workmen's tickets' early morning trains were well filled, and towards the end of its days, football matches in Luton on Saturdays would fill the trains. There were seven level crossings on the branch, unimportant in 1848, but the cause of much trouble today. The train services will be found in Appendices A5 and A6.

CHAPTER 3

THE GREAT NORTHERN

The Great Northern was a late-comer, and had to fight for both its construction and survival. The Great Northern Railway Bill was bitterly opposed by the London and North Western Railway, by the Midland and by the Eastern Counties. At the outset there were two companies, and the Direct Northern Railway and the London & York were foes in the early 1840s, but combined in the face of the formidable opposition. When the line was built it served few large cities – the first was Peterborough, 76 miles from the Maiden Lane terminus, and then there were only Lincoln and Retford before York was reached by the grace and favour of other lines. The Great Northern was superbly built, which is hardly surprising as William Cubitt was the engineer and Thomas Brassey the contractor. The company were fortunate in having an able chairman in Edmund Denison, MP, who appointed Cubitt after Joseph Locke had had to resign the appointment, partly because he was busy building lines in France.

While the Direct Northern and the London & York were still in competition, they are mentioned in the Bedford Estate correspondence. The Woburn Steward, Thomas Bennett, wrote to the Agent-in-Chief on 19th April 1844:

'I had only heard that there were two Lines of Rail proposed to York, and a branch among others to Bedford – but I have heard nothing of the merits of the competing lines – the Biggleswade people will undoubtedly make the best fight they can to obtain their line and so will the others; the 17 miles of saving distance is a trifle in favour of the short line, if the longer one should be a much cheaper one to make – as all persons (or at least the great majority) are now aware if a Line of Rail is to go through a Country the more closely it approximates their property or business the better for them. No doubt each line will have its supporters.'

The next letter, written nine days later, hints at the struggles which went on below the surface:

'I saw Mr. Fowler solicitor of Huntingdon yesterday, who appears to be interested in the direct Line of Rail to the North – he had been to Hitchin; Lord Dacre has taken the Biggleswade line favourably Mr. Radcliff holds aloof, but I suppose he will come in; Mr. Hawkins supports it. Mr. Fowler was anxious to see Mr. Tycho Wing as the proposed line will go near to Stibbington . . . '

In 1844 the Direct Northern Railway ordered their engineer, Sir John Rennie, to survey a route which went through Hitchin, Biggleswade, Sandy and St Neots. A year later another survey was made by John Miller who planned to go a mile east of Rennie through Letchworth, then to Biggleswade and Sandy, but a mile west of the 1844 route in order to serve Eaton Socon. Also in 1845 the board of the London & York instructed Samuel Hughes, their engineer, to plot a route and he chose more or less the final Great Northern path except that after Hitchin he wanted to go through Henlow, skirt Biggleswade to the west and come in again at Sandy. In this part of England then, he and Cubitt agreed very well. It was in 1846 that the two companies amalgamated and secured the Great Northern Railway Act of 1846. A letter dated 6th December 1844 from Bennett to Haedy is therefore pertinent:

'Mr. P. [Theed Pearse, the Bedford solicitor] informs me the York and the Direct Northern Lines are about to join, and thinks it is most probable the Girtford branch will come to St. Leonards. He says he has no knowledge of the Bedford and Ely promoters but thinks the professional men are respectable. I asked his opinion of it as a speculation to which he replied it would do the proprietors no good, and ruin the Navigation. He also expressed alarm at some obstruction likely to be formed to the passage of water in flood times by crossing the vale oftener than in his opinion was necessary.

'I suggested if the Navigation and Mill interests could be satisfactorily arranged and to be cleared away, whether his opinion would remain the same. He said certainly not, that he had thought of such a thing but it appeared too visionary. I laughed, and as he is of a speculative turn, I said "nothing in these days was too visionary". I then stated to him my views and opinions as to the great effect to be produced by the complete drainage of the whole vale of the Ouze and the great local and public advantage to be gained by the increased extent to land to be brought into cultivation, causing a great demand for labour and increase of food; the two grand things we must call for with so large a population. He said he had never looked at it in such a light but thought it a subject of very great importance, and one that ought not to drop without further enquiry and examination.'

When in time the Great Northern Railway obtained their Act, they rendered most of the Ely and Bedford line unnecessary, and we hear no more of this company. A letter from Bennett to Haedy dated 3rd January 1845 again shows the Estate's attitude to the various lines:

'The Duke gave me this morning all the Notices for Beds. Railways which have been forwarded to him – also the forms of Assent or Dissent. They are –

One from the Dunstable & London Branch – it touches a small piece of His Grace's land in Totternhoe. It is of little personal interest to His Grace, but as the Dunstable people are anxious for the Rail there is no objection for the Duke giving assent to it.

Four forms from the London & York. The Duke is favourable to the Main Line and has signed, or will sign, a Memorial to the Board of Trade (which Mr. Whitbread is getting up) to this effect, but these forms are in respect of the Branch from Girtford to Bedford, which is objectionable as at present proposed. I am of opinion the Duke should dissent from the Branch Line as now proposed.

Two from the Direct Northern. This branch is better for Bedford than the other. It is probable in this case His Grace will dissent or be neuter, as he cannot be a supporter of both Main Lines to York.

One from the Ely & Bedford. This may be a case in which to remain neuter.'

As the Duke of Bedford was a shareholder in the Bedford Railway (Bletchley to Bedford) which had its terminus at St Leonards, he wanted any other branch line entering Bedford to form an end-on junction at St Leonards. This would greatly increase the importance of the Bedford Railway and give an outlet to the East. The London & York Railway's branch from Sandy would have terminated in St Cuthberts which would have given passengers a long walk through the town. This explains Bennett's letter to Haedy of 12th February 1845.

'I send you a Letter which I received from Mr. Foster of Biggleswade with a copy of plan and sections of the London & York Line and Branch to Bedford . . . I think it is proper they should know any branch to Bedford not terminating in St. Leonards at the London & Birmingham Terminus will meet with the Duke's opposition.'

On 30th August 1845 Bennett wrote again. He returns with greater emphasis to the use of St Leonards station by other branch lines which might enter Bedford, and he refers to Robert Stephenson's plans for a railway linking Bedford with Cambridge. This was surveyed in 1845, and would have run through Tetworth, Waresley and Long Stow, and of course would have been an extension east from St Leonards. It was defeated in Standing Orders, and Bedford had to wait another seventeen years before a line was completed. He refers also to the Northampton Bedford & Cambridge Railway. This was surveyed by Purdon in 1845, and it would have run to St Leonards, and not to St Cuthberts as Bennett feared. The project was abandoned. The Direct London & Manchester, which also belongs to 1845, also came to nothing.

'I met Mr. Fowler of Huntingdon two days ago who is much interested in the London & York line; he professed to be (on behalf of the Company) most anxious to secure the approbation of the Duke of Bedford to their Scheme. I reminded him that Mr. Foster of Biggleswade had already had communication with us and that he had been informed that the Duke, so far as his Beds. Estates are concerned, was satisfied with their Trunk Line, but not with their Bedford Branch terminating at St. Cuthberts, and that if this was persisted in, they must expect his Grace's decided opposition to the Branch, to which Mr. Foster did not hold out any positive promise that the Terminus should be altered, but only that it *might be* . . .

'Mr. Fowler then said there was an impression that Mr. Foster was treated rather "cavalierly" by us. I said . . . he could judge for himself, and that neither disrespect nor discourtesy to Mr. Foster or the Company was meant or intended, at the same time I pointed out to Mr. Foster that by their own map . . . it did appear that Mr. Foster and the Biggleswade people only intended us to have an Eastern communication by or through their town and thence to Huntingdon and that however good a "Ruse" it may be for certain Coal Merchants to break the Line of communication at Bedford, the interests of the public are not to be sacrificed to petty Local Trade. I also said that now that the Bletchley Act was obtained, our reasons were still stronger for requiring a continued and uninterrupted communication from the West to the East, and that no Line to the East of Bedford which will not run from St. Leonards, or at least afford an easy communication with that Line, can be satisfactory to us in the west.

'You will see by the Map that a Line from Bedford to Cambridge is much better than by Huntingdon, for by Cambridge there is direct communication with Lynn, Norwich and Ipswich.

'Mr. Pearse and the Bletchley parties by their shilly shally conduct kept back their plans till the Northampton and Bedford and Cambridge Line was announced, and so far as Bedford and Cambridge are concerned we have now two lines projected. I fear if the Northampton people go on, that we may lose the continuation from St. Leonards as the Northampton will most likely act with the London & York and run into their terminus at St. Cuthberts. It is important to prevent this and an endeavour must be made to reconcile the Jealousies and Jarring Interests of the Solicitors and Engineers. This can only be accomplished by a good understanding with the different landowners interested in the Lines.

'I am of opinion from these circumstances [that] the time is now arrived when the Duke will be compelled to state his opinion and Inclinations, lest we are to be [told] hereafter "that His Grace was too late, and the time is then gone past for attending to his opinions and views".

'I learn from Mr. Sharman that negotiations are in progress for an amalgamation of the London & York, Bedford & Leicester, and Rastrick's London & Manchester. The outline is this: the London & York to make their Line to Hitchin, the Bedford & Leicester to take up from Hitchin, and the Manchester people from Leicester to Manchester, the Yorkists making a branch to Luton from Hertford, and from Shefford to Clophill and Ampthill (if Lord De Grey is so anxious to have a rail near to Silsoe as he is said to be). If this junction should proceed they will form a very strong party and Remington's Independent Line will have little or no chance of success. Provided Oakley is not more infringed upon, I believe the Junction Line is the best to support on account of its being more likely to be effectually carried out. The rest of the projected branches are originated by local Solicitors and supported by the Birmingham, or by the Yorkists, between which parties there appears to be most extreme Jealousy, but it is very foolish for parties between these Two great Lines to permit themselves to be carried away by the partisans of these contending Trunks. The best policy appears to be to avail oneself of, and take advantage of, communications on both sides.

'Interested as the Duke is in the Bletchley both by the Shares he holds and by the property he has adjoining St. Leonards, he must naturally support the Extension, unless the Northampton people have a better Line, and I think His Grace might fairly use his Influence with Mr. W. B. Higgins (who takes up the Northampton Line very warmly) to obtain his support and advise the Northampton Line to run into the Extension, unless as I said, they show a better Line, and then His Grace in that case need not hesitate to advise the Extension to give way to their opponents, securing a junction at St. Leonards.

'Mr. Pym [of Sandy] is said to dislike the Extension as it interferes with his property. I have enquired of Mr. Pearse if he knows whether the line is objectionable to Mr. Pym. Mr. Pearse says that he thinks *not* on personal grounds, but as an anxious promoter of the London & York, Mr. Pym with the Company are opposed to the Extension. If Mr. Pym's opposition is not personal but only as one of the London & York promoters, I should think that may be got over, and for the sake of securing the Extension, and for promoting the general public utility I think the Duke might be recommended to give his Sanction to the London & York; Bedford & Leicester; and Rastrick's Manchester, in preference to Remington's Independent Manchester.'

However, in spite of everything the Great Northern Railway Act was passed on 26th June 1846, and among the directors was F. Pym of Sandy. The branch line to Bedford:

'shall commence by a junction with the said main line in the said parish of Sandy and shall pass through Sandy, Beeston, Girtford, Blunham, Northill, Moggerhanger, Willington, Cople, Cardington, Eastcotts, Goldington, St. Cuthberts Bedford . . . and shall terminate at or near a street called Back Street in the said parish of St. Cuthbert.'

By the time the Bill was passed it had cost the company £432,620, and as Brassey, the contractor, said 'it cost less than this to build the whole of the Turin-Novara Railway in Italy'.

Then began the almost interminable job of negotiating with the landowners on the route for the purchase of the land and buildings. The Railway Company had, of course, compulsory powers, but they were used with discretion, for there was no point in making enemies unnecessarily. Over a distance of 14 miles, from Hitchin to Sandy, there were 126 separate parcels of land. Where the track went right through buildings, it was usual to have them re-erected nearby.

The solicitors acting for the Great Northern Railway in London were Baxter Rose & Norton of Westminster, who had their agents in this county. The first action to be taken by solicitors was to send out a statutory notice of their intention to use certain lands, which were specified on the copy plan and schedule lodged with the Clerk of the Peace at Bedford. Each owner was required within twenty-one days to deliver at the office of Messrs. Baxter Rose & Norton a statement in writing giving the particulars of their estate, and the amount of money they claimed as compensation for the value of the lands, and of any injury and damage.

The owner of the property generally consulted his solicitor, and then used an estate agent to determine the value of the land or buildings, and the injury or damage he was likely to suffer.

S. B. Edwards of Arlesey Bury Farm first got in touch with his solicitor, Mr T. Hine of Bedford, who wrote to Baxter Rose & Norton on 4th March 1847:

'S. B. Edwards, Esq., the landlord intends claiming for the farm house and homestead to the east of the intended line . . . You will therefore oblige me by stating by return of post what are the views of the Directors . . .

'I shall take it for granted that my neglect to claim for the same shall be no barrier to a claim at a future day.'

Mr Swaffield, the Ampthill auctioneer and estate agent, was called in by Mr Edwards, and he obtained an estimate from J. T. Wing, the Bedford architect, for the work to be done:

'*Arlesey Bury Farm*

I estimate the expense of building the house and homestall on the Bury Farm at Arlsey the property of Samuel Bedford Edwards Esq., providing all new materials and giving the same accommodation as at present afforded to be placed on a different site at £2,174.

For rebuilding Mr. Edwards' private homestall as above at £560.

For removing the Hermitage homestall and building one new cottage at £260.

Jos. Tacy Wing, 6th March 1847'

It is evident that the line is going right through the farm and the Company will have to provide fresh accommodation. However, while negotiations proceeded, Mr Edwards died. His claim was pressed by his Trustees, but disputed by the Company, who had appointed W. T. Nash, a valuer of Royston, to act for them on local matters. We therefore have a second estimate for the same work:

'To William Thomas Nash Esq.

I hereby propose and agree to take down, remove and rebuild the farm house and buildings, fences and gates forming the farm homestall at Arlsey held by Mr. Inskip together with all the inside fittings and including digging and bricking a well 30 feet deep and boring the same 120 feet deep for the sum of £1,350 and also to take down remove and rebuild the Hermitage Barn stable and bullock house for a further sum of £120 the whole to be left in good tenantable state of repair.

Witness my hand this 15th day of May 1847
Luke Gimson, builder, Royston'

A letter from Baxter Rose & Norton, dated 7th July 1847 refers to the difference of opinion, and the appointment of an umpire:

'3 Park Street,
Westminster

W. T. Nash, Esq.   7th July 1847
Dear Sir,

re S. B. Edwards' Trustees

Mr. Hubbard, the acting Trustee of Mr. S. B. Edwards's Estate has been with us as to the difference between your estimation of value and that of Mr. Swaffield and as the Lands Committee are very anxious to avoid having recourse to a Jury if possible they have instructed a London surveyor wholly unconnected with the Company to proceed to Arlsey to make a special report. We are directed to beg of you to furnish us by return of post with the detailed particulars of your valuation with a full statement of your views on the subject, containing such information as it is desirable to place before this gentleman to enable him to arrive at a proper conclusion.

Baxter Rose & Norton'

Nearly eighteen months later agreement had been reached between the Great Northern Railway Company and the Trustees not only on the Arlesey Bury Farm, but also on all the other parcels of land which were being disturbed by the construction of the railway.

'The purchase money for the said land and hereditaments is to be £3,280.

'The sum for the removal and rebuilding of the buildings standing upon the land numbered 72 is to be £450.

'The sum for slating and tiling of the Hermitage House and buildings (now only thatched and will be endangered by fire from the near vicinity of the said railway) and for putting up 6 feet high fence between several premises to be £250, and lastly for residential injury – £1,320 making altogether £7,000, Which it is hereby also agreed shall include compensation for damage to be done to the remaining estate which could have been awarded by a Jury under the provisions of the several Acts of Parliament made in this behalf.'

The company agreed to make and maintain several crossings.

Legal and valuation work increased considerably with the coming of a railway, and many professional people wished to share in this temporary prosperity. W. T. Nash, the Royston valuer who has been mentioned above, originally wrote to the Board of the Great Northern Railway and was told to call on Baxter Rose & Norton, but on 1st March 1847, after his visit, they wrote to him:

'Immediately after . . . seeing you . . . we received directions from the Board to forward all the notices and other information relating to the district between Sandy and Hitchin to Mr. Woolley of Collingham Manor, Newark.'

Nash wrote again to the solicitors, only to be told on 4th March:

'We duly received your favor of the 3rd but the subject is one entirely for the consideration of the Board.'

Not easily put off, Nash wrote direct to the Secretary of the Great Northern Railway, who replied on 6th March:

'I have to acknowledge receipt of your letter of 5th with an enclosure, being copies of correspondence relative to your employment as a Land Valuer on behalf of this Company, and the same shall be laid before the Directors at the first opportunity as you request

I. R. Mowatt, Secretary'

Nash's initiative was successful, and on 1st April 1847 his appointment as valuer was confirmed.

If the acquisition of privately owned land brought complications, the purchase of common land brought them tenfold. It became usual for a committee to be formed by those having an interest in the common land; thus the Arlesey Common Committee wrote to W. T. Nash on 9th July 1847 asking him to treat direct with the Committee in the future. There was also a large common at Biggleswade and the Committee appointed wrote to Nash on 12th July as follows:

'*Great Northern Railway and Biggleswade Commoners*
The following persons having been duly appointed a Committee to treat with the Company herein pursuant to the Lands Clauses Act, we shall thank you to treat with them so that a contract may be forthwith entered into:

'William Hogg. Robert Lindsell. John Nathaniel Foster. William Pope. Charles Nash.'

One of Nash's correspondents was John Ransom, a miller, and a member of the Society of Friends.

'15th April 1847

John Ransom takes the liberty of informing T. W. Nash that he has deputed S. Swaffield of Ampthill Park to settle his claims on the Great Northern Railway. S. S. will expect to hear from T. W. N. when he is to attend to the business.'

'29th July 1847

Respected Friend,
We have signed the agreement as thou wilt see after inserting a provision against any support of the bridge being placed in the mill stream. The copy having thy signature should have the same words inserted and is for that purpose returned.'

The cost of purchasing the land was heavy. In 1847 Rowley Son & Royce of Royston dealt with sixty-seven owners of land and property and settled their claims for £34,000; Samuel Swaffield of Ampthill handled the claims of thirteen owners between Little Barford and Ippolitts and settled for £23,772.

Apart from purchasing the site of the line itself, the company could, and did, serve notices on owners of adjoining land when it was necessary to make a temporary road from the highway to the railway. Heavy and bulky construction materials might be wanted and the easiest way to get them to the contractor could well be to make a road direct to where he was then working. This notice, served in 1849, helps us to realize the disturbance to ordinary life that the coming of a line could cause.

'The Great Northern Railway Company do hereby give you notice, that under the powers of an Act of Parliament passed in the session held in the 9th and 10th years of Her present Majesty intituled "An Act for making a railway from London to York . . ." the said Company intend at the expiration of ten days from the service of this notice . . . to enter upon the lands described, referred to in the plan annexed, and coloured yellow, for the purpose of forming roads thereon to or from, or by the side, of the said railway.

'The said Company hereby further give you notice, that the Company are bound, within one month after their entry on the same lands . . . to pay to the occupier thereof the value of any crop or dressing that may be thereon, as well as compensation for any other damage of a temporary nature which such occupier may sustain . . . and also to pay half-yearly during their occupation . . . a rent to be fixed by two Justices in case of dispute and also within six months after they have ceased to occupy the said lands to pay to the owner and occupier . . . compensation for all permanent or other loss damage or injury which may have been sustained . . .

J. R. Mowatt
Secretary to the G.N.R.
22nd October 1849

To William Edwards owner
Joseph Cooper occupier
0 Acres 0 Rods 11 Perches in the parish of Biggleswade.'

Although the first trains on the Great Northern ran in 1850, alterations to the alignment were constant as, for example, when it was found that traffic necessitated the construction of more sidings. Some widening of the lines was made in Biggleswade in 1851 and on this occasion the claim was not for damage to property but loss of profit. It appears that Stratton Street, Biggleswade, was blocked in January 1851, and the thirsty inhabitants of the town who had been in the custom of visiting a public house kept by one George Chessum had gone elsewhere. The brewers, Cristy & Sale of Ashwell, Herts, soon took the matter up with the Company, and the Great Northern agreed to pay £1 16s a week for as long as the street was obstructed, representing the loss of profit on the sale of beer. It was not only the area of land taken, but the loss of cultivation due to severance (i.e. the residue of the fields might be too small for satisfactory cultivation) that called for compensation. However, when Raynsford's Trustees claimed £277 10s for 1a 2r 3p of land taken and severed at Arlesey in 1857, no one can suppose that any owner undervalued his loss.

The first Great Northern train left the Maiden Lane terminus in London on 7th August 1850. It was a 'Parliamentary' and covered the 76 miles to Peterborough in 2½ hours. This was a modest start, but it was the beginning of what was to become one of the best lines in the kingdom. The Great Northern, never a rich company, had to postpone the last mile or so into King's Cross until 1852. There were expensive tunnels to bore, and the building of a terminus worthy of such an undertaking. The opening day for the terminus was 14th October 1852. King's Cross is a splendid example of 19th century functional design, surviving bomb damage during the last war, and today still serving the purpose for which it was built.

Cubitt built the line well. With less money per mile at his disposal than Robert Stephenson had had for the London & Birmingham, he had to be content with gradients of 1 in 200 (Stephenson insisted on 1 in 333). But he was helped by going through the flatter part of the countryside. Coming from London, it was hard work for the engines until Potters Bar was passed, then came an easy run down to Hatfield. Over the river Mimram and the valley at Digswell went the lovely viaduct which today carries locomotives weighing well over 100 tons just as well as it did the small Sturrock engines of the 1850s. There was a 'hump' at Woolmer Green, but some fast running was possible through Bedfordshire, with another hump at St Neots.

Each railway had its own style of architecture and it is impossible not to recognise the Great Northern touch not only in the more obvious station buildings but in the small lineside workmen's cottages. Another typical Great Northern feature was the 'somersault' signal so called because its arm swivelled about a centre pivot. This was adopted at great expense after the accident at Abbots Ripton in 1876 which was caused by signals working in slotted posts being clogged by snow and remaining in the 'clear' position instead of returning to 'danger'. The apple green livery for passenger engines and the varnished teak coaches made an admirable turn out.

The southern part of the main line was commendably free from level crossings although those at Arlesey station, Everton crossing and Tempsford station have persisted. Arlesey is now (1969) being replaced by a bridge. Arlesey, Biggleswade and Sandy were original stations, with Arlesey Siding (later Three Counties) opened in 1866 and Tempsford in 1862. Train services are given in Appendices C1, C2, C3 and C4.

CHAPTER 4

THE MIDLAND COMES SOUTH

The year 1851 found Bedfordshire served by four railways of which three were within the county boundaries. The fourth, the London & North Western, came close to the south-west of the shire and by means of its two branches was serving an area bounded by Woburn, Bedford, Dunstable and Leighton Buzzard. The only main line within the county was the Great Northern, but this did not serve the county town, and Bedfordians wished to have a main line of railway running through their town. Bedford will always be regarded as a Midland Railway preserve and it would be profitable to examine the background and then the rise of the Midland.

The Midland Railway Company began as four small provincial railways which, after joining forces, decided to reach for London. The Midland Counties Railway, the Birmingham & Derby Junction Railway and the North Midland had all met at Derby. Amalgamation was the wisest policy, and the Midland Railway emerged in 1844. The tiny fourth constituent was the old Leicester & Swannington Railway which had started its life in 1832. It owed its beginning to John Ellis and George Stephenson, and its sixteen miles were devoted to the carriage of coal. The Leicester & Swannington had the wyvern of Mercia as its badge, and this the Midland adopted.

Already, in 1845 the Midland was thinking of further expansion. Leicester-Bedford-Hitchin suggested a good geographical route, and at Hitchin either the Direct Northern or the London & York would provide access to London. F. S. Williams in his *Midland Railway; its Rise and Progress*, states that the Leicester to Hitchin route was decided upon because of pressure put on the Midland Board by landowners at Market Harborough, Kettering and Bedford. Then there was the tempting iron ore traffic near Wellingborough, and south of Bedford, William Henry Whitbread was anxious to have the railway through his estate, offering the Midland land at no more than £70 an acre. However, other promoters had the same plans in mind.

During the period known as the Railway Mania three companies sent their surveyors over the Leicester to Hitchin route, while two others did the northern and southern halves respectively. In 1845, the Leicester &

Bedford Railway, with a capital of £1,500,000 plotted a line which, in Bedfordshire, would have gone through Sharnbrook, Milton Ernest, then slightly to the east of the present Midland Road station in Bedford to Medbury Farm near Elstow, and, tunnelling under Hammer Hill, would have reached Hitchin via Rowney Warren. This company's bill was rejected in the Lords; its assets were purchased by the Midland.

George Hudson's name was connected with another attempt to build a line, also in 1845. This was known as the South Midland Railway and was surveyed by Robert Stephenson. The line would have passed close to Bletsoe and Milton Ernest and then would have run into St John's station in Bedford. The bill was mangled in Parliament, and only a small branch from Irchester to Huntingdon received sanction. Again the Midland stepped in and purchased the assets.

The Midland Railway, under John Ellis, was growing fast. In 1846 the company planned its own extension to Hitchin. Hudson was the prime mover, who chose Robert Stephenson as engineer, and the latter had Liddell as his assistant. The route is an interesting one. From Cotton End the line tunnelled under Exeter Wood, past Old Rowney and New Rowney, to the east of Shefford, south of Clifton and exactly where the *Bird in Hand* public house stands today, and on to Hitchin. The capital was £2,250,000 and the bill became law. But Hudson had also wished to see the Eastern Counties Railway, of which he was Chairman, extend from Hertford to Hitchin, and when this bill was thrown out on Standing Orders, the Midland Railway Extension Act lost its value. In 1847, when the act was passed, money was becoming more difficult to raise, and so the Midland drew back, and in 1850 their powers to extend expired.

The London & Nottingham Railway plotted a line through Bletsoe and Milton Grange to Clapham Road, Bedford, but the company was wound up. Finally the Direct Northern Railway (1845) planned to build a branch from Stevenage to Bedford by way of Shefford, Deadman's Cross and Cotton End. However, the company joined the London & York Railway, and abandoned their branch in favour of the London & York's branch from Sandy to Bedford. When both companies became the Great Northern Railway, the Sandy to Bedford branch was included in their 1846 Act, and held in reserve.

In his letters Thomas Bennett, the Woburn Steward, comments on almost every railway. He refers to an important meeting at Bedford in his letter to Haedy dated 20th September 1846:

'I am glad to find that the Railway Meeting at Bedford on Friday passed off very well and the competing parties "King" Hudson and the Midland on the one part, and the Bedford & Leicester on the other, have probably seen the folly of "war to the knife" . . . The Bedford Terminus at St. Leonard's – it is in the Duke's interest to promote those lines that must come there.'

The Duke disliked any line which would run near his house at Oakley. Bennett wrote on 22nd January 1847:

'The Duke signed his Assent to the Luton & Dunstable Railway, and to the Cambridge & Bedford by Biggleswade, but to the Leicester, Bedford and Hitchin his Grace does not feel disposed to assent, on account of Oakley, although he by no means wishes to oppose the scheme . . . [but] no amount of money can compensate him for what he may consider an intrusion on the privacy of his Residence.'

When it appeared that the Midland Railway would succeed in getting their Bill through, the Duke had second thoughts. On 24th January 1847 Bennett wrote:

'I do not think the Midland Company would wish to make a station at Oakley, but I think when the Duke may be staying there, he will not like to have to go to Bedford . . . It would be always a convenience to have Fish, or parcels left in passing by. If therefore, it is of sufficient consequence, now is the time to mention it . . . get an interview with Hudson – as I dare say we can do nothing in it without the full concurrence of His Majesty.'

And two days later 'His Grace would rather no Rail came into the parish [Oakley] but if it cannot be helped, then we would like all benefit from it'.

In 1852 the outcome of negotiations between the Midland and the Great Northern was an agreement to accommodate Midland traffic at Hitchin. The route was re-surveyed by Charles Liddell and John Crossley, and when once the Act was obtained, Thomas Brassey, the greatest of the railway contractors, began construction in 1855. It is reported that John Ellis put a limit of £19,000 per mile on the cost of construction.

By 1857 the line was ready. Although called the Leicester to Hitchin extension, the line began at Wigston Junction, 3·2 miles south of Leicester. The track between Wigston and Leicester was part of an 1840 extension to Rugby. Brassey had built the 63 miles for £1 million, a low figure, and in keeping the cost down followed the contours laid down by Liddell. The road was a very hard one to work for steam locomotives as there were four summits approached by long inclines, including for southbound trains Sharnbrook summit, after four miles up at 1 in 120. This was so severe that when coal traffic became really heavy the Midland built separate goods lines through a tunnel at Sharnbrook, thus easing the gradients. This was part of the scheme for a new line to Nottingham via Melton Mowbray opened in 1880. After Bedford there was another steep ascent from Cardington to Warden tunnel. This was at a climb of 1 in 120. Warden tunnel itself, 880 yards long, was unpopular with enginemen if the wind was blowing from the north-west. Here, heavy goods trains would be travelling at a walking pace and the wind would blow the smoke into the cab of the engine. 'The only way to breathe', said Bert Rogers, a driver from Bedford shed, 'was to get down onto the lowest step at the side of the engine and let the loco take the train through.' The footplate was resumed when fresh air was reached, on the descent to Southill station. Luckily Warden tunnel was dry. If it had been a wet tunnel the engine wheels would have slipped and then the crew would have had to stay on the footplate.

In other ways the line was expensive. From Bedford to Sharnbrook the Great Ouse was crossed seven times; the piers of Sharnbrook viaduct reached their foundations 25 feet below the clay and there was a long brick arch viaduct at Wellingborough. The passenger service commenced on 8th May 1857 but at first passengers had to change at Hitchin on to G.N.R. trains. A better service was provided from 1st February 1858, when Midland trains were permitted to run over Great Northern metals from Hitchin to King's Cross, thus saving the trouble of changing trains at Hitchin. For this privilege, which did not permit Midland trains to pick up or set down passengers between Hitchin and King's Cross, the Midland paid the G.N.R. £60,000 annually.

When the line was ready for opening, John Ellis received the following letter from the Board of Trade after the usual inspection by their officer.

'4th May 1857
I enclose a copy of the report by Lt. Col. Yolland on the Leicester and Hitchin line, and provided only one engine in steam is allowed on the branch to the London & North Western station at Welling-borough and provided a proper passenger station is erected at Bedford within a limited time, my Lords do not object to the opening of the line for public traffic.

Douglas Galton.
Captain. R.E.'

The station which we now call Midland Road was not ready in time for the opening, and the London & North Western Railway allowed the Midland to use their station – the present St John's. Much happened before the Midland station was completed. In the *Bedfordshire Times* of 12th December 1857 arguments were put forward to decide the location of the station. St Mary's was suggested by some inhabitants and strongly urged by the parishioners. This did not at all suit Bedford's tradesmen as is shown in the minutes of the Midland Railway's Board dated 17th November 1857: 'A memorial received from certain merchants, tradesmen and inhabitants of Bedford praying that the station might be constructed on the north side of the river Ouze'. It was resolved that 'provided the Town of Bedford will assist in improving the approaches, the site of the station should be on the north side of the river'.

The minutes for 6th January 1858 reveal that the Mayor of Bedford had written to say that at a Council meeting on 16th December 1857 it had been agreed 'to widen approaches to the station by 40 feet in Well Street and to appoint a Committee consisting of the Mayor, Aldermen Clifton, Kilpin, and Hurst, Colonel Mellor, Mr Jones, Mr Tansley, Mr Bull, Mr Shelton, Mr Read and Mr Eagles to carry out the widening.'

On 18th February 1858 the Midland Board recorded their pleasure to note the progress made in Bedford, and further progress was reported by the Mayor and Mr Turnley when they called on the Midland Directors. In return for what the Council were doing in Bedford the Mayor asked the Railway Company to ease the gradients on the approach to Kempston Road bridge. The Board agreed. The station was finished at the end of January 1859 and the last Midland train to use the L.N.W. station at St John's did so on 3rd February 1859. On 3rd August 1859 the Midland Board's minutes report that property was purchased in Agar Town (near St Pancras), and so it appears that the Board were even then thinking of their own line to London.

The Midland were fortunate in having as their locomotive engineer Matthew Kirtley, who had risen from the ranks and so had a very practical knowledge of the design of steam engines. It was Kirtley who designed the engines to work the newly opened route from Leicester to Hitchin, and he built his machines so robustly that one of them, No. 158A, is now in Leicester Museum. This locomotive was built in 1866 and therefore had an active life of eighty-two years before it was withdrawn in 1948.

The Midland stations between Leicester and Hitchin conformed to a standard design. The platforms tended to be rather low, presumably for economy, and the station buildings were on the small side, of yellow brick and with lattice-type windows set in a cast iron frame. These could be seen until 1962 at Sharnbrook, Oakley, Cardington, Southill and Henlow. Shefford never had good station buildings. The platforms there were of timber, as was the booking hall, until the latter was demolished and a brick-built booking hall and parcels offices were erected in the station yard. The line was commendably free from level crossings. Train services over the years are given in Appendices B1, B2 and B3.

The extension fulfilled the hopes of its originators and it throve only too well; in fact the Exhibition traffic of 1862 demonstrated clearly that the Midland must have their own line to London. When the Hitchin line was part of the main line all was well, but on the opening of the direct London line in 1868, the Bedford to Hitchin line fell overnight to the status of a branch, even though some Midland expresses continued to run to King's Cross, since St Pancras station was not ready in time to receive the new trains. As a consequence, the original double track from Bedford to Hitchin was singled in 1912, but a reasonable service of steam 'rail motor' trains was operated for fifty years thereafter. These gave way to diesel multiple unit trains in 1960 and also some very odd four wheeled rail buses were put on. But the increasing road traffic and the burden of the 1947 and 1953 Transport Acts impoverished the line. Oakley lost its passenger trains in 1958, Sharnbrook in 1960 and Cardington to Henlow in 1962.

This line had an especial debt to William Henry Whitbread who did more than anyone else to encourage the railways to serve Bedfordshire. Above all, it was he who encouraged the Board of the Midland to come south through this county to Hitchin, and because of his work an obelisk has been erected to his memory. It stands on the Whitbread Estate close to Southill station, and could be seen from the train as it left for Shefford. The inscription reads:

'To William Henry Whitbread Esquire For his Zeal and Energy in promoting Railways through the County of Bedford. 1864. Erected by Public Subscription.'

CHAPTER 5

LUTON DUNSTABLE & WELWYN;
BEDFORD & CAMBRIDGE RAILWAY.

The fact that railway connection came to Dunstable before Luton caused little satisfaction in the latter town particularly as a scheme for a railway had been mooted since 1844. There is a relevant letter from Thomas Bennett, the Woburn Steward, to C. Haedy dated 10th May of that year. The Duke of Bedford owned land in Caddington, and Bennett was concerned about severance, i.e. the line so dividing fields that the pieces of land left are difficult to farm.

'I send you a note I have received from Mr. W. Bennett with a resolution passed at Luton as to making a Railway from that place to Leighton. I think this line is a much more feasible one and more likely to pay than that proposed from Bedford to Bletchley, and of much more use to the County and the neighbourhood – for there now exists a very considerable traffic of coals and other goods from the Grand Junction Canal at Leighton to Luton: Luton is also the great straw plait manufactory and the carriage of plait Boxes to the Rail, now that the Coaches are off, must be very great.

'As far as it concerns the Duke I do not anticipate any objection on his Grace's part. I enclose a Tracing of the plot of land in Caddington – you will see that it is entirely cut off [from] the Lewsey farm by the Road from Luton to Dunstable. If therefore it should be selected as a Station the whole of the piece would be eagerly purchased at a good price, and as his Grace has no other property in Caddington it cannot be any object to keep it, if it is wanted for any other use. Should this go on, the Duke's Estate there will have all the advantages to be derived from it, without any of the disadvantages of severance or other annoyances which occupiers are subject to, until the Fences and Fields get put in proper form again, and as from the importance of the trade of Luton, they are almost sure to have a branch either to the Birmingham Line or to the Eastern or Northern if that proceeds (indeed it is not improbable they may in time have both) yet independent of any private interest to his Grace, I think for the general benefit of that part of the County, the branch to Leighton should be encouraged as far as meeting the views of the promoters in giving consent to the sale of the ground, if it proceeds, and not offering opposition to it.'

Luton did in fact have its connection with the eastern side of the county sixteen years later.

The next day Haedy replied:

'The Duke takes the same view of it as you take, and agrees that it should be encouraged to the extent you mention, viz: by meeting the views of the promoters to the extent of consenting to the sale of the ground and not offering opposition. Beyond that it is not desirable that the Duke should go.'

A survey of the route from near Welwyn to Dunstable was made in 1845 by Samuel Hughes for the London & York Railway but the scheme was dropped by their successors, the Great Northern. However, the isolation of their town was keenly felt by Lutonians and by 1854 another project was put forward under the title of the 'Luton Dunstable & Welwyn Junction Railway'. A Bill was presented to Parliament on 16th July 1855 for a line to run from a junction with the L. &. N.W.R. at Dunstable across the road now called A5 to a second station in Dunstable at Church Street. The route lay through the parish of Caddington, near Skimpot Farm and Bury Farm to Luton. Here a station was planned in Bute Street and the line, after crossing the Hitchin road was planned to go through the parish of Breachwood Green to New Mill End crossing the Hertford-shire boundary near the *Leathern Bottle* public house. Other stations were planned for Harpenden, Wheathampstead, and Ayot.

The gradients were severe in this hilly district, being up at 1 in 94 from Dunstable to Skimpot, and down at 1 in 90 past Bury Farm, Luton. A supplementary Bill was presented in November 1855 to allow the line to take a more northerly course between the stations at Dunstable later known as 'North' and 'Town'. The promoters had the satisfaction of obtaining their Act on 7th July 1856.

In view of the Duke's interest we might expect that Thomas Bennett would mention the proposals in his letters. On 21st August 1854 he wrote to Haedy, the Duke of Bedford's Agent-in-Chief in London:

'I send you a Herts. paper containing some information on this scheme. The proposed Line . . . will touch upon Lewsey. It seems to me a matter of such importance to the District, as to be deserving the notice and support of the Duke of Bedford both in a public and personal sense.

'Luton being the first Town in the County as a place of business, it is needless . . . to say how much greater it may become . . . nor, how much the Line of Country between Luton and Dunstable . . . will improve in value.'

The L.D. & W.J.R. held its first Ordinary General Meeting at Luton on 11th October 1855. The Hon. W. F. Cowper, MP, referred to the opposition offered by the London & North Western and the Great Northern Railways, which had proved unavailing. The capital was authorised at £120,000 with borrowing powers up to £40,000. A contract for the works costing £92,000 had been let to Jackson & Bean who had subscribed one third of the capital. The directors recommended that the work between Luton and Dunstable should commence at once. The board consisted of: the Rt Hon W. F. Cowper, MP, T. Chambers, MP, J. B. Lawes, J. Waller, L. Ames and H. Thomson.

Most of these gentlemen were on the board of the Hertford and Welwyn Railway which would branch from the east of the G.N.R. main line as the L.D. & W.J.R. would to the west. The ceremony of turning the first sod took place in Luton on Thursday 25th October 1855 and the day was proclaimed a general holiday. The section between Luton and Dunstable L.N.W.R. was opened on 3rd May 1858 but after this happy event, the company began to run into financial difficulties.

As many of the leading figures had interests in both the Luton and the Hertford lines it had been decided to amalgamate the Companies which was accomplished by the Hertford & Luton & Dunstable Railway Act of 1859. It might appear that this step was the right one as the line from Luton to Welwyn Junction was opened on 1st September 1860. But alas, when the new company held a meeting at the Great Northern Hotel, London, only eighteen days later, it was disclosed that they were in debt to the contractors for the sum of £21,000. Mr Parker and Mr Whitbread suggested a further meeting on 21st October but the proposal was defeated. The obvious step was taken on 1st May 1861 which was to apply for an Act to vest the line in the Great Northern Railway which duly came to pass.

In building the station in Luton the company had to purchase land from the Marquis of Bute and the following correspondence between Charles Austin, a local solicitor, and John Cumberland, a Luton estate agent, with Thomas Collingdon, the Bute Estate's agent at Cardiff, is of interest:

'Luton, 26th July 1859

On looking over these papers it appears that £1,283 has been paid on account of this purchase: vizt. £350 which for the purpose of ad valorem duty was apportioned on the conveyance of the land to the Dunstable Road, and £933 paid as a deposit to make up one third of the whole purchase money on payment whereof possession of the whole including seven acres was given to the Company. This will leave £3,500 to be apportioned as purchase money for the ad valorem duty on the present deed . . .

'The draft conveyance is forwarded by book post which we shall be glad to have returned for engrossment.

Charles Austin.'

Austin was a solicitor in the Luton firm of Williamson & Austin, later Austin & Carnley.

John Cumberland, a Luton estate agent employed by the Bute Estate, wrote to Collingdon from Luton on 30th July 1859.

'I enclose you Tracings of the Land proposed to be offered for sale on 25th next month, also a copy of the sale Bill which is now being printed.

'I could not till today arrange with the Railway Company about the altered line at the end of Guilford Street; it is now settled, setting back from the road at the extreme point of your ground 30 feet. This is very important and adds considerably to the value of the land there – the alteration near the station is likewise a great advantage, giving now some good plots with frontages to the Upper Bute Street, which are very valuable. You will see by the tracing I propose to give these a right of way at the back from Guilford Street.

'If you approve of the Lots as laid out I will put the plans in the hands of the Lithographer. Mr Hopkins has seen them and quite approves them.

'I have not drawn out the Bill of Sale of your Cottages not know-ing whether you will offer those in Park Road in one or more Lots. On hearing from you this bill shall be printed.

John Cumberland.'

On 23rd September 1859 Williamson & Austin sent a cheque to Collingdon:

'We have received a cheque as under,

Balance of purchase money	£2566
½ yrs Interest due Michaelmas	£125 12s 8d
	£2691 12s 8d'

New Mill End, the last station in the county (going east) was renamed Luton Hoo in 1892, and Luton had the words 'Bute Street' added in 1950.

The Dunstable stations bore various names. The G.N.R. station was first known as 'Church Street' but this was changed to 'Town' in 1927. At the north end, Dunstable L.N.W.R. became 'Dunstable North' in 1950.

The Luton, Dunstable & Welwyn Junction railway consisting of nearly 17 miles of cross-country line through mainly agricultural districts was particularly vulnerable after the Beeching Report (1962). It had ceased to be Luton's principal connection with London after 1868 when the Midland line opened. The first loss was goods traffic which was diverted to Luton from the smaller stations in 1963. The passenger service was maintained by diesel multiple unit trains until 1965 when these ceased to run. However, goods traffic is still handled at Luton by virtue of a connecting link made between the two stations in 1966.

For train services see Appendix C4.

Three years before the Great Northern ran their first trains to Luton and Dunstable, a very small line was opened in east Bedfordshire. This was the Sandy & Potton Railway, which despite its short length of 3 miles, and its short life of five years, has a history of unusual interest. This little line owed its origin to Captain William Peel, the third son of Sir Robert Peel. Although the latter spent most of his life in Lancashire, the second and third sons lived in Bedfordshire. William turned to a Naval career, but he was also interested in his estate, which lay between Potton and Sandy. The opening of the Great Northern Railway in 1850, so near his land, aroused his interest. It seemed obvious that a line of his own, connecting with the G.N.R. at Sandy, would benefit his estate and his tenants, and from 1852 he began to purchase land on the west side of his estate as far as Sandy. Thus when he put his plan into operation it was not necessary to obtain Parliamentary powers, as the railway would be entirely on his own land. Construction of the 3 miles began in 1855. It curved away from the south of Sandy station and ran east as far as Deepdale, where it curved sharply to the north and climbed up to Potton at a gradient of 1 in 100. It crossed over the Sutton-Sandy road on a bridge of three brick arches.

In 1854 the Crimean war broke out and it was not long before Captain Peel was ordered to the Black Sea. His courage in action, particularly in throwing into the sea a Russian shell which had landed on his ship, earned him the newly founded decoration of the Victoria Cross. At the conclusion of the war he was given the command of the frigate *Shannon* and ordered to China. In the meantime, in England, the construction of the Sandy & Potton Railway had progressed and was ready for opening in November 1857. The Board of Trade inspector having reported favourably, the railway was opened for passengers on 9th November 1857. Captain Peel's mother, Lady Peel, performed the opening ceremony and named the locomotive 'Shannon', after the frigate. There were the usual festivities. However, Captain Peel's end was a sad one. On the way to China, he received orders to go to India where the mutiny had broken out. He distinguished himself at the raising of the siege of Lucknow and when the mutiny was quelled he looked forward to returning to England. But an epidemic of small-pox broke out in India and Captain Peel died on 22nd April 1858, and never saw his railway.

The 'Shannon' was built by the firm of George England in their Surrey works and cost £800. It hauled two coaches and there was also one wagon for goods and one brake van for the guard. The train services, which were quoted in *Bradshaw* until December 1861 are shown in Appendix C5. As will be related in the second half of this chapter, the Sandy & Potton Railway was merged into the Bedford & Cambridge railway in 1862, and between 1860 and 1862 'Shannon' was used in the construction of the new line. After 1862 the engine was sent to the London & North Western Railway Works at Crewe for shunting purposes. The next move was to the Cromford & High Peak Railway, a line of formidable gradients. Later in its life the locomotive made its final move to the Wantage Tramway which ran from Wantage Road station (on the Great Western Railway's Bristol main line) to the town of Wantage, the track being laid at the side of the road. Many of us who travelled in that part of the world in the 1920s will either have seen it at work, or else, better still, have travelled in the little train. The 'Shannon' with other engines hauled passenger and goods trains until 1925, when the passenger service ceased. Goods traffic lasted through the 1930s and during the war, but the railway disappeared after 1947. Fortunately the 'Shannon' was considered by the Great Western Railway as being worthy of preservation, and it was beautifully restored in Swindon Works. Thereafter it rested on a plinth and under a tin roof on the down platform at Wantage Road station, and there it remained until the station was closed by the Western Region of British Rail in 1965. It has now been presented to the Great Western Society at Didcot, where it can be seen in steam. More fitting would be to send 'Shannon' back to Potton where its original engine shed still stands in excellent condition on Mr Marshall's farm. Although there were only the two stations on the Sandy & Potton Railway, the driver would obligingly stop almost anywhere if an intending passenger gave the appropriate signal, such as a flag, if his house was adjacent to the railway.

Although Bedford was not in direct rail communication with Cambridge before 1862, the first of several schemes for this dates from as early as 1845. Three surveys were made in 1845 and 1846. The fourth attempt was successful and the route finally adopted was the work of Liddell & Gordon in 1858.

There is some very interesting correspondence from Dr Jacob Brooke Mountain, Rector of Blunham. The letters are undated, but were probably written in the winter of 1858–59, and they show that Dr Mountain was not attracted to the railway, but he was prepared to tolerate it provided his financial interests were protected. The correspondence is with Mr Wilkinson, his solicitor at St Neots.

'Blunham Rectory,
Saturday.

My Dear Sir,

I am informed that the projected railway through Moggerhanger is likely to take place and that it will intersect diagonally the arable fields charged with the corn rent so that the landlords will alter the present boundary fences in order to make the fields available for the plough. If so, it is quite clear that the claims of the Rector will be compromised by the operation, and unless due provision for those claims is made in the Act *at the expense of the Company* I shall feel it my duty to join in petitioning against it.

Will you be so good as to communicate with Mr. Turnley on the subject.

Yours always truly,
Jacob H. Brooke Mountain.'

Mr Thomas Wesley Turnley of Bedford was a solicitor for the Bedford and Cambridge Railway.

Another landowner was Edward Henry Dawkins of Moggerhanger House, and he wrote in December 1858 to Dr Mountain:

'I thank you for sending me Mr. Wilkinson's note which I return. I had a hasty view of the proposed line of the railway as deposited with the Clerk of the Blunham Parish. It appears to intersect 21 pieces of land belonging to me – at least my name appeared in the Schedule 21 times. I think it would be very advisable to show our *teeth*. I would readily bite if I knew on whom to fasten.'

The Rector wrote again to his solicitor:

'Blunham Rectory,
Wednesday.

I send you my map on which the proposed line of railway is slightly traced in pencil. Deviations are reserved on each side and the line branches in a "Y" to north and south leaving nearly a mile between the two junctions with the G.N.R. My name does not appear at all in the schedule, though all the other owners, occupiers and parties interested are fully enumerated.

The omission may have arisen from my telling Mr. Turnley's clerks that I have no lands in Moggerhanger Parish. I shall not be a consenting party to the railway, but I shall offer no opposition provided that they give me an equivalent security for my corn rent, and clear me from all legal and other expenses.'

Another letter helps to explain why the Rector had been omitted from the schedule.

'Blunham Rectory,
Thursday.

Mr. Dawkins tells me that the projected railway from Bedford to Cambridge runs through all the lots liable to me for the corn rent. I have had no notice, though the surveyor, Mr. Cheffins, has called to inspect the hay, and two gentlemen from Mr. Turnley's office of Bedford also called with their own map to ascertain the owners of the land; but they said nothing about the corn rent and I did not think of it.'

And lastly:

'Blunham Rectory,
Tuesday.

I am quite willing to be guided by your advice in re Railway. It is personally of no importance to me and I am only desirous to do my duty to the Living. But the unpunctual payment of the Corn Rent is an annoyance.'

Liddell & Gordon, the engineers of the Bedford and Cambridge Railway, saw their line opened on 4th July 1862, and the first passenger train on the 7th. Three days before the formal opening this notice appeared in the *Bedfordshire Times*:

'BEDFORD & CAMBRIDGE RAILWAY

The Directors are desirous of negotiating Loans upon Debenture Bonds under the powers of their Act at the rate of $4\frac{1}{2}\%$ interest per annum, payable half-yearly, on 1st January and 1st July. The Railway will be worked under a Parliamentary Agreement and the interest upon the bond debt guaranteed by the London & North Western Railway Company.

Euston 29th May 1862. W. Lang. Secretary.'

The railway ran east from St John's station (then known as Bedford L.N.W.) and crossed the Great Ouse and a tributary, with four bridges in a short distance. The Ivel was crossed after Blunham. It is doubtless the number of river bridges which decided the company to have a single line only from Bedford to Sandy, although the piers were wide enough to carry a double track. In the 1939 war although so many lines were duplicated or otherwise widened, it is strange that this stretch of eight miles was left alone, and when, in 1957, the bridges over the Eastern Region main line at Sandy were renewed at a cost of £150,000, no attempt was made to provide a second set of rails. Originally the first station to be met after leaving Bedford was Blunham, as Willington was not opened for passenger traffic until 1903. So far the line was reasonably level, but after Blunham it dipped sharply to the valley of the Ivel, and just where the railway burrowed under the Great North Road, a halt named Girtford was opened in 1938. Unfortunately the 1939 war caused a shortage of staff and the halt was closed to passengers after only two years. It would have been much easier for the railway to cross the Great Northern on the level, but the latter strongly objected and carried the day.

After crossing the Great Northern, the Bedford & Cambridge line curved south into Sandy station, so that you had the peculiar position (also occurring at Trent on the Midland) where trains going to London left the station in opposite directions. The up G.N.R. train to London went south, and the L.N.W. train with passengers for London travelled north. Hereafter the line took over the alignment of the Sandy & Potton railway, curving first sharply to the east, and then to the north with the added burden of a gradient of 1 in 100 up. Just before entering Potton the traveller could see, on the right, the old engine shed which housed 'Shannon'. All the stations so far had been reasonably near the towns and villages they served, but because of the opposition of the Turnpike Trustees at Gamlingay, this station had to be located about 1½ miles from the town. Before the train reached the next station, Old North Road, it had to climb a long 'bank' up to Hayley Woods at 1 in 105 with a similar descent to Old North Road. When the line was opened, the Old North Road was more important than the Great North Road, but in the 1870s, the very narrow bridge at Tempsford was widened, and traffic began to use the Great North. The line now crosses flat but swampy ground lying between the river Granta and the Bourn brook. There was a further station, called Lord's Bridge, before Cambridge was reached.

Although Willington station was almost wholly of timber and Blunham was partly of timber, the stations at Sandy and at Potton were fine brick structures, and the brackets supporting the roof in each case, had the letters 'B – C' cast in them to denote 'Bedford & Cambridge'.

The platforms were of normal height, and no public road was crossed on the level – a well built railway. L. & N.W. locomotives and stock were used, the former being often Allan 'Crewe' type of small dimensions. Other famous types were 'Prince of Wales' and Midland Compounds, but steam gave place to diesel power in 1960.

In its prime, the railway carried plenty of traffic; it was a useful cross-country link and before the coming of the motor lorry, an enormous vegetable traffic was conducted. Fred Chapman of Potton was goods clerk at Potton sixty-five years ago and remembered working late night after night in the summer when the carts from the various market gardeners waited in the station yard to unload their vegetables to catch the night train to Covent Garden market. The London Midland & Scottish Railway was one of the pioneers in diesel traction and a multiple-unit diesel train was run as an experiment for some months on the Oxford and Cambridge lines in 1936. During the 1939 war the branch carried very heavy traffic; passenger trains were normally of four coaches from early L.N.W. corridor stock, the locomotives being Stanier Class 5 engines or his 26xx tank engines. Freight was dealt with by the G Class eight coupled, and these, after the war, even hauled passenger trains during busy summer traffic. In 1940 the Ministry of Transport put in a spur to enable trains to run from and to the Great Northern main line. A special signal box, Sandy West, was erected and lasted until 1960. The underground petrol storage tanks adjacent to the Sandy-Potton road had special sidings built for tank wagons with another special signal box – Sandy Heath.

Regarding signal boxes on the line, the first box was where Bedford St John's No. 1 stands. Later there was No. 2, just opposite the present day bus garage, and there was one called Goldington, situated near the power station, controlling a passing loop. A few years before the war, Goldington box was closed and the loop removed; in the year 1940, No. 2 box was moved from the east end of the station to its present position by the river at Newnham. When the branch was not mentioned in the Beeching plan those of us who used it deceived ourselves that it would be immune as one of the last east-west links. There was dismay when British Rail announced their intention to close, and a great fight was put up by the various local authorities. But the 1962 Transport Act permitted an appeal only in the case of hardship – the meaning of which was to be interpreted by the relevant Transport Users' Consultative Committee and the Minister of Transport. The loss of £97,000 a year could not be challenged. There were many of us on the last train which ran on 30th December 1967. For timetables, see Appendix A4.

CHAPTER 6

THE MIDLAND REACHES LONDON;
BEDFORD & NORTHAMPTON

When, in 1858, the Midland trains began to run over the Great Northern metals from Hitchin to King's Cross, the Midland management regarded their trains as providing a main line service. Unfortunately there were only two tracks in this section of over 31 miles, and the Great Northern were beginning to fill these tracks with their own trains. The Midland, despite the sum of £60,000 a year which they paid the Great Northern, were coming to be regarded as a nuisance. In 1860 James Allport (later Sir James) had returned to the Midland as general manager, and he was not one to allow his company to exist as a second best. The junction at Hitchin was under the control of a Great Northern signalman, and his instructions, to say nothing of his loyalty, caused him to give preference to the trains of his own company. In 1862, the year of the second Great Exhibition in London, the delays assumed gigantic proportions, and 3,400 Midland trains were delayed between Hitchin and King's Cross. Of this total, 2,400 were freight trains, many carrying coal, and when on 30th June the Great Northern refused to allow Midland coal trains to stand in their sidings at King's Cross, it was inevitable that the Midland would decide to build their own line to London. They already had their own coal depot at Agar Town near St Pancras.

When the Great Northern saw that they were likely to lose £60,000 a year, they at once offered to quadruple their line between Hitchin and London. Allport countered by asking for running powers in perpetuity, The Great Northern offer was only a palliative in view of their own growing traffic, and Allport was only 'playing trains' while pushing on with his real objective – the Midland Railway London Extension. Liddell and Barlow, competent engineers, plotted the route, and the Midland Board had little difficulty in convincing Parliament that their line was essential. The Bill became law in 1863. If there was any doubt at all in the mind of the Board that they were doing the right thing, such doubt was removed by the Welwyn accident of 9th June 1866. A down Great Northern goods train came to a halt in Welwyn North tunnel owing to a failure of a boiler tube in the engine. On the Great Northern, as on other lines, semaphore signals were normally at 'clear' but were placed at 'danger' after a train had passed. As traffic was regulated on the notorious 'time interval' system, the signals were lowered again after a stipulated interval, and at Welwyn a Midland goods train following the first duly entered the tunnel under clear signals. It collided with the rear of the Great Northern train, blocking the tunnel, and as if this was not enough, soon after an up Great Northern goods train laden with meat from Scotland destined for Smithfield entered the tunnel and collided with the wreckage. The live coals which spilled from the engines' fireboxes quickly ignited the wooden trucks, and the draught through the tunnel and ventilating shafts roused the flames with frightening force. Only two lives were lost but the material damage was one of the worst in our railway history. It was thirty-six hours before a train could go through the tunnel, and the delay to Great Northern and Midland trains is better imagined than described.

The construction of the London extension was handed over to four contractors, of whom the ageing but still most able Thomas Brassey undertook the northern part, i.e. Bedford to Harpenden.

The original plans show that the line would have formed a junction with the Hitchin branch near Elstow, and would then have run southwesterly towards Chimney Corner to where the existing line now runs. This would have meant that a large number of trains would have had to cross the L. & N.W. Bletchley branch on the level – a most undesirable arrangement. A wiser re-alignment resulted in the railway as we know it. After crossing the Great Ouse, the line had to climb a 1 in 176 to clear the Bletchley branch near Cow Bridge, and it dips at the same incline soon after. Powers had to be obtained to divert Ampthill Road at this point. Near Stewartby the Midland had to demolish Magpie Hall as it was in a direct line; the farm buildings of Magpie Farm were visible thirty years ago, although they have since vanished. To reach Ampthill station you pass through Ampthill tunnel, and the original bore was the eastern one; this can be seen quite clearly from the front of a diesel multiple-unit train as the track points straight to this tunnel before curving to the right to pass through the later bore. Before 1939 the *Swan* public house at Astwood was kept by John Wooding, who when young used to walk over to Ampthill to watch the workmen digging the tunnel. A new road had to be made to reach Ampthill station which, in the early days was much more important than Flitwick. The railway has been climbing, mostly at 1 in 200 to Ampthill, but now it falls to Flitwick.

The engineers' plans show the line passing through Flitwick Wood and there was no Flitwick station until 1870. The next station was called 'Harlington for Toddington', and the road between the two villages had to be diverted. The summit is reached 15·3 miles from Bedford in a cutting at Chalton about 60 feet deep. Williams relates how teeth of an immense crocodile and many ammonites were unearthed when the cutting was being made. The line now falls at 1 in 176 to Leagrave, where powers also had to be obtained for a road diversion, and on past Dallow Farm, and so into Luton. South of Luton the line again rises to Chiltern Green where the Midland obtained powers to divert the existing Great Northern branch to Dunstable seven furlongs to the west. The line then continued through Harpenden and St Albans to St Pancras. The first traffic from Bedford, on 13th July 1868, went on the Moorgate Street line, but the new St Pancras station was ready by 1st October in that year, though nearly five years were to pass before Scott's beautiful hotel was ready to receive travellers, on 5th May 1873. However, in 1872 the passenger bookings at St Pancras numbered 171,000 bringing £97,000 to the Midland Railway.

The Midland was now one of our greatest railways, setting fashions rather than following them. In 1873 third class accommodation was included in all trains, a revolutionary step. In 1874 Pullman coaches were introduced, and in fact the first trial was between London and Bedford. The next year second class was abolished and cushions fitted to all third class coaches to cover the bare boards. Nothing could have advertised the Midland better than the decision to change the livery of the locomotives from green to crimson lake in 1883 so that a Midland train was quite outstanding in its appearance. This change was made under the chief mechanical engineer Samuel Johnson, who would have been an artist if he had not designed engines. His most beautiful creation was the 'single driver' of 1896 which was stabled at Kentish Town and therefore was seen at Bedford nearly every day. No. 118 of this class has survived and can be seen at the Leicester Museum.

In 1894 the west curve was put in at Bedford station enabling express trains to pass with undiminished speed. With a view to establishing four tracks continuously from London, another tunnel was bored in Ampthill west of the first one in 1891, and three years later the four track system extended from St Pancras to Glendon North Junction, this distance of 75 miles being the longest in the country. In 1905 the bridge over Hitchin Road, Luton, was widened to accommodate more tracks. In more recent years the Royal Ordnance Factory was opened at Wilshamstead (1941) and this increased the freight traffic on the line. Timetables are shown in Appendix B4 and B5.

There were three schemes to unite Bedford and Northampton before the successful one of 1872: two in 1845 and one in 1864. Charles Liddell surveyed the route in 1864 which was practically the same as the one finally adopted, though the original plan provided for a separate terminus at Bedford. A paragraph in the *Bedfordshire Mercury* of 13th

November 1866 suggests that this idea was dropped because of the enormous demands made by the owners of property, and that by using the Midland station, the company saved £20,000.

The line was opened on 10th June 1872. The railway left the Midland main line at Oakley Junction, and after crossing over the Bedford to Northampton road by a fine stone bridge consisting of a single great arch, arrived at Turvey station – a pleasant stone building. Unfortunately Turvey itself was about one mile away. The line then ran near Clifton Reynes and crossed the Great Ouse just before Olney station, which was attractively built in stone, and conveniently situated. The trains ran into St John's Street station in Northampton, but this was closed in July 1939. There were no level crossings.

After 1945 there was a decline in traffic and services ceased in 1962. Timetables for the 19th century are given in Appendices B6 and B7. Between 1939 and 1962 the trains from Bedford ran into the L.N.W. Castle station in Northampton. Between 1923 and 1939 the London Midland & Scottish Railway used to run excursion trains from Bedford via Olney and Ravenstone Wood Junction to Towcester in connection with the horse racing there.

CHAPTER 7

SCHEMES THAT FAILED

A glance at the railway map of the United Kingdom for, say, 1910 would show so many routes that a student of railway history could be forgiven for thinking that every proposed line had succeeded. Actually many more lines were planned than those disclosed on a map – for example in Bedfordshire nine (including the Sandy & Potton) were constructed and nearly thirty failed. Several of the proposed lines have been mentioned earlier when describing the background history of successful lines, and further details can be found in my typescript account: *Railways of Bedfordshire Planned but not Built* at the Bedfordshire County Record Office.

When a railway was proposed, landowners, business men and financiers would meet and decide to issue a prospectus. This, when circulated, should bring in enough support for a company to be formed, and for engineers to be instructed to plot the route. Competent lawyers had the Bill drafted, and when this was submitted to Westminster, copies of the plans and books of reference would be deposited with the various Clerks of the Peace. In the case of unsuccessful lines, the promoters might get as far as having a Bill presented, or only as far as depositing plans. Others less fortunate would fall by the wayside. One company which did not even get as far as publishing plans was the Boston Bedford and London Railway. This was as early as 1836 and the following letter dated 16th August is from Thomas Bennett, the Steward at Woburn, to W. G. Adam, Agent-in-Chief of the Duke of Bedford at the London Estate Office.

'The Duke gave me a prospectus of the Boston, Bedford and London Railway which had been sent to His Grace, requesting his support, and the Duke desires me to enquire about it. I have, and do not think there is any chance of its being carried into effect, but it has made the Bedford people on the alert, and a Cross Line from Cambridge via St. Neots, Bedford and Newport Pagnell to join the Birmingham, is started, and I think this is likely to answer all the purposes Bedford and the adjoining country may want in that way. This Cross Line is likely to succeed, and I hope it will, as it will give an outlet both East and West. The Bedford people say very truly that if they do not get a Communication with the Main Lines in progress through the Country, they will be excluded from any benefits that are likely to arise from these increased means of traffic.'

In 1844 we begin to hear of the Ely & Bedford Railway. Plans were duly deposited and a Bill presented but in 1846 the rival Great Northern Railway obtained its Act which made nearly all of the Ely & Bedford Railway unnecessary. The following is a letter from Goodwin Partridge and Williams, agents of the Ely & Bedford, to Mr Wilkinson, a St Neots' solicitor.

'Lynn, September 14 1844

We send you a prospectus of the Ely & Bedford Railway and will send a packet as soon as we can obtain them. We have sent a prospectus to all the Provincial committee including the three Gentlemen of your Town. Our advertisements appear for the first time today, but the project has become known in Liverpool through our friend Mr. Lacy, and we have in consequence already received applications from substantial men there for upwards of 2,000 shares.

Will you be kind enough to furnish us with particulars of all public carriages passing through St. Neots mentioning the number of passengers which the coaches are licensed to carry, whether the vans and carriers carry passengers, and the class of goods carried etc. We send a prospectus to each of the gentlemen on the north side of the river upon whom we called the other day.

PS.   We are obliged by your letter respecting water traffic.'

A railway with the imposing title of the Direct London & Manchester Railway received a good deal of attention in newspapers. There is a letter in the *Reformer* (later called the *Hertford & Bedford Reformer*) dated as early as 1st August 1840:

'Sir, In resuming the subject of the London & Manchester Railway let us consider a few of the advantages to be derived therefrom. First to the town of St. Albans. Previous to the opening of the London & Birmingham Railway nearly 100 coaches passed through that town daily and there was also a considerable business doing in posting. Large sums of money were expended in the town and consequently it was in a flourishing state. After the opening of the railway, business vanished. The only inference therefore which we can draw is this – that so soon as the proposed line comes into operation the trade will not only return but increase in a tenfold degree, and what has previously prevented St. Albans from becoming a manufacturing town but the want of a railroad? Independent of this it has many attractions – its ancient Abbey, the monument to Bacon, the celebrated Holy Well, the Town Hall and various other buildings. The air is very salubrious and it is surrounded by the most picturesque scenery.

With such advantages there would doubtless be a great increase in the inhabitants, for when it is brought within an hour's ride of the Metropolis the man of business will eagerly embrace the opportunity to remove to such a delightful spot. He will be enabled to arrive at his office in town in less than an hour from the time he leaves home, and can after the fatigues of the day return to his family in one of the most delightful spots imaginable. House rent will also be cheaper and the expense of a family be considerably diminished.

The town of Redbourn will be benefited to an incalculable extent. This town, it is well-known, received its support solely from the coaches that passed through it, but since the opening of the London & Birmingham Railway everything like business has disappeared: but the time is not far distant when it will not only regain its former station but will be considerably increased. The proposed new line will pass close to it, and during the time works are about business to a great extent must be transacted. It will not however be for that time only, but will secure a permanent advantage. I am sure that every inhabitant on the line will immediately be up and coming and stirring and straining every nerve to promote the cause. The inhabitants of Bedford have already had a meeting; they have taken the matter up in a manner that reflects the highest credit upon them, and I trust that the inhabitants of St. Albans will speedily follow in their wake. It they do not they will have themselves to thank for the loss of the only opportunity of retrieving their fortunes that ever can and will occur.

It is a duty incumbent upon them to do so – the very thing which for the last two or three years they have looked upon as the only means of their salvation is about to take place – which they cannot hesitate for a moment to support.

Yours truly,
Q.E.D.'

On 29th August 1840 the *Hertford & Bedford Reformer* contained the following:

'*London & Manchester Railway through St. Albans, Luton & Bedford*

It will be gratifying to all who are interested in the commercial and general welfare of the line of country from London to the North to learn that all those parties who have taken up arms in favour of this railway are by no means relaxing in their exertions. The London Provisional Committee is formed and a most wholesome regulation has been adopted, namely that two gentlemen from each Local Committee down the line will be privileged to take seats in the

London Provisional Committee as a representative deputation from their own Committee. This will have the effect of uniting the working part of the shareholders – render the proceedings less complicated – and afford greater facility to business.

'The Bedford Borough Committee met on Wednesday; communications from the London secretary were read which put the question as to the line, at rest. It had been the opinion and fear of many parties that the projectors were vacillating between contrary opinions and had not really determined on the line; and that they were coquetting with this, that and the other interest in order to find which was the most weighty. We are glad to find that such suspicions are groundless. The projectors were anxious not to make too strong pledges till the affair was more matured; and therefore they contented themselves with simply ascertaining how far the interest upon the line would go with them in this (we repeat the phrase with all deference to the *Railway Times*) "Great National Undertaking". The projectors through their Secretary Sir Edmond Temple, decidedly affirm that they never contemplated any deviation from the line originally marked out. Great exertions have been made and private interests have been thrown in, *sub rosa*, to entice the projectors to make their line by Biggleswade and thus leave Bedford to shift for itself, and a pretty shift it would be. Indeed another line has been broached but has met with the consideration it deserved. Little spurts of this kind must be expected in all cases where there are conflicting interests, and where an innovation and improvement of any magnitude is contemplated.

'The Bedford County Committee will meet the Bedford Borough Committee at the Shire Hall in Bedford on 4th September.'

However, in due course the London & Manchester was rejected under Standing Orders, and the Board split. Two engineers, Sir John Rennie and G. Remington, launched their 'Direct Independent' railway under part of the Board, while J. U. Rastrick (who had already built the London & Brighton Railway) under the remaining directors continued work on the original route, under the original name. Thomas Bennett of Woburn wrote to C. Haedy on 24th August 1845:

'I will send you the *Northampton Mercury* which contains a Letter against "Remington's Manchester line". I think there is every reason to be satisfied that we are not yet committed to support either – probably better information will soon appear.'

The Duke had been displeased because the proposed Direct London & Manchester line ran close to his house at Oakley, and he had cause for alarm at Remington's revised plan which brought the railway even closer. Bennett wrote to Haedy on 29th July 1845:

'It appears to be proper to reply to the Manchester Line as you propose, for unless they cut through the Hill some way about where the present Turnpike Road passes over it, the property as a Country residence will be completely spoiled; the former plan went almost straight from Bedford to Bletsoe leaving the River to the West of the Line, but by this plan I should say they mean to keep more in the vale to the north of Bedford and cut through Oakley Hill somewhere between Bales farm and Hilton's . . .'

However, Bennett felt more reassured on 13th November 1845 after he had found out that the final course of both the Manchester lines would not, after all, affect the Duke's Oakley property:

'I have just seen the local agents of the amalgamation (Rastrick and Remington) Manchester Line. They have not finally decided on their Line through Oakley, on the west side of Judges Spinney at the deepest cutting through the Hill. The Line will at no place be within sight of the House, and considering that it passes so near it is perhaps as unobjectionable [a] Line as can be obtained.'

However, if the united company could not get a bill through against the bitter opposition of competitors, especially the London & Birmingham, the divided ones were even less likely to do so, and in September 1846 it was announced that both companies had been dissolved.

This was, however, an inventive age. A letter dated 26th October 1845 written by Thomas Bennett to C. Haedy shows that the level-headed Bennett had caught what was called 'atmospheric fever', and he thought that wide turnpike roads would provide ample space for 'atmospheric trains' to run alongside road traffic, to the benefit of the Turnpike Trustees, and of course without alarming the horse traffic, for the trains would be silent.

'I think there is every reason to suppose the Atmospheric principle, which is only yet in its Infancy, may work almost as great a change in the "locomotive department" as that has upon the Turnpike roads.

'I forward you the prospectus of the new London & Birmingham. The projectors reserve for future deliberation the mode of Traction, and I also send you in this a preliminary announcement of a London & Northampton, which you will see is proposed for the Atmospheric, and if this plan can be adopted to the present line of the Turnpike road, it will, I think, meet with supporters along the line of Road and particularly from owners of property in the Towns and villages –

now almost deserted. To the Turnpike Trustees and unfortunate Bondholders the scheme, if successful, will be a god-send, because the present road is generally fifty ft. in width, one Half of which can well be spared and leave plenty of Room for the present Traffic, and as the income from Tolls barely pays interest of Debt and salaries . . ., the parishes through which these Turnpikes pass have the almost certainty of being in a very short time burdened with the maintenance of the Road. Any scheme which will therefore relieve the different trusts from their liabilities will meet with local support.'

Clegg and Samuda were the engineers who patented the atmospheric system of railway traction. Briefly, the invention required the laying of a cast iron pipe between the rails, the pipe being about 18in in diameter. A piston moved along the pipe because stationary steam engines exhausted as much air as possible on one side of the piston, leaving the other side to be acted upon by the normal pressure of the atmosphere. A lug on the piston was attached to the train which often moved very fast. As this projection from the piston had to be partly inside and partly outside the pipe, the latter had a slot running along the top side and this slot was closed by leather flaps, well greased. The wear on the flaps proved to be the Achilles' heel of the system. It was tried several times between 1840 and 1847, but the upkeep was too costly, and the junctions too complicated. However, Bennett was in good company, for Isambard Brunel himself had faith in the system.

The Northampton, Bedford & Cambridge Railway planned in 1845, adopted a route which was in due course copied by the successful 1872 line, and it is the unbuilt line that is referred to by Bennett in the following letter to Haedy, and he mentions, also, another technical problem of railway construction.

'30th October 1845

A line has been last week surveyed from Bedford up the Vale of the Ouze which passes quite in front of Oakley House on the opposite side of the River. I rather suppose it must be the Northampton Line by Turvey. I enquired at Bedford but did not get any information. Our *friend* Ikey (Elger) will probably think it prudent not to be the first to make this communication . . .

We are now having applications for Larch for Railway purposes. Mr. Stephens sold one Lot of ten thousand feet at fourteen pence a foot . . . The contractors decline buying anything but Larch. This is an unfortunate change for the owners of Woodlands. When the London & Birmingham Line was making there was consumption for anything, no matter how rough or coarse, for temporary sleeper, which were taken up and replaced by Stones – now the Stone Sleepers are abandoned and the Larch, after serving the purpose for making the Road, will be relaid . . . in the Road after it is permanently made.'

There were several schools of thought on the correct way of putting down the permanent way (so called because the contractors' rough tracks were 'temporary way'). The most common and the one to be finally adopted was that of laying larch cross sleepers; it was quicker and cheaper to use these than to lay rails on rough wood, and then to have to cart away the rough timber and replace it with larch. Very early railways in the northern colliery areas had used stone blocks three or four feet apart on which to lay the rails. It was found that the blocks were expensive to cut and cumbersome to handle. In addition they had to be tied with cross metal rods, otherwise the road would 'spread'. George Stephenson and Robert Stephenson persisted with the stone blocks after lesser engineers had discarded them, but they began to discard them when working on the London & Birmingham Railway (1838).

A matter which caused a near panic in 1845 was the decision by the Government that all Bills for new railways or extensions of existing ones must be in the hands of the Board of Trade by midnight on 30th November annually, if these Bills were to be discussed in the following session of Parliament. This was because the amount of railway construction with the relevant Bills was swamping normal Parliamentary work. In 1845 30th November fell on a Sunday, and railway officials assumed that Saturday would be the closing day. Many letters arrived at the office of the Clerk of the Peace, Theed Pearse, junior, at the Shire Hall, Bedford, of which the following example is from the solicitors of the Direct London & Manchester Railway, and is dated 11th November 1845:

'As the solicitors for several new lines of railway, we should feel obliged if you could arrange to keep your office (as Clerk of the Peace) open until 12 p.m. on Saturday 29th inst., and if by accident we should be so pressed as to be unable to make the necessary deposits that evening, we should esteem it a very great favour if you would receive our plans and books of reference on Sunday 30th – the last day allowed by the Standing Orders of Parliament.

We shall be most happy to pay you any additional fee you may consider an adequate compensation for this facility being afforded to us.

Crowder & Maynard'

The same request must have been made to the Board of Trade, as the

Board sent a letter to each Clerk of the Peace stating that it was legal to deposit plans on Sunday 30th November 1845.

The south of Bedfordshire would have been served by a proposed Cambridge and Oxford railway which entered the county near Lilley, and passed through Limbury and Lewsey to Dunstable, Totternhoe and Eaton Bray. In the event, only 18 miles between Royston and Hitchin was built, and this eventually became part of the Great Northern. The proposed line crossed land belonging to the Marquis of Bute of Luton Hoo, to whom the two following letters were addressed.

'The Bury, Luton.
11th March 1846.

My Lord,
 . . . I embrace this opportunity of mentioning to your Lordship, that the Oxford & Cambridge Railway threatens somewhat to disturb my premises, and that I shall feel obliged if anything can be done (not to hinder the Company, but) to retain my holding inviolate, as there appears to be no *necessity* calling for interference with the buildings and land I hold.

I am my Lord, Your obliged and humble servant,
[the Rev.] Henry Burgess.'

'St. Margarets,
Ware, Herts.
18th April 1846

To the Marquess of Bute.
My Lord,
 Having with Messrs. Ray & Collingdon just left the solicitors and agents of the Cambridge & Oxford Railway Company, I beg to forward your Lordship before leaving Town the substance of our meeting subject to your Lordship's approval, and in so doing I am inclined to think your Lordship's objection to the proposed line will undergo some change when it is considered that *none* of the buildings at The Bury will be touched excepting a cart shed on the east side of the said Farm Buildings, and that the sum of about £10,000 will be paid as a compensation for crossing your Lordship's Estate taking altogether about 10 acres of land including the Villas. I hope your Lordship will think favourably of this proposed arrangement which I cannot but recommend provided the Company will accede to it . . .
Wm. Heard'

The Bill was rejected in the Lords except for the little Royston to Hitchin stretch, but while its fate was uncertain, the following letter shows some of the problems it caused to people living along the proposed line. Thomas Hyde wrote on 22nd March 1847 to F. Chase, Steward of the Manor of Luton, which went with the Bute estate:

'I shall be much obliged any time when you write to me, for information concerning the Rail Road, as there are so many conflicting rumours concerning it at Luton, we do not know who or what to believe. There is an Oak Tree, 2 Ash and 4 or 5 Elm standing in 7 Acres close to the proposed line of Rail. Please to say would you like the Elm fell and kept for our own use, and the Ash and the Oak sold, but the Oak if it could be left standing about 3 weeks longer would be more valuable as the Bark would then strip.'

No one could forecast accurately what would happen to a Bill in its course through Parliament. Active support by Members of the Commons could be defeated by interested landowners in the Lords. If an Act passed, there could be financial difficulties, or the line might be abandoned through changed circumstances. Often the outcome kept both shareholders and landowners in suspense.

However, even though a railway might not materialise, the presence of a skilled engineer in the district could be of some local benefit. For example, in 1845 M. Borthwick was surveying the extension of the Bedford Railway to Cambridge (which did not come to pass), but his professional skill was employed in connection with 'The New Cut' which can be seen today at Goldington, and which resulted from collaboration between Thomas Bennett and Captain Polhill of Howbury.

A list of Railway Companies which deposited plans with the Clerk of the Peace in Bedford, but whose projected schemes collapsed from one cause or another, is shown in Appendix D.

CHAPTER 8

RAILWAY OPENINGS

The opening of each of the nine railways in this county has been mentioned, but nothing said about the official ceremonies. The Victorians did these ceremonies well; the tables sagged with food and the speeches were verbose. To paraphrase the speeches would be to lose the atmosphere, and so a few are therefore given as reported in the Bedfordshire newspapers of the day.

The *Bedfordshire Times* 21st November 1846:
> '*OPENING OF THE BEDFORD & LONDON & NORTH WESTERN RAILWAY*
>
> *EXCURSION TRIP TO BLETCHLEY 17th November 1846*
> The long-deferred ceremony of opening this railway took place on Tuesday when the shops were closed, and a general holiday was given in Bedford. Throughout the morning there were arrivals from different parts of the country; and some thousands of persons made their way to the station at St. Leonard's, until, at length, every other part of the town appeared deserted. At 12 o'clock, a large party who had received the excursion tickets, entered the station, and shortly afterwards the formidable train of upwards 30 carriages, crowded by nearly 600 passengers, and drawn by two powerful engines, started amidst strains of music from the Bedford brass band, and shouts from the assembled multitude – the bells of the parish churches toning aloud their merry peals. The banks on each side of the line were crowded with spectators and at every crossing of the roads large numbers of persons were assembled to witness the passage of the first train.

> 'Mr. Randle, the chief agent of the contractor, Thomas Jackson, Esq., Mr. Storey and the other gentlemen who have been engaged in the superintendence of the works, were on the engines, pointing out the gradients on the line, which was necessary in consequence of the tremendous train, and from the circumstance of the rails being somewhat slippery from the rain which began to fall soon after the train started. Large parties were assembled at the several stations on the line, and appeared to take great interest in the event. On arriving at the famed Brogborough-hill, where the gradient is steep (namely,

1 in 127) the train went slowly, but on reaching the open fields again it went on at a rapid pace, and eventually reached the station at Bletchley about half-past one o'clock. Here the passengers alighted and viewed the extensive works which are in progress, and which are intended to make Bletchley station the most important first-class station on the great line. The engines were turned on one of the new tables invented by Mr. Handcock, which may be termed the perfection of ponderous machinery, and at that moment a train arrived from London bringing Mr. Scott, the engineer, and a party from the London and North Western Railway Directory, to join in the opening celebration of the Bedford branch. About two o'clock the train left Bletchley, and a very pleasant journey was made back to Bedford. The excellence of the arrangements was generally remarked, and particularly the improved mode of laying the rails, whereby the least possible vibration is caused to the carriages in their transit.

'On their return from Bletchley, the travellers were delighted to see waiting at the station, her Grace the Duchess of Bedford, who was anxious to do honour to the party assembled, by gracing it with her presence; as well as to testify the great interest her Grace took in the completion of a work she had so auspiciously commenced – a work so important to the town and county of Bedford, with which her noble family is so intimately connected. Her Grace expressed her extreme satisfaction with all she saw around her; and it gives us great pleasure to add, that with the kindest consideration requested to be specially introduced to Mr. Jackson, the contractor, to convey to him her Grace's congratulation upon the successful completion of his contract . . . . Her Grace, in company with Mrs. S. Whitbread, Miss Whitbread and Miss Payne then retired to the refreshment room which was tastefully and elegantly arranged by Mr. Brashier, who in his usual admirable style, had provided, by order of the directors, a most excellent dejeune. Champagne having been handed round, the Duchess took the opportunity of proposing success to the Bedford Railway, to which all the ladies present most cheerfully responded.

'Her Grace having desired to see the preparations for the dinner to be given to the party at the Bedford Rooms, then retired for that purpose, and, having viewed the whole arrangements was extremely pleased, and conveyed the hope to Mr. Elger, who accompanied her Grace that the party might pass off with every enjoyment . . . .

THE DINNER

'At 3 o'clock a party of upwards of 200 persons . . . sat down to a splendid dinner at the Assembly Room, in Harpur-street, where there was a profusion of turtle, game and almost every other luxury of the season, and it was served up in the best possible style by Mr. C. Higgins of the Swan Hotel . . . After the company had done ample justice to the dinner, the Rev. Dr. Mountain said grace. T. J. Green, Esq., the Chairman of Directors, presided, supported by H. Stuart Esq., M.P., A. Sharman Esq., the Mayor of Bedford, the Rev. Dr. Brereton, H. Littledale, Esq., Robert Newland, Esq., John Astell, Esq., Robert Lindsell, Esq., Chairman of the Leicester & Bedford Railway Company, the Rev. B. C. Smith, M. Prendergast, Esq., the Recorder of Bedford, Sir Harry Verney, Bart., the Chairman of the Oxford & Bletchley Company, – Tootell, Esq., Director of the London & North Western Railway, Capt. Huish, etc. etc. The Vice-chair was ably filled by Theed Pearse, Esq., the Secretary of the Bedford Railway, supported by Dr. Witt, T. A. Green, Esq., Thos. Jackson, Esq., the contractor of the works. Thomas Barnard, Esq., and Isaac Elger, Esq., acted as Vice-chairmen at the long tables on either side of the room. Henry Bruyeres, Esq., the able director of the locomotive Department of the London & North Western line, and Mr. Long, the intelligent assistant secretary, were also of the party.

'The Chairman gave the toast of The Queen, which was loyally received. He said they had never had the light of the royal countenance in Bedford, and why? Because hitherto there had been no railway (hear, hear). Who would care to come to a town without a railway (hear, hear and cheers). Now, however, they had a railway, and perhaps Her Majesty in the course of the royal progresses, would delight her loyal subjects in Bedford, by paying them a visit . . . The Chairman then said "The next toast I am about to propose to you is one which your attendance today assures me will meet with your cordial acceptance: it is a sentiment which I am sure throbs in every bosom, and, I trust, will find utterance on every lip – Success and Prosperity to the Bedford Railway (cheers). First, allow me to express the heartfelt gratification my brother directors and myself experience at the sight of this magnificent assembly, testifying not only your kind feelings toward ourselves, but the warm interest you take in our great undertaking, for great it undoubtedly is; though small in geographical extent, great in the results which must flow from it – great in the benefits which it will confer (hear, hear). It is now eleven months since our railway commenced; in that interval has been performed, I may say, the work of years, with an efficiency which does infinite credit to the contractors, and with an order and propriety of conduct on the part of the workmen engaged, which has been highly satisfactory to the country around. At that time many

mists hung round our undertaking, many doubts and difficulties were
in our way; – now, those doubts and difficulties have been dispelled,
the mists have vanished, and the horizon is clear on every side (hear,
hear).

'At that time we had two formidable antagonists on either flank –
the Midland & Eastern Counties Company on the north, and the
Oxford & Cambridge on the south, either of which would have
materially damaged our cause; they are now happily *hors de combat*,
peace be to their manes. At that time our ally – the Oxford &
Bletchley Company, the next most important link in our chain – was
but a project, it is now a great fact, having received the sanction of the
legislature, thus forming a continuous line from Bedford to Oxford
under one management. It is true that our Cambridge Extension Line
fell through in the last session on account of an engineering blunder;
but that which seemed a loss is in fact a gain, for the project will be
renewed in the ensuing session by the powerful Eastern Counties
Company, with far greater chances of success, and a far more evident
necessity for its allowance than before existed . . .

'As members of the vast commercial empire we know the great
advantages arising from the cheap and rapid interchange of agricultural produce, the minerals, and the manufactures of different
parts of the country, with the prosperity and happiness that result from
it. And as members of this enlightened community, we must feel how
the cause of morality is advanced, how science is promoted and how
society improved by the quick and easy communication thus afforded
between all its members . . . I now heartily call upon you to drink –
Success and Prosperity to the Bedford Railway (loud and long-
continued cheers).'

Of the local people who attended, T. J. Green, the Chairman of the
Bedford Railway, was a prosperous Bedford coal and wood merchant,
with an estate at Pavenham; the Member of Parliament, H. Stuart, lived
at Kempston, and was related to the Stuarts of Tempsford; the Rev Dr
Brereton was Headmaster of Bedford School; H. Littledale was at Kempston Grange, John Astell of Everton and Moggerhanger; Dr Witt lived in
Potter Street (now Cardington Road), and was a former mayor of Bedford; Isaac Elger of St John Street, Bedford, a surgeon.

It is evident that the navvies had behaved well during the construction
of the railway and belied their reputation. It is therefore pleasing to record
that they were also feasted, as we learn from the *Bedfordshire Times* of
28th November 1846:

'We omitted last week to mention that on Wednesday Mr.
Jackson, the contractor of the works, regaled the workmen employed

at the Bedford Terminus. The supper was provided by Mr. Austin of St. Leonards Farm, which is more generally known as the "Old House at Home", and consisted not only of good old English fare, roast beef and plum pudding, but the table was supplied with game and other delicacies, stranger to the palates of the assembled *gourmands*. Mr. Mitchell, the superintendent of the works, presided and Mr. Scott the sub-contractor of the brick laying ably supported him as vice. It was a strange contrast to see 63 hearty fellows assembled in jovial carouse and reflect that some centuries back, the same room was used by the monks of St. Leonard. After the men had done ample justice to the viands, Mr. Mitchell in a manly speech proposed the health of Mr. Jackson, the response to which made the walls of "St. Leonard's" tremble, and certainly if, as is reported, any unearthly visitants dwelt therein their ghostships must have awaked from their reverie.

'The health of Mr. Randle and the other gentlemen engaged upon the works having been drunk, the same compliment was paid to Mr. Mitchell, the police at the terminus, host and hostess etc. Time being called, the men left, preceded by a band of rather a novel composition, we should say, to*Jullien's ear, viz. one drum, one tambourine, one violin and three fifes. To the credit of the men, not one was intoxicated, although ample opportunity was afforded.'

It is not possible to cover the opening of every Bedfordshire line. The Dunstable Railway from Leighton Buzzard to Dunstable seems to have begun very quietly. The Great Northern attracted more notice. The *Bedfordshire Times* of 10th August 1850 has this paragraph:

'*BIGGLESWADE*

Opening of the Great Northern Railway. This event was celebrated with great rejoicing at this town. The day was ushered in by the ringing of bells; all the shops were closed, and everything betokened a general holiday. The Ampthill Brass Band was in attendance and paraded the streets. At 4 o'clock about 300 navvies were escorted through the town to a capacious tent where a substantial dinner was spread out. At 6 o'clock a large party consisting of the gentry of the town and neighbourhood sat down to a sumptuous dinner at the Town Hall.'

A leading article in the same issue described the run to Peterborough on a special train for the company's directors to view the line.

Bedfordshire had to wait seven years for the next ceremony, when the Midland Railway opened the line from Leicester through Bedford to Hitchin. On this, the first normal passenger train left Hitchin station for Leicester at 7.33 a.m. on 8th May 1857. The Midland paid £500 rent for

Jullien was a teacher of music in Bedford in 1846.

the original facilities at Hitchin station, but this was increased to £60,000 when from 1st February 1858 they obtained running powers from the Great Northern for its trains to go on to King's Cross.

The opening day, 7th May 1857, was declared a public holiday in Bedford, and an excursion train left Hitchin at 7.30 a.m. calling at Shefford 8.00; Southill 8.15; Bedford 9.00; Sharnbrook 9.30; Wellingborough 10.15; Kettering 10.35 reaching Leicester at 12.00 noon. The *Bedfordshire Times* of 9th May 1857 described the day:

'*OPENING OF THE LEICESTER & HITCHIN RAILWAY*
This interesting event took place on Thursday under circumstances which will long be remembered by the inhabitants of Bedford . . . Shops were closed, streamers waved from buildings in different parts of the town . . . crowds of people were flocking to the station to secure their places several hours before the time fixed for the departure of the trains. The Mayor, aldermen and councillors, assembled at the Shire Hall at half past 8 o'clock and accompanied by Mr. Barnard, M.P., several magistrates and other gentlemen walked in procession to the station, preceded by the band of the Bedfordshire Militia . . .

'The procession having arrived at the arrival side of the London & North Western station, no time was lost in taking possession of the carriages, and at a few minutes past nine the whistle sounded, the band, occupying an open carriage in front of those occupied by the town council, striking up a merry tune, and the train, numbering thirty-three carriages, first and second, started slowly on its journey . . . Several bridges, and each side of the line from Bedford to beyond Bromham-road were thickly studded with human beings waving their handkerchiefs . . . The Mayor and Corporation were met at [Leicester] station by Mr. Ellis, Chairman of the Midland Railway Directors . . . Shortly after the passengers of the first Bedford train were disposed of, the third class train came in sight consisting of 35 carriages . . . The first train left soon after 2, and arrived in Bedford at half past 4. The second train arrived about five o'clock.

'The Dinner took place at the Bedford Rooms, under the direction of Mr. C. Higgins of the Swan Hotel. About 174 sat down. W. W. Kilpin, Esq., (mayor) presided; supported by Sir George Osborn, Bart., the High Sherriff, J. Underwood, Esq., the Mayor of Leicester, T. Barnard Esq., M.P., S. Whitbread, Esq., J. Ellis, Esq., the Rev. J. Wing of Leicester, . . . Captain Polhill Turner and Captain E. Thornton . . .

'The Rev. E. G. Bayly [said] . . . The time for talking about the advantage of railways had long passed; the increase of population and increase of commerce had made England very great . . . Had Russia possessed the same means of communication . . . England might have been carrying on the war still . . . The advantages of rapid communication had been witnessed that day . . . many had been enabled to go 50 miles and back comfortably in time for dinner . . .

'The Mayor said "When the Bletchley branch opened the traffic brought to the town averaged 200 tons a month: the average was now 2,000 tons a month: coals 1,600 tons a month . . . The Midland Company was one of the most extensive in the kingdom . . . passing from Rugby to Derby, 57 miles; from Derby to Leeds, 74 miles; from Derby to Birmingham, 48 miles; from Birmingham to Bristol, 95 miles [and] several other lines making 333 miles, which give a total of 600 miles [and] lastly, from Leicester to Hitchin 62½ miles, making altogether a grand total of 662½ miles . . . The capital of the company is 21 millions. The staff list numbers 9,000 persons. [There are] 400 locomotives [and] 1,000 passenger carriages . . . The carriage he had the pleasure of riding in today . . . was one of the most beautiful he ever saw . . . There were also 10,000 carriages for stock and 10,000 for minerals." '

The Midland station in Bedford was not yet ready, and so the train started from St John's, the L.N.W. station. Not until 1st February 1859 did passengers begin to use the station we now call Midland Road. The journey from Bedford to King's Cross therefore had three phases. From 8th May 1857 trains from Leicester ran into and out of (St John's) L.N.W. station and passengers changed at Hitchin. From 1st February 1858 the trains continued to use the L.N.W. station but went through to King's Cross. At last on 1st February 1859 the Midland trains ceased to use the L.N.W. station and ran from the Midland (Road) station on the journey to King's Cross.

Something has already been said about the opening of the Sandy & Potton Railway on 9th November 1857. After Lady Peel had named the engine 'Shannon' there were the usual festivities. One report said that the dinner cost 2s 6d with an unlimited quantity of beer. The Market Square, Potton, was gay with banners, one reading 'Perseverance and Industry will join us with Cambridge'. Five years later Potton and Cambridge were indeed linked, when the little line was swallowed up in the Bedford and Cambridge Railway, though in the meantime the Great Northern branch across from Welwyn Junction to Luton and Dunstable had been opened with very little fuss. However, the *Bedfordshire Times* of 8th July 1862 contained:

'BEDFORD & CAMBRIDGE RAILWAY

We are informed that the new line from Bedford to Cambridge was opened on Friday last. A large train started from Bedford in the morning taking shareholders and other inhabitants of Bedford and the vicinity, free passes being issued by the directors . . .

'The agreeable manner in which the trains glide along and the comfortable style of the carriages are no mean recommendations in these days of general locomotion. At Blunham, the first station on the line from Bedford, the trip train on Friday stopped for the shareholders to make a brief inspection of the offices; the journey was then resumed and in a few minutes Sandy station reached. Here the line crosses the Great Northern Railway and then along the railway which was constructed by the later Captain Peel to Potton. Up to this point there was no demonstration on the part of the population living on the line, but the inhabitants of Potton turned out in great force to testify their delight at the success of a line of railway calculated to be of very great service to all classes. At this station there was a large influx of passengers, and the train then moved on through Gamlingay and Hatley, and at length reached Cambridge . . .'

The Bedford and Cambridge railway seemed to have completed the links that it was thought Bedford needed with the outside world. In the *Bedfordshire Mercury* for Monday 14th July 1862:

'Railway accommodation for Bedford may now be considered complete – Bedford now being intersected by excellent lines of iron road from East to West, and from North to South . . . Any part of the island can now be reached by the traveller with the utmost facility.'

However, building proceeded. In 1868 the new Midland extension from Bedford to London was opened. There was a ceremony but no dinner. This was partly because the Midland Railway had not been able to complete St Pancras station, and even more because they were stretched to the financial limit. They had opened services from Kettering to Huntingdon in 1866, to Manchester in 1867 and most serious of all was the enormous expenditure facing them to drive their line from Settle to Carlisle (opened 1876). As regards Bedford, the arrangement was for suburban trains to run from this town via Luton and St Albans to Moorgate Street as from 13th July 1868, while main line trains continued via Hitchin to King's Cross. When the great St Pancras station was ready on 1st October 1868 the main line trains and most of the suburban ones ran in and out of it, but a few trains still used the Metropolitan widened lines to Moorgate Street.

The *Bedfordshire Times* of 7th July 1868 carried this notice:

'*MIDLAND RAILWAY*
OPENING OF THE NEW LINE BETWEEN LONDON
AND BEDFORD THROUGH LUTON AND ST. ALBANS
FOR LOCAL PASSENGER TRAFFIC.

This railway will be open for local Passenger Traffic on Monday, July 13th, from which date the Midland Company's trains will run through between Bedford and Moorgate Street, calling at Aldersgate, Farringdon Street, and King's Cross Metropolitan stations. For Particulars of Train Service see Time Tables which may be obtained after July 6th at the Metropolitan Railway Stations, at any of the Stations between London and Bedford, or on application to the Chief Offices at Derby.

'Applications for Season Tickets to be made to Mr. C. Mills, Midland Agent, Great Northern Station, King's Cross, London. The Main Line Through Trains will continue to run to and from the Great Northern station at King's Cross until further notice.

James Allport,

Derby, July 1868 General Manager.'

The *Bedfordshire Times* leading article on 14th July ran:

'The official announcement of the opening of the Midland Extension Line from this town to London, already published in these columns, has been received by the inhabitants of Bedford, Luton, and the other towns along the line, with a satisfaction that only the removal of grave inconvenience of long standing could give rise to. It is difficult to imagine anything more annoying to business men than to travel between Bedford and Luton, for instance, by the circuitous route via Bletchley, Leighton and Dunstable, taking at least two hours and a quarter by a through train. We have known instances in which the journey has occupied even five hours, owing to unavoidable delays at the junctions above-mentioned. This want of adequate railway accommodation between Dunstable, Luton and Bedford has acted very prejudicially on the development of local commerce; and in addition to this we must mention the serious annoyances experienced by jurymen summoned to attend the Courts of Quarter Sessions and Assizes, many of whom have been fined for not being punctual in attendance. All this is now happily removed by the opening of the Midland Extension Line, and we have no doubt that a remunerative traffic, passenger and otherwise, will reward the exertions of the Company to provide railway facilities for the important district through which they have carried their extension line. The ordinary trains from Bedford are timed to reach Luton in 48 minutes, stopping at the intermediate stations of Ampthill, Harlington, and Leagrave. About 20 trains are to run each way on week days to and from Moorgate-street station of the Metropolitan Railway, calling at Aldersgate, Farringdon, and King's-cross Stations, to suburban and other stations on the Midland Railway, including St. Albans, Luton and Bedford. On Sundays it is proposed to run ten trains each way. The time-table will be found on our third page. Bedford, which was for a long time isolated from other towns for want of railway accommodation, is now, we are happy to say, one of the best served towns in the Kingdom and mainly through the enterprise of the Midland Company.'

More praise came from the *Bedfordshire Times* when on 21st July the new Midland station at Bedford was described:

'The station arrangements are most admirable, and the buildings of red brick and white stone facings have a very pretty appearance. In addition to the platforms in front of the booking-offices, waiting-rooms, and other offices, there is . . . a long platform, with one or two supplementary waiting-rooms and a signal-box, where one man has the entire control of the block signals . . . The table of fares appears to be very moderate.'

Public approval was complete with the opening of St Pancras station, the most beautiful in London. It is difficult to say which was the first train to run on the new line. If we mean the first passenger train of any kind, then it was the humble 7.35 all stations from Luton to Bedford on 1st October 1868; if we mean the first express to use St Pancras, then the 3 a.m. from Leeds arrived in St Pancras at 9.55 on that day. In the down direction the 10 a.m. Manchester express was the first, and it is convenient to regard this train as opening the service.

The L.N.W. had been operating the train service on the Bedford & Cambridge even before they took the line over completely. In 1871 the single line between Sandy and Cambridge was doubled, leaving only Sandy to Bedford (St John's No. 2) as a single track which it remained to the end. When the L.N.W.R. Chief Mechanical Engineer, the great Francis Webb, started the manufacture of steel rails at Crewe, they were tried out on the Cambridge branch, and at Blunham a new electrical apparatus was tried for the safer working of single line traffic.

The promised rail connection between Northampton and Bedford by a direct route at last became an accomplished fact on 10th June 1872. There was the usual rejoicing, but the official celebration was delayed until 26th July, because of the death of the Duke of Bedford.

On 3rd August 1872 the *Bedfordshire Times* contained the following account:

'OPENING OF THE BEDFORD & NORTHAMPTON
RAILWAY
Banquet at the Assembly Rooms
On Friday afternoon 26th July the opening of this new railway was

celebrated at Bedford, a number of gentlemen from the counties of Bedford and Northampton being accorded the invitation of Lt. Col. Higgins of Picts Hill, Chairman of the Directors of the Company, to a banquet which was held in the Assembly Rooms. The large hall was effectively arranged for the occasion, and handsome decorations in the form of a variety of greenhouse plants from the nurseries of Mr. Sheppard being judiciously placed at the end of the room, and on the tables and along the frontage of the gallery. The hall was also carpeted for the occasion and flags were displayed from the front of the building. The Chair was taken by Colonel Higgins who was supported by the following gentlemen: The High Sheriff of Northampton Mr. Nethercote; the High Sheriff of Bedfordshire Mr. W. F. Higgins; Colonel Gilpin M.P., the Mayor of Northampton Mr. Marshall; the Mayor of Bedford Dr. Coombs; Mr. James Howard M.P.; the Rev. Sir H. J. Gunning Bt. of Horton; Lt. Col. W. Stuart jnr. of Tempsford Hall; the Recorder of Northampton Mr. Brewer; Mr. G. Gunning; and Mr. Joseph Palmer. Other guests were Colonel Cole, Cardington Mills; Mr. Charles Longuet Higgins of Turvey Abbey; Mr. Harry Thornton of Kempston Grange; Mr. R. Orlebar of Hinwick House; the Rev. G. F. W. Munby of Turvey; Mr. Henry Allport; the Rev. J. W. Haddock of Clapham; Mr. E. Ransom of Kempston; Mr. Carpenter of Kempston; Mr. Price; the Rev. W. Suthery of Clifton Reynes; the Rev. C. C. Beatty-Pownall of Milton Ernest; Messrs. A. E. Burch, James Pearse, W. Smail, M. Whylley, W. J. Nash, H. Sharpin of Bedford; Mr. Stephenson of Woburn; J. Garrard of Olney, Aldermen Bull, Jessopp, Sergeant, Carter and Robinson of the Bedford Corporation, and Councillors W. Harrison, Young, Sturges, Colburn, Lester, Wilson, Barrard, Scoles, Roff, Roe, also of the Bedford Corporation, and T. W. Pearse, Town Clerk. Caterer – Mr. Gunter of Belgravia, S.W., Band of the Coldstream Guards under Mr. F. Godfrey.

'The Chairman regretted the absence of Mr. Charles Howard of Biddenham due to the sale of his celebrated flock of sheep. Had he known he would have postponed the gathering . . .

'In proposing the toast of the Bedford & Northampton Railway the Chairman said, "In 1845 we had the Northampton Bedford & Cambridge Railway – a Bill was procured, but all at once came one of those peculiar panics which have happened in this country almost periodically, and which put a blight on this undertaking. The concern was wound up . . . Then came the period of more recent date when the new line was taken up. A Bill was introduced and passed both Houses, but then came one of those unfortunate periods when the money market got into a sinking state . . . In the course of two years there occurred a better state of things and we were enabled to enter into an agreement with that distinguished firm Messrs. Clark and Punchard. When I spoke of Mr. Whitbread I was lamenting that he could not have lived to see the accomplishment of the object he had so much at heart . . . I offer you gentlemen of Northampton the right hand of friendship (enthusiastic cheering)."

'The High Sheriff of Northamptonshire said in reply: "I recollect the coach between Bedford and Northampton of the days gone by which absorbed three mortal hours in accomplishing the distance and how long it might take that tortoise among vehicles – the carrier's cart – I don't pretend to say (laughter). One afternoon passing that carriage I said to myself:

'The way is long, the wind is cold,
The carriage is infirm and old.' (much laughter)." '

CHAPTER 9

CONTRACTORS AND NAVVIES

'I have no fear but the work will soon be done. In that part of the country there are a great many men known by the name of "navigators" who have much experience in work of this description.' So spoke H. C. Lacey, Chairman of the Ely & Huntingdon Railway at the half-yearly meeting of the company held on 29th July 1845. These words are of interest because they show that the term 'Navigators' was coming into general use, soon to be shortened to 'navvies'.

An enormous number of workmen was needed to build a railway, and they were concentrated in a small area. When the line was finished, the men were turned adrift, and might live as vagrants until a new scheme was advertised, and this would seldom be in the same neighbourhood as the last. These figures give an indication of the scale on which work proceeded:

Total railway route mileage completed 1825–44	2,235
Total of new mileage completed by 1845 ..	2,523
Total of new mileage completed by 1846 ..	3,157
Total of new mileage completed by 1847 ..	3,870
Total of new mileage completed by 1848 ..	5,123

Hamilton Ellis, is his work *British Railway History* says:

'The engineering contractor was a new figure in British commercial life. With the coming of the railways the country saw the largest programme of heavy public works which it had known since the building of the great cathedrals and abbeys in the middle ages. The only thing which anticipated railway construction had been that of the canals, and from this stemmed the navigators, quaintly named for they had nothing to do with working any sort of craft – the navvies, the cream of British heavy labour and perhaps the most ferocious and voracious race of men to be let loose on the land since Cromwell produced his Ironsides. They formed the contractors' armies and the king of contractors was Thomas Brassey. The Grand Junction Railway gave Brassey his real start. One fact that emerged from Brassey's Grand Junction contract was his extraordinary ability to deal with the navvies. These wild men who were a law unto themselves, each of whom was reckoned to lift about twenty tons of earth a height of six feet in a day, whose staple food was beef, beer and spirits in enormous quantities, whose principal relaxation was gambling, whose dalliance was with polyandrous female camp followers, who lived "Box and Cox" twenty together, in turf hovels, followed and obeyed the gentle spoken Tom Brassey with the same sort of devotion as the Grande Armeé had given Bonaparte . . . Brassey loved them.'

The *Railway Record* was one of the early periodicals of the railway age. The first issue appeared on 13th April 1844 and by 3rd August it found itself obliged to say something about the navvies. In a leading article headed 'Railway Navigators' it says:

'The improvident habits of the class of men known as navigators are alluded to in a report to the Poor Law Commissioners appended to the fifth report of the Select Committee on Railways. It appears that, during the winter of 1842 as many as fourteen of these persons were admitted in one night into the Abingdon Workhouse. It is stated that they usually receive wages varying from 3/- to 4/6d for every ten hours' labour, but are required by their gang of fellow workmen to subscribe a gallon of beer daily and another gallon at the time the ganger or sub-contractor pays the wages. As the works approach completion employment is difficult to be obtained, and then the labourers, having previously spent their earnings in the most lavish manner, undergo the severest privations, frequently subsisting for a whole week upon the wages of a single day. Ultimately there is no longer any prospect of employment upon that particular undertaking and then the workmen remove, seeking shelter and food in the Union workhouses on their route, to some other locality where employment is more abundant.'

From the newspapers one has the impression that Bedfordshire did not suffer unduly from the navvy invasion. Our first railway from Bletchley to Bedford, opened on 17th November 1846, was only 16 miles long, and so the labour force was small. However, between that date and 10th June 1872, when the last railway (Northampton to Bedford) was opened, there were occasional incidents.

In 1854 the Midland Railway was extending their system, and building the line from Leicester through Bedford to Hitchin. The contractor for the work was the great Tom Brassey, but as the army of navvies moved into the county, it is easy to understand that some concern was aroused. The following is an extract from the register of the Michaelmas 1854 Quarter Sessions Minutes:

'In consequence of the great number of workmen employed in the works of the Leicester & Hitchin Railway which intersects the County from north to south, ORDERED, subject to the consent of one of Her Majesty's Principal Secretaries of State, that the number of constables first appointed under the Act of 2 & 3 Vict. c. 93 be increased by one additional constable to act during the ensuing half year, and that application be made by the Clerk of the Peace to the Secretary of State for his consent as required by the second section of the same Act.'

There were, too, many accidents, as we see from the minutes of the board of the Bedford Infirmary, dated 1st January 1855:

'The Secretary having reported that several very severe accidents have been received from the Leicester to Hitchin Railway now being made it was RESOLVED that Mr. Brassey and Mr. Knowles the contractors be applied to for an annual subscription or donation to the Infirmary and that representation be made to them of the heavy expense which such cases are to the Institution.'

If several were injured, fortunately few were killed. The Coroner's register of inquests has only one entry at this time:

'27th December 1856, Richard Street, navvy age 26, Killed at Souldrop.'

Another leading contractor was Samuel Morton Peto, and from his books a comparison can be drawn as regards the wages paid to navvies just about the time the Bedford Railway was built, and again when the Midland Railway extended their line from Bedford to London:

	1843	1869
Mason	21s	27s
Bricklayer	21s	25s 6d
Carpenter	21s	24s
Navvy	16s 6d	18s

Railway construction continued in the county on and off between the years 1857 and 1890. Scarcely had the last beer bottle been thrown away on the completion of the Midland Railway's extension from Leicester to Hitchin in 1857, when the sound of the pick and shovel was heard in the south of the county. However, the event which affected Bedfordshire the most was the building of the main line from Bedford to London, linking the county town to Luton and St Albans directly for the first time. The line attracted general interest, and three views in F. S. Williams's *The Midland Railway* show scenes in Bedfordshire near the line: Elstow Church; Dallow Farm, Luton; and a view of the countryside just to the south of Luton. Two tracks only were laid and the engineering works became more difficult as the line progressed toward London. Liddell and Barlow had surveyed the route in 1862, and the undertaking was so extensive that it had to be awarded to four contracters. From Bedford going south, A. W. Ritson and Joseph Firbank were selected to carry out the works, and nearer London the contracters were Thomas Brassey and Stephen Ballard. At Ampthill the tender submitted by John Knowles of Shefford was successful and he was awarded the contract to build the first (eastern bore) tunnel. Knowles was experienced in tunnel work, but nevertheless two of his men were killed during operations. One was overwhelmed by a fall of earth and another, Charles Bell of Luton, aged 65, was run over by a contractor's wagon.

With the opening of the new trunk line to London on 13th July 1868 there was a brief lull until the construction of the Northampton & Bedford line. The route had been surveyed twice in 1864, by Charles Liddell and by Sir Charles Fox. Liddell's line, with small variations, was the one finally built. When the work was put out to tender, the contract was awarded to the contractor Harrison, but as the weeks went by he showed no inclination to sign the papers and finally he withdrew. The work was then offered to the firm of Waring Bros who had done so well on the main line to St Pancras. They at first agreed, but later withdrew. The line involved some heavy earthworks, but nothing which could really have daunted such an able firm. Finally Clark & Punchard agreed, on 25th May 1870, to do the work, and the first train ran on 10th June 1872. Although this was the last new railway to be opened in Bedfordshire, the navvies remained.

There was intense competition between the various companies, and the Midland became aware of the fact that the London & North Western Railway was planning to lay quadruple track from Euston to Roade. The idea was to give a separate road to the coal trains, and to leave one line free for passenger trains. In 1872 the Midland secured Parliamentary powers to widen the line between Rushton and Bedford, and further powers were granted in 1876 for more detailed work just north of Bedford. The engineer was J. S. Crossley in both cases. This meant a return of the navvy, but by now public opinion could no longer accept the conditions in which he lived.

Charles Magniac of Colworth, a magistrate and Member of Parliament, brought the matter before the Quarter Sessions. The report in the *Bedfordshire Mercury* of 7th January 1882 reads:

'A NAVVY ENCAMPMENT: WYMINGTON

Mr. Magniac said that he should like to mention a matter which had some connection with the Police Committee business. At his end of the County the owners of property were at the present time practically at the mercy of bands of navvies who are employed on new works in that neighbourhood by the Midland Railway Company. These navvies take possession of any part of the adjacent property which they choose, and go about in bands of 18 or 20 with guns or dogs, breaking down fences, taking railings off, and, as a matter of course, poaching, but of this he did not wish to say anything. The damage, however, which they do in his own neighbourhood was becoming very serious indeed and very considerable. He made no complaint whatever against the police; on the contrary he had great pleasure in expressing now, in the presence of Col. Josselyn [the Chief Constable], the appreciation with which the efficient performance of their duty by the police was regarded by the inhabitants of the locality, for the police do their utmost to protect property. The state of things at Wymington was a perfect disgrace to a civilised country. From 300 to 500 navvies are gathered and encamped upon a swamp, with green water lying in holes and ditches in front of the houses or huts of these people, and not the slightest attempt had been made by the Company to introduce sanitary arrangements or to make religious provision for those people. Such a thing did not seem to have entered into the minds of the Company, and the amusement of the boys and many of the men was to assault the clergyman who went amongst them and to disfigure the building which some gentlemen had erected there in order that divine worship might not be neglected. For himself, he would bring the matter before the Directors of the Midland Railway Company, but it was a disgrace to a civilised country to see men, women, and children, numbering altogether from 300 to 500, huddled together in a space of 2¼ acres. The misery of the worst Irish cabin was nothing compared with the state of things amongst these people. Only yesterday he tried to see about a man who had been seriously injured, but the state of filth and mud was such that it was impossible for him to get there. The medical attendance also was complained of. The fact was that these people were brought there and as much work as possible was got out of them, but as to their moral or religious comfort it was far from the thought of the Company . . . Poaching he would say nothing about, but the damage done to property, to the fences and hedges, was so great that when stock are taken out into the fields they stray all over the country.

'Mr. Barnard asked on whose property are the cabins built.

'Mr. Magniac said that part are built upon land taken by the Railway Company for the purposes of their traffic, and part are upon a small field which has been leased from a proprietor of land in Wymington parish . . .

'The Chairman asked if Mr. Magniac suggested an increase in the number of police in that locality.

'Mr. Magniac replied in the negative. Such a step would have no appreciable effect. He hoped the Court would excuse him for trespassing so much, but the fact was that the condition in which these people are placed renders it impossible that they could do anything but stray all over the place. The filth and dirt of the place where the houses are situated was so excessive that not only did he not prevent these people from going on his land but actually encouraged them. It was hardly to be expected that they would spend an hour in that filth if they could get anywhere else.'

The result was that Quarter Sessions 'RESOLVED that the Chief Constable be instructed to put himself into communication with the Midland Railway Company and the Sanitary Authority of the Wellingborough Union respecting the condition of the huts used by the navvies employed in the Midland Railway works at Wymington, and the conduct of the navvies.'

Newspapers for the two following years disclose nothing further, so we must presume that conditions improved. In 1893, when the second (west) tunnel was bored at Ampthill, the men included five hundred miners from Lancashire. By the end of the century railway expansion had ceased, and quiet once more descended on the countryside.

1. *Building the embankment of the London & Birmingham at Hillmorton, near Rugby, 1837, by Edward Rudge.*

2. *Excavating the Tring cutting on the London & Birmingham, by J C Bourne, 1837.*

3. *Leighton Buzzard's first railway station, 1838.*

4. *St. John's station, Bedford, opened 1846, with train, circa 1870.*

5. *Lidlington Station, opened 1846, as it was circa 1890.*

6. *Sandy Station, opened 1850. People waiting to welcome wedding party, circa 1890.*

7. The 'Shannon' engine built for Captain William Peel, for the Sandy to
Potton railway, 1857.

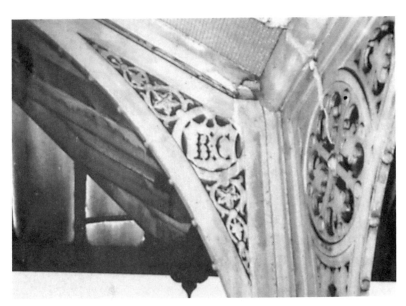

8. Cast iron bracket with letters 'BC' (Bedford & Cambridge) at Potton
Station, built 1862.

9. *Bedford Midland Road Station with Kirtley engine, circa 1870.*

10. *Train leaving Sandy hauled by Webb 18 inch goods engine, circa 1900.*

11. Market gardeners' carts outside Potton Station in the potato season, circa 1900.

12. Hat boxes ready for loading on Bute Street Station, Luton.

THE ANNUAL

TEMPERANCE EXCURSION

TO THE

SEA-SIDE.

EARL & Co.'s BOOTS FOR THE MILLION.

NINE HOURS AT THE SEA-SIDE.

The Luton and District Temperance and Band of Hope Union have made arrangements with the GREAT NORTHERN RAILWAY, and intend running Special Trains to

YARMOUTH

AND

LOWESTOFT,

On Wednesday, July 6th, 1892.

SPECIAL TRAINS WILL LEAVE

	A.M.
LUTON, G.N.R. -	- 6 30
New Mill End -	- 6 35
Harpenden, G.N.R. -	- 6 40
Wheathampstead -	- 6 45

RETURN FARES.

1 Day.	3 and 4 Days.	6 and 7 Days.
4/6	8/-	9/6

Children under 12 Half Fares.

Day Excursionists return from Yarmouth (Vauxhall Station) at 8 p.m.; Lowestoft (G.E.R.) 8 p.m.
Passengers for more than 1 Day return as per Co.'s Time Tables.

Parties of 8, by giving early notice to Mr. W. H. COX, can secure Reserved Compartments.

It is requested that an early application for Tickets be made to any of the following Gentlemen :—

Mr. W. ORD, 80, Chapel Street.
 „ J. GILLAM, 28, Windmill Street.
 „ J. GILTROW, 37, Havelock Road.
 „ W. WALSH, Jun., 9, George St. West.

Mr. J. DOCKRILL, Barber's Lane.
 „ H. BURNET, 54, Collingdon Street.
 „ F. STRATFORD, 54, Pondwicks Road.
 „ W. BRYANT, 6, Vicarage Road.

Mr. W. H. COX, 57, Waller Street.

The Committee recommend GOATES,
168, King Street, Yarmouth, for good
accommodation on reasonable terms.

PLEASE LOOK THE OTHER SIDE.

GEORGE DALTON, Crown Printing Works, Chalfont, Luton.

13.   Temperance excursion poster – Luton to Yarmouth, 1892.

14. Dunstable North Station showing Stirling mixed traffic engine on passenger train, circa 1900.

15. Johnson goods engine at Bedford Midland Road Yard, loaded with Longhurst & Skinner's removal vans, circa 1900.

16. *Luton Midland Station, demolished in 1937, as it was circa 1900.*

17. *Bedford Midland Station southbound platform and canopy shortly before demolition, 1978.*

18. *Poster – preparations for the opening of Captain Peel's railway, 1857.*

19. L.N.W.R. Webb Cauliflower *goods locomotive on a train just south of Bedford St. John's Station, circa 1914.*

20. Female cleaners at work on a Class 3 Belpaire *at Bedford Midland sheds, 1941.*

Midland Railway.

SEASON TICKET.

T—181.   **FIRST CLASS.**

FROM

JAN. 1, 1877, to JUNE 6, 1877

ALLOW

MR. W. LIGHTBOUND,

OF BEDFORD,

TO TRAVEL BETWEEN

**BEDFORD AND BIRMINGHAM
(Via DERBY OR NUNEATON.**

This Ticket is not Transferable, and is issued
conditionally, on its being given up on Expiration,
and on the holder being subject to the same Rules
and Regulations as other Passengers, the Ordinary
Fare to be paid if the Ticket is not produced when
required.

GENERAL-MANAGER.

Entd...

*21. Midland Railway first class season ticket between Bedford
and Birmingham, 1877.*

22. *Oakley Station, circa 1907.*

23. *Commemorative postcard for the Sharnbrook accident, 1909.*

24. Woburn Sands Station, circa 1885.

25. Steam railmotor, bound for Bedford, at Woburn Sands, 1908.

BAPTISMS folemnized in the Parifh of _Souldrop_
in the County of _Bedford_ in the Year 18**82**

When Baptized.	Child's Chriftian Name.	Parents Name.		Abode.	Quality, Trade, or Profeffion.	By whom the Ceremony was performed.
		Chriftian.	Surname.			
1882. Jan.y 29th No. 601.	Sarah anne daughter of	John & ann Elizabeth	White .	Railway Huts - Souldrop	Stone Mason	Digby Newboll Rector
May 7th No. 602.	Rose Mary daughter of	Samuel & Sarah	Chickley	Tunnel Works Sharnbrook Summit	Railway Labourer	G. Digby. Newboll Rector .
May 28 No. 603.	alice maud Mary daughter of	James & anna Sophia	Stone	Tunnel Works Sharnbrook Summit	Railway Labourer	G. Digby. Newboll Rector
May 28 No. 604.	Elizabeth	Frederick & Mary Jane	Fuller	Tunnel Works Sharnbrook Summit	Railway Labourer	G. Digby. Newboll Rector .
May 28th No. 605.	Herbert Son of	Jesse & Eliza	Headland	Railway Bank Cottages -	Plate - layer	G. Digby. Newboll Rector.
May 28th No. 606.	Elizabeth Sarah daughter of	Frederick & Elizabeth	Timson	Railway Bank - Cottages	Signalman	G. Digby. Newboll Rector
July 21st No. 607.	Lilly daughter of	William & Martha	Walton	Sharnbrook Huts	Time Keeper	G. Digby Newboll Rector
July 21st No. 608.	Bertha daughter of	William & Martha	Walton	Sharnbrook Huts -	Time Keeper	G. Digby Newboll Rector

26. Baptism entries for railway workers in the Souldrop parish register, 1882.

27.   Totternhoe lime kilns, 1912.

28.   Arlesey Station level crossing, circa 1914.

CHAPTER 10

TRAVELLING BY RAIL

When once the speed had been accepted and the cheapness realised, train travel became the accepted means of moving about the world, but some people took a little time to trust the new devices. The London Brighton & South Coast Railway had opened their route to Portsmouth in June 1847 but this did not attract Mrs Hester Dawson (*née* Gery) who wrote to Mrs Hester Wade-Gery of Bushmead on 4th December 1847: 'Have taken lodgings at Portsmouth; have seen Ada and Freddie. Little Henry was tired. I came in the coach which rattles very much but not nearly so much as those vile cars.' Another member of the family had the opposite opinion. W. H. Wade-Gery wrote to his parents on 30th November 1847:

'Will come to see you and Mary Hannah on Saturday next. I shall take a day ticket by the ¼ before 10 o'clock from Bedford and be at Ramsgate in the evening, return on the Monday morning.'

The 9.45 from Bedford (L.N.W.) reached Euston at 12 noon. Mr Wade-Gery would then take a cab to London Bridge for Ramsgate. The South Eastern Railway had built the line in 1844. A train journey in 1847 would seem spartan to us. Mr Wade-Gery would arrive at the (St John's) station by horse-drawn vehicle and might have to wait while his paper ticket was written out by the booking clerk. Edmondson's invention of printed cardboard tickets (1839) had not been universally adopted by 1847, and until then the clerk booked you in his book of paper tickets. From the low platform it would be quite a step up into the four-wheeled vehicle, lighted, if first class, by an oil lamp. This was a November day but there would be no heating in the carriage. If he had a good deal of luggage, much of it would be strapped on to the roof. At the head of the train would be a diminutive 'Bury' engine which would jerk the train into motion as all the carriages were loose coupled. The short coaches would clatter over the wrought iron rails, which only 20 feet in length would give a bumpy ride. The time of thirteen minutes to the next station, Marston, would seem agreeably fast, as the distance of six miles gives an average of 28 m.p.h. and the maximum was probably nearer 40. No smoke would be seen as the engines consumed coke fuel. The stop at Marston would be effected by the fireman and the guard each screwing down a hand brake. The loose coupled coaches would come together, the shock being diminished by buffers stuffed with horsehair. The ascent from Lidlington to Ridgmont would be slow, after which good speed would be made to Bletchley where arrival was timed for 10.26. If the platform road was not clear a policeman in frock coat and top hat would signal to the driver to stop just as he does today on the road. Although signalmen have replaced policemen for over 100 years, they are still referred to as 'bobbies'. If the platform were clear, the train would draw in, leaving our friend time for a cup of coffee before the London train arrived.

Even the elderly often preferred rail travel to coach for long journeys, since it was far less tiring. C. Haedy, the Duke of Bedford's Agent-in-chief in London wrote to the Woburn steward on 23rd May 1839, when Bedfordshire's only link was the Leighton station of the London & Birmingham, opened the previous year.

'I am exceedingly sorry to hear of poor Robert's misfortune, and I fear it is not unlikely to be attended with serious consequences. He appeared to have come very ill provided with Information . . . He had been, as I understood him, to the Woburn Coach Office, but had refused to go by the coach, on understanding he should have to go between forty and fifty miles . . . As he . . . seemed disposed neither to return back to Cornwall [nor] go by the Coach, I advised him to go by the railway to Leighton and there hire a Gig or chaise-cart or any other conveyance, by means of which I told him he might get to the Abbey and see Mr. Hitchins that evening, and he set off with the Intention of doing so. I gave him a direction . . . and sent the office Porter with him, who paid for his place (with Robert's money) and saw him safe to the carriage, and gave particular Directions to the Guard to look to him and see that he was set down at Leighton. I thought him a very old man to be sent so great a distance. I asked him if he wanted any refreshment, but I understood him to say that he didn't and he said he did not want any money. I hope he will not have a serious illness.'

It isn't clear how Roberts had become ill – possibly he became confused and lost his way when he arrived at Leighton – but he had been sent for from Cornwall to work on the grotto which the 6th Duke was having built at Woburn.

Two years later, in July 1841, the steward at Woburn wrote to Haedy on a matter of much greater importance, for the Queen was to visit Woburn, and extra police were being sent down from London for the occasion.

'The four Policemen can start on Monday morning by the six

o'clock train, get over from Leighton, refresh themselves and be with me by ten o'clock (or eleven would do) to get their assistants assigned to them, and the places for their stations pointed out.

'When you see the Duke about the regulations for lookers on, will you also consult him as to the procession, viz. as to order in which the Queen is to be received – the road to the Abbey, whether by the Basin Pond and West Front, or the Back Road – and the *pace* at which to travel – some of the Cavalry will be rather heavy.

'I expect we shall muster about 150; I have confined the request of attendance to the Tenantry who entirely or for the chief part get their living by the Duke's estate, this is the Farmers, and have made the distinction between those and the people holding only accommodation land etc., but there is some difficulty as regards the house tenants in Woburn, and therefore I have said that those who have horses and like to join us may, those who have not horses or cannot ride are not expected to put themselves out of the way. It is thus left an open question.'

A Colonel Cavendish wished to buy a horse from the Duke, and so Haedy wrote from London to Charles Burness of Park Farm, Woburn, on 26th April 1845: 'The Duke of Bedford wishes you to send the black filly to meet at Leighton the train which leaves London at 11 o'clock on Monday morning, and which I believe reaches Leighton at about half past twelve. A person from Colonel Cavendish will meet it there at that time and will decide whether it will suit or not.' The filly did suit, and the reply said 'the gentleman has taken her with him'.

An amusing scene is created by a letter from W. Grant of Harrow Road, London, to a Leighton Buzzard solicitor. Grant had been asked to sign the text of the Leighton Buzzard enclosure award, a large heavy volume, about 2½ feet by 2 feet. Grant said that he was travelling north by a train that would stop at Leighton.

'June 1848

I intend coming down by the train that arrives at Leighton at 33 minutes past one on Wednesday, so if you will be at the station with the Award and a pen and ink ready I will sign it. I shall probably be in a second class carriage. I do not intend staying at Leighton beyond the time of the train's delay.'

Much later, we find Anthony Trollope using Leighton Buzzard station. In his autobiography he mentions that after returning from Australia in 1872 he sent three horses from his house at Waltham Cross, Essex, to stables at Leighton Buzzard. He used to travel down by an early train from Euston, and ride to the meet from Leighton Buzzard, and so get in some hunting, which he loved. We are not, therefore, surprised to find at least one of his heroes doing the same thing.

The new method of travel gave rise to a new etiquette which is referred to in several journals of the time. The *Bedfordshire Mercury* in its issue of 23rd March 1861 has this to say:

'The Higher etiquette proper to be observed in railway carriages forms a most important part of this subject. It is not alone sufficient to avoid treading on a fellow passenger's toes, or sitting on his hat, or incommoding him with gusts of wind from the open window. The social amenities of railway intercourse should embrace many acts far more thoughtful and unselfish than these, and opposed to the first come, first served principle which governs so many travellers. It is very delightful for two or more intimate friends to be able to retain the whole compartment to themselves during a long journey without paying the Company for that luxury, but they should not grasp at this unfair privilege by filling each seat in their carriage with portmanteaus and rugs or by acting the old rather exploded game of the lunatic and his keepers. They should not attempt to block up the carriage windows at the side of the platform nor should they commit themselves so far as to say that several seats are engaged by passengers who have just gone to purchase a newspaper. Such tricks are sure to be exposed by some determined station superintendent before the starting of the train, and they often lead to unpleasantness. The travellers who are forced into such carriages by the arm of authority are not likely to prove very agreeable companions on the journey, while the greedy firstcomers can never remove the impression caused by their deliberate lies. The soft seat in such cases becomes hard and unbearable, and the carriage is turned into a cage, a round house or a dungeon.'

The *Bedfordshire Mercury* (24th August 1861) reported that on the Paris, Lyons & Mediterranean Railway experiments were being carried out to provide some heat in carriages. 'Waste steam' from the engine was circulated through pipes, the coaches being connected by india rubber tubing, and the temperature in the first class was said to reach 60° Fahrenheit. At this period first class passengers in England were given footwarmers which were metal containers filled with hot water; ten years later the London & North Western Railway brought out a footwarmer containing acetate of soda which generated heat after a porter had given it a good shake-up. It was not until 1874, thirteen years after the report of the experiments in France, that the Midland Railway introduced the Pullman coach, and we find the beginning of the modern method of steam heating pipes supplied from a boiler.

Some of the county's early travellers kept diaries. One was the Reverend R. A. Williamson of Kempston Manor. His father had been rector of Campton and the family was well-to-do. The diary covers both the years before railway travel was general, and the railway age, and allows an interesting comparison between horse and rail transport.

'28th May 1840. Posted down from town to . . . Kempston fare (Barnet to Kempston)   £4 6 3

15th June 1840. Trevor's carriage took us to station at Leighton to meet the "train". Gave coachman and footman   7 6
Arrived Euston 9.20 leaving Leighton 7.30.

13th August 1840. "Fast train" [on London & Southampton Railway] to Winchester. fares . . .   £1 15 0
Reached Winchester at 2 p.m. $\frac{1}{2}$ hour after time. Reached "station" at 5$\frac{1}{2}$ but train was again late . . . started not before 6. fares   5 0
Reached Southampton in 20 minutes [13 miles]

15th July 1842 [Paddington] for the mail train $\frac{1}{4}$ [to] 9, fare   £1 7 6
Started at 9, reached Bath 20 [minutes] before 1

10th August 1842 Two Railway guides (Bradshaw) . . .   2 0

11th August 1842 Two 1st class fares to Leeds . . .   £5 4 0
From London thro' Rugby to Derby and Leeds in less than 9 hours

15th August 1842 Fares from Leeds to York (2) 1$\frac{1}{2}$ hours   12 0

28th September 1842 Coach fare from Alnwick to Darlington . . . 64 miles, by mail, $\frac{1}{4}$ [to] 8 to 3$\frac{1}{2}$ . . .   £1 0 0
Railway fare from Darlington to London in first class carriage, 3$\frac{1}{2}$ to $\frac{1}{4}$ [to] 5, 13$\frac{1}{2}$ hh. [231 miles] fare . . .   £3 8 0
Stopped $\frac{3}{4}$ h. at York, crossed ferry to see Cathedral 1 [hour] Letter at Newcastle . . .   4
Stopped $\frac{1}{2}$ h. at Derby, cup of tea   6
Stopped 10 m. at Wolverton, a bun   1

2nd January 1844 Set off [from Bath] 9 for Sutton Coldfield [by coach] 2 inside and 1 outside places to Gloucester   £1 14 0
[Saw] Cathedral at Gloucester from 1 to 2   1 0
Railway Gloucester to Cheltenham   3 0
Biscuits at Station   6
Fares, three in [side coach] from Chelt. to Birmingham, 2$\frac{3}{4}$h. [fare] . . .   £1 16 0

Carriage, Birm. to Sutton . . .   17 0

9th November 1844 Trip with A. and L. to Colchester, started at 8½ from Shoreditch, Colchester at ¼ [to] 11, fly to Greenstead, Hithe . . . seeing St. Botolph's priory, St. John's Gate [and] Castle . . . Started home at 6 and reached Shoreditch at 8½, home at 9.

18th December 1844 Down to Sutton [Coldfield], by 9 o'clock train: great bustle and crowd: second engine required: detained 40 [minutes]: fares (each)   £1 5 0
Soup at Wolverton 1/- did not make up our lost time, Birmingham at 2.

24th April 1845 [In London] by water with A. and others to see model of new atmospheric railway: much pleased with it: simple and intelligible . . .

5th August 1845 Guide Book for Birmingham Railway   3 6

[4th January 1846 Married Anne Grey]

21st January 1846 . . . Started in Mr. T's carriage for Leighton: found that only a 3rd class train went at 5, and we had to wait till 7 – walked about the town, tea at ¼ [to] 6   5 6

15th August 1846 . . . to "George & Blue Boar", to reach the Bedford Times coach . . . travelled outside . . . reached Shefford safely [fare for 2]   £2 1 0

[16th September 1846 Times coach Bedford to London 5½ hours]

15th March 1847 . . . In the little carriage to Tamworth at 6¼ a.m. thence by railway to Derby, York, Darlington and Stockton, in second class to save the difference for the Irish (this was 29/-) . . . to see Robert at Stockton [fare for 2]   £3 11 3
[Robert was going to the Cape as a Bishop]

19th May 1851 [Worcester] to London [to see Great Exhibition] [three tickets on Great Western Railway] £4 5 6'

The eleven years of travel end here. The Reverend R. A. Williamson was headmaster at Westminster School, and on 8th September 1851 was installed as Hon. Canon of Worcester Cathedral. He died in 1865. The journey to Colchester in 1844 shows that day trips were by now possible, and he visited the Great Exhibition six times.

Another Bedfordshire diarist was J. T. Brooks of Flitwick House. Both he and Mr Williamson were men of substance and both discovered that it was possible to make long day trips by train, returning to their own beds at night. J. T. Brooks is a family man travelling mostly to London, whereas Mr Williamson, having places where he can stay in Kempston, London and Sutton Coldfield, travels further afield, and if there is no line of railway on his route, does not hesitate to hire expensive horse conveyance. The diary of J. T. Brooks covers only the year 1843. Brooks has to make the journey from Flitwick to Leighton Buzzard, the nearest station:

'13th January 1843 At 5 o'clock a.m. dearest Johnnie and George left us on their return to Town. They rode to Leighton for the 7 o'clock Train and arrived in Town soon after 9 – a horrid ride – dark as pitch – very heavy rain and sleet and yet (from the frost of last night) the Roads so slippery the Horses could with the greatest difficulty be kept up. Bob Adams sent to the Station (at 2 a.m. he started from here with carpet bags) to bring the Horses back. A disagreeable day – miss our dear Lads whose company we have enjoyed much the last fortnight.

26th January 1843 . . . dearest Johnnie came home today – sent the carriage for him in the morning to Leighton and he arrived there at ½ past 3 and reached home at ½ past 5, quite well thank God.

1st February 1843. Rose early, left home this morning at a quarter past 9 a.m. (our time) and proceeded (at half past 8 a.m. real time) in the carriage to the Leighton station (for the Train at 20 minutes before 11). Reached London 20 minutes before 1. *A miserable morning* [Johnnie was going to Portsmouth for India]

3rd February 1843 [At] one o'clock I took a cab to the Railroad [in London]. . . . At half past one the train started and reached Leighton at ½ past 3 where the Carriage was waiting and arrived at home at half past 5 o'clock (6 o'clock our time).

17th March 1843. Rose at half past 4, breakfast at five, and at half past 5 (five by the real time) left home for the Leighton station, to take Mary Ann to Town on a visit to the Williams and other friends. Got to Williams . . . (Guildford Street) at ¼ past 9 o'clock . . . Left for home by the 6 o'clock train from Euston Square. Got to Leighton at 8 where I found the Carriage waiting . . . and got home at 10 o'clock. Very cold coming home.

[Thursday 11th May 1843. Trotter and his family (with us for 24 years) left by Ellis and waggon to go to New Zealand]

13th May 1843. Rose at 4 o'clock a.m. (half past three by the real time) and at quarter past 5 set off in the carriage (accompanied by dear Willie) for the Leighton station. Reached London . . . at 10 minutes past 9. Trueman Tanqueray also accompanied me; we three got into a Cab and went to . . . Guildford Street. [They went to the British Museum to see the Elgin Marbles and mummies, then to the National Gallery and Burlington Arcade, Piccadilly. Then by carriage to the Horticultural Gardens at Chiswick, where there was a band of the Coldstreams and Grenadiers. They left Turnham Green at $\frac{1}{4}$ past 4, and arrived at Guildford Street at 5.10, cost 16s.] Got to the Railroad at 10 before 6, went to Leighton (Mary Ann, Willie, I and Tanqueray) in the first class, having come from it in the 2nd class. Arrived at Leighton at 5 minutes before 8, and home 5 minutes before 10 (25 minutes after 10 by our time) after a very pleasant day, the cost . . . being £3 10 6, but it was a treat for all the children . . . The day was fine and no rain.

24th May 1843. Rose at 4 a.m. at 5 started for Leighton station and got to London at 9 . . . Breakfasted . . . Walked to the Fete of the Botanic Society in the Regents Park – enjoyed it very much . . . equal to the Chiswick – walked to the station at 6 (40 minutes) got to Leighton at 8, home . . . thank God! at 10.

25th May 1843. At home all day.

15th June 1843. Left home at $\frac{1}{2}$ past 8 (eight by the real time) got to Leighton at $\frac{1}{4}$ past 10 (10 by the real time) for the Train at $\frac{1}{4}$ past 10 and got to town at $\frac{1}{4}$ past 12. After luncheon walked in Regent Street.

Sunday June 18th – evening to St. Pancras [church] service . . . splendid.

30th June 1843 Returned . . . by 6 o'clock train got to Leighton at 8, home at 10.

19th July 1843 Spent a delightful day in London. Left at 5 returned at 6.

13th October 1843. Went to Town . . . to bring home Mary Ann . . . Rose at 4 o'clock, started at 10 minutes before 5 o'clock a.m. in the carriage to Leighton, for the train at 10 minutes past 7 . . . Reached town at 10 minutes past 9. Breakfasted with the Williams . . .

15th November 1843 Rose at $\frac{1}{4}$ before 4 o'clock a.m., at $\frac{1}{4}$ before 5 a.m. set out to Leighton for $\frac{1}{4}$ past 7 train.

6th December 1843 Rose at quarter before 4; breakfast at half past four. Set off in the carriage for Leighton – quarter before five arrived at Leighton before 7. Arrived in Town 10 minutes past 9.

7th December. Euston Square 6 o'clock. To Leighton at 8 o'clock and home at . . . 10 o'clock.'

The phrase 'our time' obviously means that the clocks at Flitwick were kept half an hour fast.

The great protagonist on the railway scene in Bedfordshire in the 19th century was W. H. Whitbread, and Southill station was opened in order to serve the Southill estate. As the mansion and park are most attractive, many excursions were organised to visit the park, for this was the age of the great railway excursions. On Friday 21st June 1861 several corps of rifle volunteers assembled in Southill Park at the invitation of Mr Whitbread for drill. According to the *Bedfordshire Mercury* the men left by the 2.25 p.m. train from the Midland station. A heavy rain continued throughout the afternoon, but after having partaken of refreshments the men gave three cheers for Mr Whitbread. The bands then struck up and the men marched back to Southill station. On 17th July 1866 a great fête was held at Southill Park, and 2,000 passengers travelled from Bedford station. Another passage from the *Bedfordshire Mercury* reads:

'On 18th August 1868 the teachers of Bunyan Meeting Sunday School and a few friends numbering 53 proceeded by the 11.58 train from Bedford to Southill station, tickets having been issued at single 2nd class fare for the double journey. The party proceeded to the Park by the kind permission of S. C. Whitbread Esq. and were conducted through the beautiful gardens. Tea was prepared on the banks of the lake.

'Innocent games were indulged in and then came a stroll to Warden church. The party returned on the 7.39 train to Bedford having enjoyed the rural picnic exceedingly.'

The total number of railway excursions advertised in the *Bedfordshire Times* and the *Bedfordshire Mercury* is enormous. One is given below, and others are to be found in Appendix E1 and E2.

'*L.N.W.R.* Excursion. London to Edinburgh, Glasgow, Dublin, Wales, Liverpool, Chester, Birmingham, etc., etc.

Monday July 1st or 8th 1850, offering a choice of 9, 12 or 15 days.

London to Edinburgh or Glasgow and back		...	42 0d
,, ,, Dublin	,,	...	42 0d
,, ,, Bangor	,,	...	28 0d
,, ,, Windermere	,,	...	32 6d
,, ,, Liverpool or Manchester and back		...	21 0d
,, ,, Shrewsbury & Chester	,,	...	20 0d
,, ,, Leeds & Huddersfield	,,	...	25 0d
,, ,, Birmingham	,,	...	12 0d

ENCLOSED CARRIAGES

Thus affording an opportunity at a small cost of visiting the Highlands, Dublin, and the romantic lakes of Killarney, North Wales and its charming scenery; the greatest wonders of the world – the Britannia and Menai bridges and Conway Tube; Snowdon, the Vale of Llangollen, the ancient City of Chester, Eaton Hall the magnificent seat of the Marquess of Westminster, the lakes of Cumberland and Westmorland, the Isle of Man, the manufacturing districts of Lancashire and Yorkshire.

Monday July 1st at ¼ before 6 punctually, returning to London on or after July 10th.'

We have referred above to the awkward journey from Luton to Bedford before 1868, which caused the following entry in the Bedfordshire Quarter Sessions minute book for Midsummer 1861:

'Mr. Smart presented an estimate of the comparative expense of the conveyance of prisoners by the Turnpike Road or by the Railway from Luton to Bedford. There appeared to the Committee no question as to the matter of expense – the Railway affording the cheapest mode of travelling, but the change of rail and the return of the constables has hitherto presented the greatest difficulty. Mr. Smart has, however, entered into a correspondence with the General Manager of the L.N.W.R. which he will lay before the Court on Tuesday next. Mr. Smart will also be prepared to lay before the Court the comparative expense of sending prisoners by the above railway, or by the branch line which communicates with G.N.R. from Luton.'

Timetables show that if the constables and prisoners caught the 7.25 a.m. from Dunstable, and then changed at Leighton Buzzard and Bletchley, they would arrive in Bedford at 10.15.

Although the Midland trains were running direct to Hitchin in 1857 to connect there with the Great Northern, this was in competition with a horse-drawn bus which ran between Bedford and Sandy. A notice in the *Bedfordshire Times* of 7th November 1857 reads:

'A bus leaves the "Red Lion", High Street, Bedford daily at 7 a.m. reaching Sandy in time to meet the up train which arrives in London at 9.30. Returns to Bedford on the arrival of the Parliamentary train leaving London at 6.30 a.m.

'Leaves Bedford again at 1.45 p.m. to meet the mixed train due London 5.30 p.m. Returns to Bedford on the arrival of the 1.45 p.m. train from London, due Sandy 3.20; arrive at Bedford 5 p.m.'

When the Bedford to Cambridge line was opened in 1862 it was supposed to provide a connection at Sandy. Presumably by that time the horse bus had disappeared, but it seems that the new train services left something to be desired. The letter quoted below appeared in the *Bedford-*

shire Times on 22nd July 1862 (shortly after the opening of the Bedford and Cambridge Railway) and it is very much to the point:

'Is the Cambridge line intended as an accommodation of the public? If so they must arrange their timetable and keep such time as their trains will meet certain ordinary trains on the Great Northern. I had anticipated the 8.5 train would meet the down Parliamentary train from London due at Sandy at 8.28; and so it would, had more energy and punctuality been shown on leaving Bedford. Being 8 minutes behind time on starting the consequence was I lost the "Parly" and had to return to Bedford, disappointed at the cheapest mode of transit to the North. Lest any other unlucky wight should be caught in the same trap, I write this as a caution.

VIATOR'

Reference has been made to the pioneering in luxury travel by the Midland Railway in 1874. On 21st March of that year, three new Pullman cars named 'Midland', 'Excelsior' and 'Victoria' went from St Pancras to Bedford and back for a trial run. The passengers were directors and friends and lunch was served on board by Spiers & Pond. The experiment was considered successful, and on 1st June a Pullman car was added, as a regular feature, to the 8.30 a.m. from Bradford reaching St Pancras at 2.05 p.m. Generally you bought refreshments at the stations. The *Bedfordshire Mercury* of 15th April 1876 contained a complaint from a hungry traveller, and since the Midland station had a refreshment room which always received favourable mention in the local press, the station referred to must have been the L.N.&W. (later St John's).

'I do not know who is to blame but certainly travellers who find themselves called upon to stop at Bedford station are in a somewhat sorry plight as far as refreshment is concerned. Possibly by roaming round the neighbourhood all that could be required might be obtained, but at the station itself not a bun or a glass of lemonade is to be had.

'Surely there is sufficient energy in the town to establish a refreshment room of some sort so that travellers may not be compelled to regard Bedford as a likely spot in which to be.

STARVED OUT'

A coffee stall was opened in the station yard at St John's from 1940 to 1949, but this seems to be the only period when any facility was available.

Last, we come to the 'Dickens Episode' which produced a good deal of correspondence, and refers to the involuntary stop which the famous

writer made on Bedford station in 1867. The train which Dickens caught –
the 9.35 a.m. from Leicester, was one of the fastest trains of the day in
1867. It ran without stopping to Market Harborough, a distance of 16·15
miles in 24 minutes, an average of 40·4 m.p.h.; the next stop was Bedford,
the time for the 33.1 miles being 45 minutes, giving an average of 44.1
m.p.h. The speed from Irchester to Sharnbrook summit would have been
quite low owing to the gradient of 1 in 120, but once 'over the top' the
driver would take advantage of the falling gradient of 1 in 119 and his
speed would rise to 60 or 65 m.p.h. A Kirtley express engine of the No.
100 class could have done so easily. If he had been delayed at stations or
by signals he would certainly try to make up time. (Modern diesels
exceed 90 here.) The most likely explanation of Dickens' conduct is that
his nerves were in a bad state. He had had a miraculous escape from death
when his train was wrecked at Staplehurst on 9th June 1865 and it is often
suggested that he never really recovered and that his death on 9th June
1870 was hastened by this harrowing experience. A brief account of the
Staplehurst episode will enable us better to appreciate Dickens' appre-
hensiveness. He was travelling from Folkestone to London by 'The Tidal',
that is to say, a train whose departure varied daily according to the time
of high tide in Folkestone Harbour. The train took passengers and goods
off the packet boat, and of course it was the arrival time of the boat which
governed the running of the train. John Benge was foreman in charge of
a gang engaged in renewing the timbers of a bridge over the River
Breult near Staplehurst, and he planned to do part of the work between
the passing of the 2.51 up train and the 4.15 down. He knew there was
'The Tidal' but he had misread his working timetable and thought it
passed at about 5 o'clock. This was sufficiently unfortunate, but he then
acted in a most negligent manner. He knew that the regulations stipulated
that a look-out man should post himself 1,000 yards from the scene of
the operations, having clipped a detonator to the rails every 250 yards as
he walked. Benge told the man to walk only 500 yards and not to use any
detonators. He then proceeded to remove two lengths of rail and the
wooden baulks below, when he heard 'The Tidal' in the distance. The
man posted at 500 yards did his best to warn the driver, but the inadequate
brakes of the period did not permit the driver to stop in time. The train
plunged into the river below the bridge, and Dickens was badly shaken.
He got out of his carriage and helped those who were injured. Later he
wrote to a friend 'A perfect conviction against the senses that the carriage
is down on one side comes upon me with anything like speed.'

Two years later came the Bedford incident. On 5th February 1867 the
Bedfordshire Times published a letter from Mr Andrew Wright referring
to earlier correspondence which had appeared in *The Times*, and in the

same issue of the *Bedfordshire Times* was a long leader much of which is quoted below.

'A ride in a Midland Railway fast train has so operated on the nerves of our good friend Mr. Charles Dickens that he determined to pull up at Bedford, wait for a slower train, and write to *The Times*. His letter which was published on Tuesday and the discussion it has provoked will no doubt produce good results if there is anything wrong. Mr. Dickens wrote as follows:

"As it is better to prevent a horrible accident by a timely caution than sagaciously to observe after its occurence that anyone acquainted with the circumstances out of which it arose could have easily forseen it, I beg most earnestly to warn the public through your columns against the morning express on the Midland Railway between Leicester and Bedford.

"I took the train this morning leaving Leicester at 9.35. The reckless fury of the driving and the violent rocking of the carriages obliged me to leave it at Bedford rather than come on to London with my through ticket. When we stopped at Market Harborough general alarm was expressed by the passengers and strong remonstrances were urged on the officials, also at Bedford. I am an experienced railway traveller at home and abroad; I was in the Staplehurst accident; I have been in trains under most conceivable conditions, but I have never been so shaken and flung about as in this train, and have never been in such obvious danger.

"The very obliging authorities suggested that the road was 'rough' from the thaw and that I was in a light carriage. As to the first suggestion, I am certain from experience on other railways since the thaw set in that there is no such roughness on other railways. As to the second, one of the passengers whc protested the most strongly was a gentleman in a heavy carriagᵉ next to my own. I may add that my companion in the carriagɛ (who left the train with me) is most certainly constantly on English railways and fully confirms what I have here written (January 26th)."

'To publish the whole correspondence from *The Times* would occupy too much space and therefore we give a summary of the chief suggestions offered. Fear is as contagious as the small pox. A number of persons begin now to share the nervousness of Mr. Dickens, who is probably by them regarded as a high authority on railway matters since his last work on "Mugby Junction". Accordingly there are letters from several persons who have passed through the dangers of a ride by express on the Midland Railway. A "Captain R. E." felt the oscillation but his alarm was qualified by his wit and logical reasoning, and he came to the conclusion that the fantastic dance of a drunken character which the carriages were performing could not be accounted for except for the fact that they were in the "Shires" and that the presence of some pink coats and tops in the train might possibly have sent the carriages mad on that pleasant hunting morning. "A Shareholder" followed suit by declaring his belief that the unpleasant oscillation was due to the reckless driving of the express train, and that it is always so when he goes by it. The "Another Traveller on the Line" says that the express rolls and tosses on the Midland Railway but runs smoothly on the Great Northern Railway although at an increased pace. From the general tenor of his letter we glean that an alleged rocking arises from some defect in the permanent way. Then a Mr. G. C. Masters, who says he is a regular traveller on the same line daily, and that Mr. Dickens who is described as the above well-known individual is probably but a casual, adds his testimony that the speed had become "frightful" and that the oscillation was so great that we were rocking about scarcely able to keep our seats. He thinks there are two considerations; that which other correspondents appear to anticipate, *viz.* being killed by a smash on the line, and one which he suggests is nearly as bad "being frightened to death". Mr. W. P. Collins writes to say that Mr. Charles Dickens is right. He adds that the Company drive their light carriages with reckless fury and he is careful to avoid the Midland Railway expresses. Somebody else says that this is not a regular mode of procedure of the expresses and thinks the oscillation complained of might have been caused by the thaw altering the level of the rails. Mr. Alfred Ellis travelled by the train of which Mr. Dickens complains, read one of his books all the way in great comfort, and felt neither rocking nor shaking. He thinks that Mr. Dickens' discomfiture was "due to the imperfect coupling of the carriages and not to the condition of the road". Mr. James Howard of Bedford, who uses the same train very frequently writes as follows:

"I have read with surprise Mr. Charles Dickens' account of the perils of the Midland Railway. I constantly travel by the morning express referred to, which although very fast, runs as smoothly as any I have ever journeyed by. I am an experienced railway traveller like Mr. Dickens having travelled in three-quarters of the globe. The line from Leicester to Hitchin is considered by engineers one of the best pieces of permanent way in the kingdom. I have been a constant traveller on this line since its opening, and never having met with the slightest accident, I think it is only due to the Midland Railway Company with which I am entirely unconnected to assure the public that Mr. Dickens' experience is very different from mine and that they are as safe on the Midland Railway as on any line I am acquainted with."

'Mr. M. T. Bass writes that for his sins (we presume he means political sins) he has to travel some 7,000 miles in the course of the Session on the Midland Railway, principally between Leicester and London. He has given formal notice to the Company's servants of their liability for bumping their passengers about in the express trains. Probably the Company will think this complaint about speed by Mr. Bass as somewhat ungrateful, for if we mistake not, this gentleman at one time brought charges against the Directors at General Meetings for not taking him up to London fast enough. Mr. J. F. Halford testifies that the express trains run a portion of the way at a rate of 60 m.p.h., but that although they have done so on this line for many years there has not been the slightest accident.

'There is much to be said on both sides. Many persons like to go fast and the Midland Railway Directors try to oblige them. In doing so they give them a little more shaking than if they take them gently along by the slow trains . . . It is curious when one knows the persons who compose the Midland Railway Board of Directors, to hear them charged with recklessness, furious driving and generally being "too fast". The public expect to go at the maximum speed, and demand that the trains shall keep time, and in such a case must endure a little more rocking than they would have by slow trains . . .

'We have understood that all persons employed by this Company are well paid and therefore the line should be well worked. The Directors will be benefited by the discussion, and the public will receive a greater assurance of safety when the real cause of the oscillation has been ascertained. Mr. Dickens has so far, done good service by his letter and we hope his next visit to Bedford will be taken under more agreeable conditions.'

CHAPTER 11

ACCIDENTS

Railway accidents never fail to command attention, partly because of their comparative rarity (contrasted for example with road accidents) and partly on account of the massive damage which ensues. An express train in rapid motion possesses a kinetic energy which is frightening in its proportions, and is hardly matched in its destructive power. At first there were few accidents as the railway was little more than a line from A to B and trains were few and widely spaced, but as the system became more complex and trains multiplied in numbers, so did the number of accidents increase. The first locomotives were feeble enough, and the attention of the engineers was concentrated on obtaining more power. The braking of trains was of secondary importance. The method used on road vehicles was adapted, that is to say a train was brought to a stand by the friction of a block of wood against the iron tyre of the locomotive or vehicle. The pressure on the block was increased by a lever, and later more so by a wheel. The normal points of braking were the locomotive tender and the brake van at the rear, helped by brake vans marshalled in the train if necessary. Obviously, braking power was governed by the strength of the operator. In the 1840s and 1850s the number of collisions due solely to inadequate braking power caused engineers to seek some improved method, but another fifty years were to elapse before the ideal – continuous automatic brakes – was to be evolved.

Personal injury on the railway can be divided into two classes (1) accidents to fare-paying passengers arising from a mishap to the train in which they are travelling, and (2) the less spectacular, but no less tragic, accidents to persons crossing the line or straying on to the track for one reason or another.

The absence of accidents on the early railways gave rise to the following eulogy in the *Railway Times* of October 1840:

'The superior safety of railway travelling over that of any other system is established. For example on the London & Birmingham, which was one time dragged before the public more than any other Company for its management, the travelling from September 17th 1838 since it was opened throughout to August 31st last, has been no less than 81 millions of miles, and there have been carried $1\frac{1}{4}$ million of passengers with but a single fatal accident. It is true that there have been a few cases of contusion, but only one serious, and one case of simple fracture.'

Equally enthusiastic was the coroner of Southall who had fifteen miles of the Great Western and fourteen miles of the London & Birmingham in his district. 'During the period 1838 to 1845', he reported, 'I have not held a single inquest. During the same time several inquests on passengers by stage coach have been held – a fact which showed the superiority of railway travel.'

Unfortunately these halcyon days were to come to an end because the very success of the railways resulted in mushroom growth and a far greater density of traffic. The Railway Mania burst upon the country in 1845 and in that year 288 route miles of railway were constructed, to be followed by 634 in 1846 and 712 in 1847. There were two bad accidents in 1847, the first being at the Dee bridge on the Chester & Holyhead Railway, when a cast iron girder broke, tipping the passengers in the leading coaches into the river. Three were killed and sixteen injured. Later that year the tyre of an express engine on the Great Western broke into pieces at Southall, and two drovers travelling in a cattle train on an adjacent line were struck and fatally injured. These misfortunes so preyed on the nerves of Catherine Welby, that she wrote to Mrs Wade-Gery of Bushmead Priory on 1st July 1847:

'Returning by Derby, Northampton and St. Albans to London, now a much better road to traverse than the old North one for accomodation as I found no want of horses and the Inns well kept and arrived the second day after quitting [her sisters] at 6 o'clock. One of the drivers who had the day before conveyed the Duchess of Sutherland, told them there was no doubt but the posting business will be again revived. You may easily believe what joy to my cowardly heart such news was, and I think not less to yours, as I hope after these last two fatal accidents you will no longer venture your Life to such fragile chances, particularly as every year it will be more dangerous all things having been built by contract that alone endangers the case . . .'

Miss Welby's fears were not unreasonable, for avoidable accidents continued to occur for the next forty years. Improved materials and methods of inspection went a long way towards reducing the number of boiler explosions and derailments, but it was the human element which was the principal factor in causing disasters, chiefly because points and signals did not interlock, trains were not worked on a space interval system, and brakes were weak and unreliable. The Board of Trade inspectors, capable men drawn from the Royal Engineers, issued reports after each serious accident emphasising the necessity for 'Lock, Block and Brake.' They meant, of course, interlocking of points and signals, train movements by the block system, and automatic continuous brakes. As the companies were slow to act, Parliament finally tired, and by a series of Acts, notably the Regulation of Railways Act 1889, forced the companies to improve their methods. Often, railway managers spoke of 'interference' by the Board of Trade, and no doubt some boards of directors with an eye to profits, considered the cost of adopting all the precautions would be greater than that of settling claims and repairing damage after an accident. Although there were fifty-three serious accidents between 1847 and 1890, conditions improved considerably in the 20th century, when it could be said that the safest place in Britain was the inside of a railway carriage. Thus as recently as 1964 British Rail carried nearly 1,000 million passengers without a single fatality.

Turning now to accidents on the railway involving members of the public, excluding passengers and workmen, records show that there were thirty-nine inquests on persons killed on the Bedfordshire railways during the thirty-three years from 1854 to 1886. In the early days it is evident from local newspapers that people had not become accustomed to the new high speed of the trains, high that is, in comparison with horse-drawn vehicles. On Monday 28th January 1861 at 7.30 a.m., George Chappel, a platelayer on the Great Northern Railway was making his usual walk along the track between Luton and Dunstable examining chairs and rail joints, when he discovered the body of an old man lying in the 'four foot'. He carried the body to *The Balloon* public house where an inquest was held by Mr Ezra Eagles junior. The victim was Richard Gibbons, who when refreshing himself in that same public house on the previous day, had informed the landlord that he had just had an eight mile walk. Obviously he was healthy enough, but in the semi-darkness of the January morning he misjudged the speed of the train. In this case there was no evidence of alcohol taken to excess, but the same cannot be said of James Cherry, brickmaker of Biggleswade. He entered the *Brickmakers' Arms* public house at 7.30 p.m. on Saturday 23rd March 1861 and drank heavily for two hours. Staggering out of the inn, he made the fatal decision to take a short cut across the Great Northern main line. As he had not arrived home, a search was made early on Sunday morning and the body found near the railway. Despite the fact that Cherry had contributed to his own death, the jury strongly recommended that the G.N.R. should 'adopt means in the future to prevent trespassing on the rails'.

Two years later, at Sandy, drink again seems to have been responsible for a fatality, which happened on the occasion of Sandy Feast. James

Brittain, aged 26, was determined to do justice to the feast for there was an extension of drinking hours. At two o'clock in the morning his friend George Ball happened to meet him near *The Stone Axe* and seeing his helpless state, tried to persuade him to go home by way of the common. Brittain's obstinacy increased, and he closed the conversation by saying 'I'll see you damned first'. Well after midnight George Smallcombe, driver of the mail train, was about 1½ miles from Biggleswade and Thomas Putman, the fireman, thought the engine had struck an object but he did not say anything to Smallcombe until they arrived at King's Cross. The driver immediately examined his engine and what he saw made him notify a station official. In the meantime, John Walden, guard of the following train had seen an object on the line near Biggleswade and had stopped his train. The coroner's jury returned a verdict of 'Accidental Death'.

Deafness could be a contributory cause, because a train coming up-wind is quite noiseless and can trap even people with keen hearing. Possibly that is why Susan Jackson, aged 26, who was crossing the Great Northern main line near Arlesey Siding station early one March morning was knocked down and fatally injured, despite the frantic cries of Mr Walters, the stationmaster. She seemed to hear neither train nor voice. Mr Whyley, the deputy coroner, agreed with the verdict of 'Accidental Death', when the inquest was held at the *Lamb Inn*. When John Bates, labourer, 55 years of age, was killed near the same spot the following year (1865), the jury, on learning that about 800 people crossed the line daily, recommended that the Great Northern Railway should erect a footbridge.

In the case of Thomas Hanger the weather played its part. He was walking to Biddenham when he called at the *Barley Mow* in Bromham Road for three pennyworth of gin and water. It being a cold snowy night, he asked for another, but six penn'orth of gin and water cannot be regarded as out of the ordinary. At 11.30 p.m. warmed by the fire, he set off for Biddenham but made the fatal decision to walk partly along the railway. He had already been struck by one train when the driver of a down goods train passing Bedford just after midnight saw an object lying in his path and found it quite impossible to stop his train before running over the object. Footmarks in the snow showed that Hanger had crossed the line once and had then changed his mind. It was on the stepping over the rails for the second time that he met his death.

However, one inquest shows clearly the difference between then and now. To be poor in the 19th century was to be poor indeed. On 28th July 1861 John King, a builder living in Shefford, saw a man whom he took to be a tramp wandering about the town. In the early hours of the following day the poor wretch was killed by a Midland goods train near

Henlow. His name was never found out, and at the inquest, which was on an unknown man, evidence was given as follows:

John Joyce, who was the fireman on an engine between Shefford and Henlow on Tuesday morning said 'I am a fireman in the employ of the Midland Railway. At 4.25 I saw a man kneeling on the left hand line . . . he seemed to drop. The laff guard of the engine caught him'. (Joyce must have said 'life guard' which today is called a 'guard iron'.) P. C. Reuben Pepper said that he had searched the clothes of the deceased and had found an empty tobacco box, two short pipes, two crusts of bread, part of a boiled potato, no money and two pieces of old newspaper. The inquest did not determine why he died. There was no doubt in the case of James Spring of Sandy, who was charged with 'casting and throwing himself on the line of rails of the Great Northern Railway when a train was due and expected, with intent feloniously wilfully and of his malice afore-thought to kill and murder himself on 6th July 1877'. Spring was arrested before the train arrived, but subsequently was found not guilty and discharged.

Not all accidents were tragic, and for this reason one to a passenger in the 3.40 p.m. Euston to Birmingham express is worth relating. On Monday 23rd January 1871 a young man was travelling alone in a second class compartment when, near Leighton Buzzard, the floor of the carriage suddenly dropped out. He sprang up on the seat, and leaning out of the window, tugged at the communication cord which ran to the guard's van. He said that he heard the bell ringing but the train went on. One or two floor boards, in contact with the rapidly rotating wheels, emitted sparks and splinters and 'jerked about like parched peas in a frying pan'. At length the train slowed down and the young man jumped out without waiting for it to stop, fortunately without injury. His hat and luggage had fallen out with the floor and were found considerably the worse for wear on the track at Leighton. On another occasion at Wolverton, some wagons containing pig carcases were shunted on to the main line by mistake, as the points leading to the siding had been left open. The 5.30 p.m. Liver-pool to Euston express ran into the wagons, splintering them and scattering pork all over the tracks. Willing hands gathered the meat off the lines, and many families in Wolverton dined off roast pork.

So far, the recommendation by the Board of Trade inspectors for the universal adoption of 'lock, block and brake' was meeting with little response. Interlocking would have prevented the approach of the express while the siding points were open. Continuous brakes would have avoided a collision. The Midland Railway had already equipped a train with a new invention – the Westinghouse brake, and on 10th April 1874 a Midland train fitted with this air brake ran to and fro, experimentally, between

St Pancras and Bedford. Unfortunately the brake was not adopted, partly because of disputes between George Westinghouse and certain British railway companies. Thus by 1880 the Midland Board had still not made a decision on the fitting of automatic continuous brakes, and again we find the Bedford to London line the scene of brake trials, this time with Barker's non-automatic vacuum brake, which turned out to be ineffective.

It is remarkable that only two serious accidents occurred in Bedfordshire during the period covered by this book, and in only one could speed be regarded as the relevant factor. In the other the proximate cause was a signalling defect.

The Bedford Accident, Friday 12th March 1875

When the Bedford Railway was opened in 1846, the signalling system then common in England was adopted. A signal had been placed opposite where St John's No. 1 signal box is today, and this signal was intended to be the up starting signal for Bedford. Normally the semaphore arm is located at the end of the station platform, in which position it can more closely control the movement of trains. The disadvantage of the Bedford up starting signal was that, even if at danger, a train could move forward as far as the signal. This was of comparatively little importance between 1846 and 1857, but in the latter year, the Midland Railway extended their line from Leicester to Hitchin, crossing the L.N.W.R. tracks on the level. Rail and road crossings on the level are a nuisance, but when rail crosses rail on the level, danger is added to inconvenience. The Bedford starting signal was now in a position which invited an accident, as a train which stopped in obedience to the signal would stand foul of the Midland lines. However, the L.&N.W.R. made no effort to alter the position of the post. It became the accepted practice at Bedford for a train to wait in the station platform (always referred to as the London platform) until the starter signal was lowered.

On 12th March 1875, the 7.15 a.m. train to Bletchley was standing in Bedford station. The driver received the 'right away' from the guard who had not troubled to see if the signals were 'off'. Although John Perkins was familiar with the road and knew the procedure at Bedford, he unaccountably moved the train forward towards the signal. As he crossed the Midland line he was alarmed to see a green Midland engine and its train of crimson lake coaches speeding towards Bedford. The *Bedfordshire Mercury* relates:

'The signal at the crossing was against the L.&N.W. train, the signalman having lowered the signal for the 6.45 a.m. from Hitchin to cross to the Midland station. As the signal was clear, the driver of the Midland train was coming at his normal pace, but when near the bridge on the Elstow Road, he saw steam rising from the engine of the L.&N.W. train, and thinking this could not be right, he shut off steam as he came through the bridge, and at once applied his brake. Though he did all in his power to avert a collision, and the North Western driver hurried on, the Midland engine caught the last carriage of the L.&N.W. train broadside and went completely through it. The North Western carriage was shivered to splinters. The occupants of the smashed carriage were the Rev. William Sprott of Glasgow, 45, Charles Wilkins, 32, a bricklayer of Bedford, and Mrs. Stimson also of Bedford. Of those seriously injured, the Rev. Mr. Sprott was decidedly the most so. A stretcher was fetched from Britannia Ironworks on which the reverend gentleman was conveyed to the Infirmary; the man Wilkins also. Several persons saw the accident happen and the alarm was given to the Midland and London & North Western stations. A telegraphic message was sent to Bletchley for a breakdown gang. The L.&N.W. train proceeded to Bletchley at 7.45.

'The Midland train sustained little damage; the passengers were uninjured but the engine was derailed. By dinner time the lines were clear. The signalman Bishop is confident as to signals and said to our reporter – "Why, our driver was wrong, the signal was against him. A porter on the L.&N.W. station says the signal was against Perkins".'

Unfortunately Mr Sprott died and at the inquest the signalman, Richard Bishop, said that when he saw the L.&N.W. train going against the signal he ran with a red flag, but the driver was on the left-hand side of the engine. (On most railways the driver stood on the right, but on the L.&N.W. he was on the left.) Bishop also said that the Midland train was travelling at 6 m.p.h. and the L.&N.W. train at 12 m.p.h. at the time of the collision. James Warren, station master at the L.&N.W. station (it was not called St John's until 1924) said that a bell was rung to indicate that the duties at the booking office were completed and the foreman then told the guard he could go. Captain Tyler, the Board of Trade inspector, said that both the L.&N.W. and the Midland signals were on the wrong side of the crossing, and had not been altered since 1857. The verdict at the inquest was one of 'Manslaughter against John Perkins'. He had been dismissed from the railway service after the accident, and was now arrested. Perkins appeared before the Bedford assizes on 26th July 1875 and pleaded, in mitigation, that sleet was falling at the time of the accident. He was fined £20. It is interesting to note that Perkins was defended by the Associated Society of Railway Servants of which he was a member.

One unusual point emerged at the inquest and that was that both drivers were named John Perkins.

The main reason for the accident was the negligent placing of the L.&N.W. signal, but if better brakes had been fitted to the Midland train, the driver could have stopped before the impact. G. P. Neele, superintendent of the L.&N.W.R. in his book *Railway Reminiscences* states that his company was at fault, and that the signal was moved to the end of the up platform (its present position) soon after the accident.

The Arlesey Siding Accident, 23rd December 1876

The year 1876 had begun badly for the Great Northern Railway. On Friday 21st January, there had been a double collision at Abbots Ripton caused by one of the worst blizzards in the records of the time. The G.N.R. had used semaphore arms working in slotted posts and the slots had become filled with snow, preventing the correct aspect being displayed. In December came a somewhat similar accident.

Saturday 23rd December 1876, was a day of biting cold, and the afternoon became prematurely dark with heavy clouds and snow flurries. The 2.45 p.m. express to Manchester was waiting to depart from King's Cross. The competition for Manchester traffic was very keen, and only picked men were found on the Manchester express engines. On the day in question the driver was Thomas Pepper, a man with twenty-five years of excellent service behind him. His mate was George Smith. Pepper left the terminus promptly, but the engine was inclined to slip on the wet rails. The slipping proved troublesome, and by the time the train had passed Potters Bar summit, it was several minutes late. Therefore after Potters Bar Pepper opened the regulator wide. There was a slight rise at Woolmer Green, but thereafter the gradient would be favourable to well past Hitchin. The train would be travelling at 65 m.p.h. at this point.

At Arlesey Siding station (later called Three Counties) a pick-up goods train of twenty-five wagons had arrived from Peterborough. The driver had to attach some more wagons standing in the western siding before going on to London, and this manoeuvre involved crossing the down main line. It was already 3.30 p.m. but Graves, the signalman, unwisely decided that there was time for the goods train to reach the siding before the express was due to pass. He kept the down distant and home signals at danger, and felt safe with this slight protection as the signal lamps had just been lit. If all had gone well, the operation would have been foolish, but as things turned out it was more than foolish. As the train was crossing over to the down line, three wagons became derailed, and Walters the station master frantically summoned some platelayers to assist in re-railing the vehicles. They had just decided that the task was impossible when the distant roar of an express was heard. It was then that they realised that they were to be witnesses of a terrible accident. On the engine, Pepper had been running under clear signals for mile after mile, when, to his surprise and consternation, he saw the red eye of the Arlesey Siding distant signal. This meant that the home signal was also at danger, so he immediately shut the regulator and whistled for the guard to apply the brakes in his van. Smith had already screwed down the tender brake with all his might. But at such a speed the train slid forward on the slippery rail and soon the home signal came in sight, and what was worse, a goods train sprawled across two roads. Pepper told Smith to jump, but he stayed on the engine until just before the collision when he also jumped. He landed on his head and was killed outright. According to the *Bedfordshire Mercury* the engine jumped over one wagon before embedding itself in the next, and five coaches were wrecked. Monk, a railway policeman, went at once to the signal box to have 'obstruction danger' sent by telegraph to the neighbouring boxes. Walters asked for the breakdown train to be sent from Hitchin and for another from Peterborough. He also sent messengers on horseback to Biggleswade for doctors. By 10 p.m. on Saturday the up line was cleared, and the down line by the same time on Sunday. The fatally injured were Thomas Pepper, driver; John Lovell; Abigail Longstaffe of Dulwich, passenger; Lucy Thompson of Grantham, passenger; Maurice Mitchell of London, passenger.

Captain Tyler presided at the Board of Trade enquiry on the accident, and Mr Graham, a Secretary of the Amalgamated Society of Railway Servants was also present. The former deplored the type of brake fitted to the G.N. trains, and he thought that this railway's method of operating the block system was most unsatisfactory. When an express is concerned, it should be signalled several block sections ahead. As Graves decided not to accept the express he should have blocked 'back' to Hitchin, so that the train could have been held there. Both accidents show how right were the Inspectors of the Board of Trade to insist on the interlocking of points and signals; the division of the line into block sections with one train only in any one section at a time; and the necessity for automatic continuous brakes.

Originally the control of the movement of trains was by the time interval system. If several trains were waiting to start, one would be despatched and then after an interval of five or ten minutes, the next would be sent out. If a train stopped through engine failure, then there was nothing to prevent the second train from colliding with the first, unless a railway policeman gave a warning signal. Even then the crude brakes would not always stop the second train in time. Railways therefore began to evolve a better means of control based on a space interval. This was known as the 'Block System' because a line of railway was divided into block sections each under the control of a signal box. The system should mean that only one train is in one block section at a time, which ensures maximum safety. Sections can be many miles long in the country, and only a few yards at a busy junction; although in the latter case there may be modifications, yet the basic principle remains the same.

Growth has been gradual. To replace the railway policeman we find the London & Croydon Railway using Gregory's semaphore signals in 1841. Two years later, the South Eastern Railway began to use interlocking near Bricklayers' Arms. This means that when signals are lowered to permit a train to pass, other signals which might permit conflicting movements are locked in the danger position by mechanical means. About this time the first explosive detonator was used on the rail to warn a driver in foggy weather that his signal was at danger. Further improvements were made when equipment became reliable. For example, the L. & N.W. Railway used the electric telegraph between Wolverton and Tring as early as 1849, and it was useful when a train carrying the Prince Consort travelled up from Northampton.

Signalmen were still, however, having to run some distance from one lever to another, which could be dangerous, particularly in fog or at night. In 1861 the Eastern Counties Railway adopted the idea of grouping the levers in one frame, which is the beginning of the modern type of signal box. The Board of Trade Inspectors were becoming interested in signal interlocking, especially when an accident occurred which would have been prevented by such a device, and in 1873 the Inspectors started to put pressure on the railways to interlock all junction levers. Another step forward was made in 1874 when W. J. Williams of the London Brighton and South Coast Railway invented the notched 'distant' signal which could be passed at danger, but which indicated the position of the next 'stop' signal, thus giving the driver much more space in which to stop his train. The notched arm showed red at night, the same as the stop signal, which could be confusing, so in 1908 the Metropolitan District Railway introduced the yellow arm and yellow light at night. This obvious advantage became general from 1925.

The Regulation of Railways Act (1889) compelled all lines to adopt 'lock and block', i.e. the interlocking of points and signals in signal boxes, and the movement of trains under the block system. In 1892 the Board of Trade required all semaphores to have counterweighted arms to ensure a positive return of the signal arm to danger. It was as late as 1893 before the railways agreed that red should signify danger, and green 'all clear'. Although many railways had already standardised these colours, some persisted with the use of purple for some signals to indicate danger, and white as 'all clear'.

When in the end the automatic continuous brake was adopted, the safety factor on British railways became something of which we could be, and still can be, proud.

CHAPTER 12

RAILWAYS AND RAILWAYMEN

In the world of commerce every corporate body can be divided into the shareholders who provide the capital; the employees who do the work and take something out of it; and finally the public, who form the customers, and therefore put in money to pay the wages and provide a dividend. The employees can be subdivided into two parts – the management who steer the company to provide greater efficiency and profits, thereby increasing their salaries; and the wage earning workers who are concerned mostly with the manual effort to supply the goods. This book would be incomplete unless some reference were made to the relationship between management and employees.

The attitude of the management was to keep a firm hand on the army of employees, and, indeed, no one will quarrel with the maintenance of discipline when public safety is at stake. The railways offered permanent employment to their men, and the specialised work and the security gave rise to a sense of vocation. Generation after generation served on the iron road so that you had 'railway families', who had railways in their blood, and the companies and the public benefited from the men's devotion and their pride in their own particular line.

From the start, the public enjoyed better protection than the employee; if their goods were lost or damaged in transit they were covered by the Carriers' Act of 1830, while in the case of personal injury they had rights at Common Law for compensation. But what of the railwayman? His work whether as driver, shunter or lengthman was dangerous and personal injury was frequent. In the event of accident he could rely only on his rights under Common Law which meant that he had to prove negligence by the company before receiving a penny. In 1837 his rights were further reduced by the text book case of Priestley v. Fowler which established that a workman was deemed to accept the risk of accident caused by the negligence of any one working for the same master, i.e. a fellow employee. With regard to discipline the strictness of the régime can be gauged from the case of John Hewitt, a driver on the Liverpool and Manchester Railway, who was dismissed on 10th February 1836 for being disgruntled and threatening to join a strike. He had no Union to rely upon. On the London & Birmingham Railway in 1838 a porter named John Brand was dismissed for accepting a 6d tip.

It is not surprising, therefore, to find that a modest society was founded in 1839 mainly for the purpose of providing some financial benefit for men injured at work or falling ill, and also to organise men into a fraternity which could deal better with managements. This was the Locomotive Steam Engine Drivers' and Firemen's Friendly Society. The society had plenty of work, for example it seemed desirable that engine drivers should receive more than 8s a day for their exacting and responsible work which extended over 80 hours each week. The Society would not interfere, however, when a gross breach of discipline occurred, and their membership was limited to drivers and firemen.

The year 1848 was unsettled in Europe, and the attempted revolutions in many countries adversely affected trade here. Managements tended to harden in their attitude during times of bad trade when profits were reduced and unemployment increased. Thus the period 1848–50 is one in which several strikes occurred and organised resistance from the men may be said to date from this time. The Locomotive Steam Engine Drivers' and Firemen's Friendly Society called out 240 men, but a strike of this size had little chance of success. But in 1853 business on the L.&N. W.R. was good, so that when porters at Liverpool asked for their wages to be increased from 18s to 19s a week, their request was granted. Station masters were considered comfortably off at £2 a week, and were men of importance in their localities.

However, among railway servants lapses did occur, as when a porter at Sharnbrook was drunk on duty. The *Bedfordshire Mercury* reports:

'23rd August 1858. Sharnbrook. Committal of railway porter for being drunk.

On Friday week, Heley Abbey, a porter on the Leicester & Hitchin Railway, stationed at Sharnbrook, was taken by Superintendent Graham before J. Gibbard Esq., on a charge of having been found drunk and incapable of performing his duty while in the employment of the Railway Company. Mr. J. Jeffrey, Inspector from Derby, attended on behalf of the Company to prefer the charge. Mr. T. Sheel, station master, proved the offence. The defendant admitted he was guilty and asked the magistrate to deal leniently with him. He was committed to gaol for seven days with hard labour.'

The company would have little difficulty in replacing the porter as they had long waiting lists.

In the matter of accidents, the law could appear unfair in its attitude to employees. In April 1865 a pick-up goods train had stopped at Southill on its way from Leicester to King's Cross. Thomas Charlton the guard informed William Oldham the driver that in the shunting they were to put off one wagon and pick up four. The first operation was carried out, but when Charlton went to hook on the four wagons he tripped and was crushed by the buffers. The inquest was held at *The White Horse* public house, and a verdict of accidental death was returned to Mr Whyley, the coroner. In November 1866 Thomas Adams, a lengthman, was walking towards Bedford along the 'four foot' on the down main line with his back to the trains, instead of following the normal practice of walking so that one faced the trains. Just as it was getting dusk he was run down and killed by an express. Again the verdict was accidental death. In both cases the dependants received not a penny. The law does not award damages in the case of a pure accident, that is to say, an accident not arising out of someone's negligence. But even if it could have been proved that the accident at Southill had been caused by Charlton tripping over material left near the track by a platelayer and that Adams was run down because the driver was not looking ahead, then the company would still have sheltered behind the doctrine of Common Employment. The employee was thus worse off than the fare paying public, as a passenger injured through the negligence of a railway servant would always be able to obtain compensation. It was not until 1880 that public opinion, acting through parliament and press, brought about the Employers' Liability Act (1880) which abolished the defence of Common Employment.

The 1860s therefore saw the men disunited and unable to bring pressure to bear on the managements to redress the main evils which beset their work: inadequate pay; excessive hours; and inherent danger. The footplatemen had a small society but support was weak, because many men had been nominated for employment by directors of the company and therefore considered themselves under an obligation. Others had had to deposit a sum of money as security, while yet others lived in companies' cottages at nominal rents. Some lines like the London Brighton & South Coast Railway gave an annual bonus of £5 to drivers and policemen. Furthermore, wages paid to engine crews compared favourably with those of other trades (1865) as follows: driver 45s a week; fireman 35s a week; farm labourer 11s 6d.

Excessive hours were commonplace. Investigation into an accident at Daubhill in January 1865 showed that a signalman had been working daily from 5.30 a.m. to 9 p.m., and in addition to his signalling duties had had to open and shut level crossing gates.

There was no danger for those on clerical work, but they too had long hours and low pay. On 11th October 1865 the second of the great unions was formed – the Railway Clerks' Association (now the Transport Salaried Staff's Association). The year 1867 was one of financial depression and it is not surprising to read of an outbreak of strikes, which on the whole were unsuccessful. In cases where the strikers won, the negotiations had taken place between themselves and the Directors, since the latter refused to recognise the unions. Where a strike collapsed, the unions lost members. The Locomotive Steam Engine Drivers' and Firemen's Society did not survive this year and was dissolved.

The Reform Act of 1867 meant that more railwaymen were entitled to vote, and more candidates were able to go to Parliament as railway members. The Railway Clerks' Association was becoming stronger, but could not assist the great mass of manual workers, who, since the end of the Locomotive Society had no unifying body, and had to rely on the protection afforded by the law. The inspectors of the Board of Trade, always vigilant for the safety of passengers, continued to deplore the excessive hours of work. In 1871 an increase in trade resulted in a demand for extra efforts by the railway workmen. Drivers were working $19\frac{1}{2}$ hours a day, and pointsmen 15 hours. Mr Bass, the M.P. for Burton on Trent, revealed in the Commons that a guard in 1870 had worked from 6.35 p.m. on 23rd December to 2 p.m. on 25th December without a break. At the same time a signalman had worked for $102\frac{1}{2}$ hours in a week. The men needed protection, and the Amalgamated Society of Railway Servants was formed in 1871 with W. Chapman as Secretary. Help came too from Gladstone with the Trade Union Act of 1871 which gave the society legal status, though strikes were still considered illegal. The first Great Delegate Meeting of the A.S.R.S. was held in London on 24th June 1872, and J. Abbott was the delegate from Bedford.

Board of Trade returns for 1872 showed that fifty-four railwaymen were killed while working, especially when shunting. The Board forced the Railway Companies to have destination tickets and brake levers on both sides of the wagons to save the shunters having to dodge between buffers to read the tickets or apply brakes. The membership of the A.S.R.S. was 17,247 in 1872 and this had fallen to 6,321 by 1882 largely because the provinces distrusted London. Nevertheless the Committee were able to open the Railway Orphanage at Derby in 1875. The next year Disraeli introduced a Trade Union Act which gave yet more strength to the Union movement.

The locomotive men had always considered themselves apart from the general railway workers, and claimed that their work required more skill and carried more responsibility. Previously they had had their own society, and in the last month of 1879 they created the Associated Society of Locomotive Engineers and Firemen, which is still active.

The last year of the decade saw the passing of the Employers' Liability

Act which abolished the doctrine of 'Common Employment', and there was now some redress when a man was injured or killed.

Bedford was chosen as a meeting place for the Associated Society of Railway Servants on 3rd April 1885, and the *Bedfordshire Mercury* reported:

'The Associated Society of Railway Servants held a meeting in Bedford on Good Friday 3rd April 1885 at Roff's Rooms, 34 High Street, Bedford, supported by Mr. Meredyth (Chief Constable) and presided over by Alderman Coombs. Mr. Ellis, Secretary of the A.S.R.S. was present. A band played music including the Caliph of Baghdad. The report for 1884 said that 214 orphans were in receipt of weekly payments costing £872 per annum. The proceedings ended with a toast of H.M. the Queen.'

In the same year Bedford was chosen by the Railway Temperance Union for their annual meeting, which was held in the Assembly Rooms on Wednesday 14th October 1885.

In 1889 came the Regulation of Railways Act which enforced the adoption of continuous automatic brakes, the block system of train control and the interlocking of points and signals. In the same year a split occurred in the Amalgamated Society of Railway Servants. At the A.G.M. the motion that lower grades of railway staff should contribute only 3d a week was defeated, and the disgruntled lower grades broke away and founded the General Railway Workers' Union.

As the century came to an end Parliament passed the first of the Workmen's Compensation Acts, and the Act of 1897 introduced the principle of compensation irrespective of negligence. Only certain trades were included, but railways were among them. Thus railway workers now had fair security, in addition to their pride in their job.

CHAPTER 13

CRIME

Not many people would have sympathised with Ruskin's denunciation of the railways, but even those who disliked them were happy to use the facilities the railways offered. Among the first eager customers were citizens both good and bad, and a petition to Quarter Sessions in 1860 from some leading Luton townsfolk asking for more police constables, shows how the railway there was used. The petitioners stated:

'That numerous attempts at Burglary and Housebreaking have been recently made at Luton some of which have succeeded and property to a considerable amount has been taken away and that very recently Two well known and experienced Thieves were apprehended in the Vestry Room of the Parish Church who made a desperate resistance but fortunately the Police were on the look out . . a complete set of Skeleton Keys and Housebreaking Implements were found in their possession . . That since the opening of the Railway from Luton to Hatfield, Thieves have much greater facility in disposing of their plunder by taking an early morning Train to London in little more than an hour and before the Police are aware of the Transaction . . .'

But trains were not just convenient for escaping, but also suitable for some sorts of theft. The modern corridor coach did not become common until the end of the 19th century, and the ordinary compartments were an ideal medium for the criminal, especially if they contained only one person. Thus the most common form of crime, during this period, was personal assault with robbery as the motive, for there was no communication between carriages.

Public opinion gave H. Sheridan the opportunity to introduce his Railways (Guards' and Passengers' Communication) Bill in May 1857, which though good in conception, did not go far enough. Railways could adopt any form of communication they wished, and the result was that many companies fitted unreliable systems to their coaches, which were in effect useless.

A murder by an immigrant called Muller in 1864 caused the greatest outcry, but the railways' response varied from gradually fitting Harrison's external cord, to fitting of 'Muller's lights' on the London & South

Western Railway. These were circular 'portholes' cut in the compartments so that what took place in one compartment could be heard in the whole carriage. Although there may have been an increase in safety, the holes met with mixed reception. The Harrison type of alarm had certain basic defects. For example, when attacked by a thief, the victim had to arrange a temporary truce while he let down the window, stood on the seat, and groped for a cord which ran outside the carriage. The cord could be imperfectly connected to the guard's van, and when the guard heard the bell he might choose to do nothing. Thieves, ignorant of the common courtesies of life, seldom complied.

Meanwhile annoyance and assault continued. As was often the case, it was the smaller southern railways who showed the most enterprise, while the large northern lines held aloof. In 1865, on the South Eastern Railway, many coaches were fitted with the Walker electric alarm system, and the London & South Western adopted the Preece system. Both were worked from batteries, and both gave the alarm by ringing a bell in the guard's van. Unfortunately, in practice, it was found that the contacts became corroded, and the alarm proved unreliable.

Railway crime was not, of course, confined to assault. There is a report in the *Bedfordshire Mercury* for 16th October 1865 of an attempted burglary at Leighton Buzzard station.

'Very early in the morning of Sunday 8th October 1865 a rough looking fellow was seen loitering about the station. Mr. Maltby, telegraph clerk, heard a crash and taking a light saw that someone had broken the window of the ticket office. He saw two men standing at the corner nearest the bridge crossing the line and called to them. They ran off. He went for assistance but they had decamped in the meantime. At the corner of the bridge were found a cudgel, a muffler, a whistle, a knife and a taper and matches.'

Fortunately on this occasion there was no loss and no one was hurt.

Meanwhile, the larger northern railways were beginning to show a belated interest in passenger-guard communication, and a meeting was arranged at Euston for Wednesday 17th January 1866 to see a demonstration of Howell's Patent Communication, a somewhat complicated device. The *Bedfordshire Mercury* reports:

'Among those present were G. P. Neele, W. Cawkwell of the London & North Western Railway, J. Smithells of the London & York (Great Northern), Mr. Yoekney of the Sirhowy Railway and E. M. Needham of the Midland. *System.* A brass tube to run the length of the train with india rubber connections between cars, closed at one end, the other connected to the blast pipe of the engine, and so all the air is exhausted. A ball (numbered) is placed in an upright pipe in each compartment, covered by an airtight cap. By pulling a cord the cap opens and the rush of air sends the ball to the guard's van where it moves a trigger and explodes a detonator. The guard examines the ball and knows by the number from which compartment it came.

The rush of air also blows an external whistle to attract the attention of the driver. If the balls were hollow a message could be written and placed in. The experiment was completely successful.'

This ingenious arrangement would not have operated if the train stopped in a tunnel (a very likely place for an attack) as the engine would have no steam exhausting through the blast pipe. As for the message to be placed in a ball, the thief might show signs of impatience if the message were a long one.

The Great Western Railway was still content with the outside cord as late as 1874, when a bad accident at Shipton on Cherwell, on Christmas Eve, proved once more, if further proof were needed, that the outside cord was futile. It was now the turn of the Midland Railway to be the scene of a crime, unusual in some of its details.

Early in 1875 the Midland, always to the fore in the question of passenger comfort, had introduced Pullman coaches on some of its trains. These became immediately popular. Just before midnight on 14th June 1875 a young man named Harry Gustavus Hamilton took his seat in the Pullman coach attached to the train which departed punctually at 12 o'clock. He found his travelling companions genial, and their address was reassuring – they were the Reverend William Spragg, Herbert Willes, and Samuel Freeman. Soon after the train left St Pancras the three strangers suggested a game of cards, but when they found that they were unable to swindle Hamilton out of his money, they descended to assault and robbery. Hamilton put up a strong resistance, and had the coach been fitted with the modern alarm chain, he would have been able to put the guard on the alert and perhaps to have saved his life. As the train sped towards Flitwick he was thrust out of the carriage, and his body was found near the track next morning. Subsequently the three were arrested and charged with feloniously killing Harry Gustavus Hamilton. Herbert Willes had been too drunk to do much, but his companions received the maximum term of imprisonment. Spragg's clerical collar had been assumed merely to inspire confidence in his victims.

Although newspapers campaigned for better passenger communication, nothing much could be done until automatic continuous brakes were fitted to trains and this took place in the last decade of the century. With the Westinghouse system, pulling the alarm chain opened a valve in the train pipe and caused a slight application of the brake. The driver would feel a check to his speed, and the air pressure gauge on the locomotive would register a drop in pressure. The gauge in the guard's van would tell the same story. It was then for the driver to stop at once or proceed to the next station according to circumstances.

Once again, it was a small railway which led the way to safer travel. The Manchester Sheffield & Lincolnshire Railway (later the Great Central) evolved the modern system and it won immediate approval from the Board of Trade, and it was not long before every passenger train in this country, running on tracks of normal gauge, was suitably equipped.

CHAPTER 14

THE RAILWAY AGE – A SUMMARY

In 1838 when the first train on the London & Birmingham Railway passed through Rugby, Dr Arnold is reported as saying 'There goes the death-blow of feudality'. The editor of the *Railway Record* saw this clearly in July 1846 when he wrote in his leading article:

'Railways have effected a great social revolution. Brighton, the favoured retreat of Majesty . . . can now be reached by 2,000 passengers in a single train of 44 carriages, and at a cost of 5s return. The stage coach fare had been £1 and it took all day. The train left at 7 a.m. and arrived in Brighton at 9 a.m.'

After the Napoleonic wars, the country had entered a period of depression and unemployment combined with a rapidly rising population. The conditions in Bedfordshire are seen in the Woburn correspondence. There is a letter dated 15th September 1833 from Crocker, the Duke of Bedford's steward at Woburn, to W. G. Adam, Agent-in-chief in London:

' . . . there are so many unemployed in . . . Westoning, Flitton, Toddington, etc. and the feeling among them appears to reckless . . . There was a fire at Eaton Bray yesterday morning which destroyed the Tithe barn.'

In another letter (20th September 1834) Crocker mentions that farmers have lowered wages from 9s to 8s. Shortly afterwards, a new steward, Thomas Bennett states that 'at Steppingley . . the few farmers there are terrified out of their wits'. Well they might be, for Bennett reports that an outbuilding belonging to the Overseer of the Poor was set on fire, and glass broken in the houses of the Reverend Mr Green and Mr Cook. The burden of the losses by fire fell on to the insurance companies, and Bennett reports on 6th February 1835 that the County Fire Office have sent a police officer to Wilden to try and trace the incendiaries. Bennett saw before most people that the only permanent solution was mass emigration. in a letter to Adam written on 30th November 1834 he said ' . . . We have a surplus population . . . without some means . . . to dispose of this redundancy the Workhouse system will fail . . . If this is admitted we must turn . . . to emigration. [The demand for agricultural labour is only seasonal] and there is always plenty of Irish . . . The owners of the soil can never look to any permanent relief until a considerable part of the population will leave the Country altogether. We cannot expect to get many of the married people to go . . . and the single man is so much better off [on relief than a married man] that he will not look for anything better . . .'. The railways therefore played a part in ameliorating unemployment, though the large numbers of men needed when a line was being built were needed for too short a time. But any relief was welcomed. The *Bedfordshire Mercury* reported on 9th March 1863 that the Midland Railway was proposing to open a railway plant at Bedford capable of employing 1,000 persons. In fact this proposal came to nothing, but the railways did give steady employment to thousands of men throughout the last century.

The thirty years of comparative peace after Waterloo allowed an accretion of capital in Great Britain, and the growing railways system gave investors a use for their accumulated wealth. However, the capital could be used either for steady investment in sound railways, or in hasty speculation in unsound ones. The new industry made possible a new crime, and even the honest Buckinghamshire Railway was involved being the victim of scrip forgeries. Here is what the *Railway Record* said on 27th June 1846:

'Scrip Forgeries. The trial of Faulkner and Fabian on a charge of issuing forged scrip of the Buckinghamshire Railway has been postponed to the next sessions of the Central Criminal Court. The Recorder said "The enormous capital now invested in railways renders it necessary to take the greatest possible care to prevent fraud as much as possible".'

However, most railway stock was a very sound investment. A notebook kept by Francis Wythes of Ravensden House, near Bedford, shows a characteristic railway share list between 1846 and 1878. He had shares in 1878 in the Great Eastern Railway, London & North Western, Great Northern, North Staffordshire, London & South Western; Somerset & Dorset; and North Eastern Railway Company, lessees of the Whitby Redcar and Middlesboro' Union Railway Company.

The demand for land had tended towards inflationary prices, and both landowners and railway men accused the other side of unscrupulous behaviour. A letter from Thomas Bennett to Haedy of 4th January 1846 refers to the Bedford Railway and also to the Bedford and Cambridge Railway (1845). Mr Theed Pearse was the Bedford solicitor who worked for the Bedford line.

'I will communicate with Mr. Wing on the Bedfordshire Railways. As far as Bedfordshire is concerned, the lines in connexion with the

Birmingham & London, the Eastern Counties, and the Midland Counties, are those which are the most worthy of the Duke's support, but there may, on examination, be exceptions and some of the schemes may likewise not suit the Thorney Estate.

'I am sorry to find that Mr. Cuming and Mr. Sandars do not at all hit, and [are] not likely to agree. Mr. Pearse having lately bought land (subject to be flooded after every heavy rain) at £200 per acre, they are using this as a lever and are taking the high hand bullying tone, which appears to be Railway manners . . . I saw Mr. Pearse . . . and I said that Sandars had used his name as an authority for land being to be bought for £200 an acre close to Bedford, and I pointed out to him the difference of value in the estimation of practical builders between ground above reach of water, and that subject to be flooded and I also said that the bullying system would not go down with us and Mr. Sandars had now got our final offer. I further said that if the system was pursued, the Duke had not given assent to the Cambridge Extension and to the seven acres they meant to take from him for a station. They must therefore be prepared to encounter his Grace's opposition unless the price shall be agreed on beforehand. This appeared to alarm him, and he said he trusted the two would meet and agree and save any unpleasant proceedings between the Duke and the Company as the time is gone past for giving anyone else notice. I think we are safe in applying the screw. They must either buy the Duke's land or wait another year for their Act.'

In 1854 it is the Hitchin extension of the Midland which calls for a letter from Bennett and the following was written on 1st January:

'As the amount to which the land belonging to the Duke of Bedford is only some £1,500 or thereabouts, it cannot be of much avail, to the Directors, whether paid for at once or converted into shares, but I can easily imagine they may expect that the Duke's name along with other influential landowners on the line, will be of service to them, by such support.'

Bennett again refers to the Midland extension, and sighs for the happy days of 1846 when he writes to Haedy on 21st January 1855:

'No doubt the days for giving £1,000 an acre for Railway uses are past and gone – we must now be content with the pleasing reminiscence of those sunny times.

'The Hitchin and Leicester take about 1½ acre on the south of Elstow Road, which I sold some months ago at three hundred pounds an acre . . .'

Sunday travel caused trouble. and the Church of England found itself in alliance with sects with whom it normally had little in common, over this vexed question. Excursions were the main target. Sir John Easthope, Chairman of the London & South Western Railway, was not a man to be easily intimidated. Archdeacon Hoare of Winchester perceived with the most unfeigned regret that the day of religious rest was constantly desecrated by the running of trains upon the railway and suggested that the Divine blessing could scarcely be expected to rest upon the South Western Railway in consequence. Sir John Easthope rebutted the statement, and imputed that the Diocesan authorities were concerned only with preventing the movement of common people on the day when labour did not keep them in their place. This was in 1846.

The London & North Western Railway was one of the few to discourage Sunday excursion trains. This rule was enforced while Captain Huish was General Manager. The *Bedfordshire Mercury* quotes his remarks in 1862:

'Sunday Railway Work

Captain Huish, for 18 years Chief Manager of the London & North Western Railway bears the following business testimony on the subject:

"In answer to your enquiry and your desire to have my opinion in regard to Sunday excursion trains, gathered from my 18 years' experience as General Manager of the L.N.W.R., I can only say that during that time no excursion trains ever ran on a Sunday; and I am satisfied that while the interests of the proprietors did not suffer, the discipline and character of the Company were promoted.

"I have had a large experience of excursion traffic and was always favourable to its development, but I believe no Company ultimately benefits by working its system to the extent of seven days a week, and that by a well arranged system of Saturday trains returning on a Monday an equal pecuniary return at a much less cost is produced. Putting the question therefore on the lowest ground of argument, I have no hesitation in saying that a railway Company consults its true interests in restraining Sunday work within as *narrow* limits as possible. The Scotch railways as a whole pay better than the English ones and there the work on a Sunday is reduced to a minimum.'

The Captain, writing from his Isle of Wight home after retirement, puts the case well, but he overlooks the fact that many people want a one day excursion and not three, as he suggests, particularly if you take into account the additional cost of two nights' lodging. From the railways' point of view, Sunday excursions have the merit of occupying tracks which are free from the more crowded weekday services. If it were true that Scottish railways were more profitable than English ones, it does not follow that the reason is the banning of Sunday excursion trains.

More opposition came from hunting people, who were afraid that the railway would interfere with their activities. When the Midland line from Leicester to Hitchin was being built, there were protests from the Shires, and in his letter to Haedy of 1st January 1854 Thomas Bennett is probably referring to the Oakley Hunt.

'I believe many of the Hunting people think the Rail will be injurious to their sport; whether it will, or no, may be known from the experience of other hunting districts through which Railways pass, but this cannot much signify, from the low ebb to which fox-hunting has come in Bedfordshire . . . But there can be no doubt that any line going through a district, must eventually, indirectly or directly, tend to its improved value.'

The railways brought a new threat to the welfare of farm animals because of the speed with which livestock could be moved from place to place. The cattle plague, or foot and mouth disease, had always been a scourge, but it could be confined within known geographical limits up to, say, 1850. But now animals could be on a farm in Kent one day, and be detrained in Cumberland on the next, and disease was spread quickly over the countryside. Also, despite some hesitation to begin with, the railway companies had begun to develop a traffic in truckloads of stable manure, and this also could carry infection. There was a virulent outbreak of cattle plague in the years 1865–66, and the Bedfordshire Quarter Sessions minutes reflect local concern. At the adjourned Epiphany Session on 19th January 1866 the Clerk of the Peace read a copy of the following letter sent by the Clerk to the Toseland Justices to the Home Secretary.

'Saint Neots
Sir,   18th January 1866
Cattle Plague

I am directed by the Justices of the Peace for the Toseland Division of the County of Huntingdon to inform you that in the Petty Sessional Division of Toseland and to a much greater extent in the adjoining County of Bedford many acres are annually sown with Onion seed in the month of February – for this crop a large quantity of manure is used which is not ploughed in but is spread upon the surface and is sometimes harrowed in but often only raked over so as to make a level surface and the greater part of the manure remains on the surface.

The Justices are informed that the gardeners in this neighbourhood are bringing down large quantities of manure from London by the

Great Northern Railway to the Saint Neots Station which will be used for the Onion crop as above stated and they think that there can be no doubt that much of this Manure will come from cow sheds where animals have been kept which have died of the cattle plague and that there is great danger of the plague being extensively spread by means of this manure.

The Justices are informed that in several instances parts of animals (supposed to have died of the plague) have been sent down in the manure trucks.'

As a result, the Chairman of the Bedfordshire Quarter Sessions had an interview with managers of the Midland and of the Great Northern Railways, and gave his report on 3rd February:

'The Great Northern send nothing but horse manure from King's Cross so far as they are aware.

'The Midland Company the same.

'The Great Northern employ a man to inspect the loading of manure to see that it does not contain any portion of carcases.

'The Midland Company's representative undertook to do the same.

'The Great Northern suggested a form of Certificate to be handed to them by the senders of manure which they and the Midland agreed to adopt provided the Metropolitan authorities agreed to give their Inspectors instructions to sign them.

'Failing this Certificate the Great Northern and Midland expressed their willingness to refuse manure which they suspected as coming from infected stables or places.

'RESOLVED . . . that unless the London and North Western Railway Company consent to the same conditions as have been agreed to on behalf of the Great Northern and Midland Railways the Court may be compelled to prohibit the conveyance of manure etc. into this county by the London and North Western Railway.

'RESOLVED that whereas . . . the Justices of Bedfordshire have agreed with the Directors of the G.N.R. and Midland Railway that no manure shall be sent into that county by the said companies unless the sender produce to the agent of the said company a certificate signed by an Inspector of Police of the District from which the manure is brought stating that to the best of his belief such manure does not come from any infected premises.

'The said Justices do hereby request that Sir Richard Mayne will give orders to the Inspectors of the Metropolitan Police to sign such certificates when they can with truth do so . . .

'that the said Justices . . . have resolved and determined to declare and do hereby declare

'That it is expedient that until the 1st day of March next ensuing no raw or untanned hide, skin, hoof or offal . . . shall be brought from any place in Great Britain into the county of Bedford . . .

'That it is expedient that until the 1st day of March next ensuing no dung, hay, straw, fodder or litter likely to propagate infection shall be removed from any place in the said county where the cattle plague exists . . or has existed within a period of 42 days next previously thereto, to any other place within the said county,

'That it is expedient that until the 1st day of March next ensuing no sheep, lamb, goat, or swine shall be removed from any part of the county of Bedford where the cattle plague exists at the time of such intended removal or has existed within a period of 42 days next previously thereto, to any other place within the said county . . .'

The outbreak lasted until late in the year, for on 31st July 1866 proceedings were taken against a farmer and a railway goods clerk who had apparently collaborated to defeat the law. It appears that the L.N.W.R. had removed some cattle, seven cows and a calf, from Winslow in Buckinghamshire to Leighton Buzzard without a magistrate's licence. A licence had been obtained to move the beasts from Winslow to Granborough, two miles away, but Bailey, the farmer, wanted to get his beasts to Leighton market, so he told the goods clerk at Winslow that the word 'Granborough' was a clerical error, and should be altered to 'Leighton'. The clerk did so, without troubling to verify the statement, and both were fined the sum of 2s 6d.

The very nature of a railway company's business, that is, the carriage of goods and passengers at high speeds for long distances, and the use of machines which could emit sparks, soon meant that they were hedged in with legal liabilities. The type of locomotive used made the emission of sparks an everyday occurrence, and claims for compensation were pressed home by owners of property damaged by fire. At Kempston Hardwick, on 2nd August 1858, the 4 a.m. train from Bedford set fire to some growing corn, consisting of 10 acres of barley belonging to John Emery and 5½ acres of wheat the property of Robert Whitworth, on the other side of the line. The fire hazard was particularly great in August when the corn was dry and ripe and ready for harvesting. The *Bedfordshire Mercury* reported an incident at Sandy on 4th May 1863:

'A serious fire occurred at Warren Farm, the property of Arthur Peel Esq., in the occupation of Mr. Robertson, on Monday 27th April, between 9 and 10 a.m. The fire was caused by a spark thrown from an engine of the Bedford & Cambridge Railway. The Sandy,

Potton and Biggleswade engines were quickly on the spot, but nearly the entire newly erected farm buildings were destroyed, and a large quantity of potatoes and some farm implements. The total damage is £800.'

An attempt to obtain money for lack of reasonable care was disclosed in a case against the L.&N.W. Railway heard at the Luton County Court in 1859. Mrs Oliver was the owner of a Turin vase and some wax flowers which she was taking from Liverpool to Luton. She changed trains at Leighton Buzzard. She said that she examined the vase and flowers on arrival at Luton station and found them damaged. She stated that she had carried the parcel on her lap from Liverpool to Leighton, but she entrusted the parcel to the guard when she entered the local train at Leighton Buzzard. Unfortunately for her, she made contradictory statements under cross-examination, changing her story to having placed the parcel in the care of the guard at Liverpool. Mr Justice Coe was not impressed and found for the defendants. On hearing that his wife had lost her case, Mr Oliver, in a fury, stated that the judge had called him a liar, and that he kept company with better people than the judge. He then left the court 'in a dreadful rage'.

The increasing liabilities placed upon the public gave insurance companies their chance and they soon had schemes for policies of every description – Personal Accident in case of a train smash; Life Assurance so that dependants would be protected; Baggage and Parcel Insurance to cover loss and damage. The first company to embark on accident insurance was the Railway Passengers' Assurance Company, which commenced business in 1849. The following letter, an advertisement in the *Railway Times*, shows the benefit of insurance cover:

'Dunstable,
28th November 1849

I was travelling by railway from Penrith to Preston on the night of the 1st inst., and having occasion to go out of the train at the latter station, by the carelessness of the porter I was led over the edge of the turntable and seriously injured on the head and ribs, and three of my teeth force out, which laid me up for several days. I had previously effected an insurance against railway accidents, with the Railway Passengers Assurance Company, and when sufficiently able to get up to London, I at once gave notice to the officers of that Company, in Old Broad Street, that I had met with an accident. They immediately sent their medical officer to Mullins Hotel where I was staying, and in the course of a few days I was well enough to make my claim in person at the offices of the above Company.

I adduced evidence of my costs, both for medical attendance in the country and in London, and my hotel expenses, and within three weeks after the day of the accident received the compensation which I thought fit to demand, without demur or the loss of an hour's time.

William Good'

The railways naturally did what they could to avoid losing money. One way was the public's desire to travel without payment, which is no new thing. One William Pepper was convicted in Bedford in 1858 of travelling in a Midland train to Shefford with intent to avoid paying the fare. He was convicted, but the conviction was quashed on appeal. The railway companies have always been worried by the amount they have to pay for the occupation of land and buildings, particularly as in more recent years, some of the money which they have paid has gone to improve the roads, their great competitors. The L.&N.W. Railway appealed on 19th October 1870 against the rates levied on property at Kempston and Goldington. The appeal was 'respited' no fewer than eight times, and finally on 1st January 1873 was dismissed for both places. The company had better fortune in 1878 when an appeal was lodged on 10th April in respect of railway buildings in Lidlington, Marston, Willington, Cople, Cardington, Eastcotts, Wootton, Kempston and Elstow. It was respited until 4th June of the same year, when the railway managed to obtain reductions for six of the stations.

When the first railways opened, each station used its local time, and when the line was short, or ran from north to south, there was no confusion. But railways like the Great Western and also the London & North Western extended across several lines of longitude, and Plymouth time, for example, was about 20 minutes after Paddington time. The Board of Trade inspectors were the first to complain and to ask for uniform time. So when the L.&N.W. opened their Trent Valley line (Rugby to Stafford) in 1847, they compelled all the stations to use London time and this applied to all L.N.W.R. stations. Other lines followed suit in due course.

Advertising spread to station platforms, although the newspapers still held first place. The *Bedfordshire Mercury* in 1847 had the following:

'Joseph Manning of Threadneedle Street, London, who supplied the drink for the opening of the Bedford Railway, offers Champagne 54s a dozen, Single Stout 4s 6d a dozen.'

A more usual advertisement in this paper was:

'COALS! COALS!! COALS!!!
The best and cheapest coal supplied by Joseph Firbank, address: Head Office, North Western Station, Bedford.'

Not only did the railways themselves stand high in public esteem, but railway officials enjoyed considerable social standing. The station master of 100 years ago wore a frock coat and a top hat, and was well-known in his town, for he would make it his business to call on everyone who could provide custom for the railway. He was a person who would be asked for references. Therefore when Mr John Robinson was about to leave Sandy (L.N.W.) for Rugeley, a well-deserved promotion, he was presented with a silver cup with the inscription:

'Presented by the inhabitants of Sandy to John Robinson as a mark of their high estimation of his merits and general attention as station master of the London & North Western Railway station at Sandy from August 1862 to February 1867.'

The staff of a large station was much more numerous in the 19th century and from such large numbers it was easy to pick a cricket eleven. Friendly matches were arranged, such as that between Kempston and the Midland Railway, Bedford, on 4th September 1869. The Midland team won by an innings, and had two excellent bowlers in King and Stanley.

What did the railways do for Bedfordshire? Very much what they did for the country as a whole. People were given the benefit of fast, cheap and safe travel, and so the travel habit was started which has never stopped. People now know more about their own country. Employment was given to thousands when the railways were built, and to thousands more who ran them. Bedford became the hub of a wheel with six spokes radiating from it, and so was easily in touch with all the neighbouring towns. Luton would not have developed its industry without the railway, and until 1948 there was no town in England more than 10 miles from a station. Against these advantages there was the smoke nuisance near engine sheds, noise of shunting in sidings, and the depreciation of property near railways. But when once the embankments and cuttings have grassed over, it is often difficult to see where a line crosses the countryside, and as a train carries people in the mass, there are fewer trains. In contrast, the motorways bring a roar of vehicles that does not cease day and night.

Despite press criticism, our railways today (in the field of technical efficiency) were never better. Speeds reach 100 m.p.h. daily with the latest electronic equipment at the lineside and in signal boxes. Foreign railway executives, who are the best people to judge, marvel at the density of our traffic, and the speed allied with punctuality. Turbine driven trains (tried here in 1959 but found unreliable) in an improved version will be able to run at 125 m.p.h. in a few years. The aeroplane has to lift everything before it can transport it, so heavy traffic is ruled out, and although road traffic carries many passengers and much of the most profitable freight, it does so at a frightening cost in human life and limb. One of the strange facets of 20th century society is that the sacrifice is tolerated. As an American writer has said 'People are no longer interested in safety'. Although many branch lines have been cut off, because the last four Transport Acts have insisted on the railways balancing their budget, and the total route mileage has dropped from 19,000 to 13,000, what is left is the cream of the system, and it is encouraging to find that receipts from the all important freight traffic increase each year. We can therefore regard the railways' future with sober confidence.

Appendix A

Timetables for L.N.W.R. and branches

A.1 *November 1846 Bedford Railway* (worked by L. & N.W.R.)

Euston .	dep.	7.15 a.m.	10.45	4.00 p.m.	5.30
Bedford	arr.	10.15	1.15 p.m.	6.30	8.00
Bedford	dep.	7.15 a.m.	10.00	2.10 p.m.	5.50
Euston	arr.	10.20	12.30 p.m.	5.00	8.15

A.2 *June 1848 Bedford Railway* (worked by L. & N.W.R.)

		Weekdays					Sundays	
Bedford	dep.	7.05	9.45	11.45	2.05	5.55	8.20	3.00
Marston	arr.	7.18	9.58	12.00	2.20	6.10	8.35	3.15
Lidlington	,.	7.19	—	12.01	2.21	6.11	8.36	3.16
Ridgmount	,,	7.21	—	12.03	2.23	6.13	8.38	3.18
Woburn Sands	,,	7.36	10.13	12.20	2.40	6.30	8.55	3.35
Fenny Stratford	,,	7.44	—	12.28	2.48	6.38	9.03	3.43
Bletchley	..	7.51	10.26	12.35	2.55	6.45	9.10	3.50
London	..	10.10	12.00	3.00	5.00	8.30	—	6.00

London	dep.	7.15	11.00	12.30	3.45	5.30	7.30	—
Bletchley	arr.	9.08	12.47	2.20	5.20	7.12	9.08	4.00
Fenny Stratford	,,	9.35	1.20	3.20	—	7.20	9.35	4.08
Woburn Sands	,,	9.45	1.30	3.30	5.33	7.30	9.45	4.18
Ridgmount	,,	9.51	1.36	3.36	—	7.36	9.51	4.24
Lidlington	,,	9.53	1.38	3.38	—	7.38	9.53	4.26
Marston	,,	10.03	1.48	3.48	5.48	7.48	10.03	4.36
Bedford	,,	10.15	2.00	4.00	6.00	8.00	10.15	4.48

A.3 *September 1860 London & North Western Railway*

		Weekdays					Sundays
Bedford	dep.	7.15	9.50	4.10	6.50		7.27
Ampthill*	arr.	7.26	10.01	4.20	7.00		7.37
Lidlington	,.	7.32	—	4.26	7.06		7.47
Ridgmount	,,	7.39	—	4.32	7.13		7.55
Woburn Sands	,,	7.45	10.15	4.38	7.20		
Fenny Stratford	,,	7.53	—	—	7.28		8.05
Bletchley	..	7.58	10.25	4.48	7.33		8.10
Leighton Buzzard	.,	8.19	10.46	5.18	9.07		8.27
Euston	..	10.05	12.00	6.35	9.30		10.20

Northampton	,,	9.10	11.30	6.20	8.35		10.35
Oxford	,,	9.50	12.50	6.30	10.10		12.55
Rugby	,,	9.50	11.35	6.50	9.12		11.06
Birmingham	,,	11.10	12.25	8.15	10.25		12.30

[*Name of station changed to Ampthill (Marston).]

A.4   *July 1890   London & North Western Railway*

Weekdays .... *Sundays*

		a.m.								a.m.	p.m.
Cambridge	dep.		7.50	11.25		1.48		4.40	7.00	8.45	6.50
Lords Bridge	,,		8.00	—		1.57		4.50	7.12	8.57	—
Old North Road	,,		8.10	11.43		2.06		5.00	7.23	9.08	—
Gamlingay	,,		8.18	11.54		2.14		5.09	7.33	9.18	7.15
Potton	,,		8.24	12.01		2.21		5.15	7.38	9.23	7.22
Sandy	,,		8.32	12.10	12.25	2.27		5.23	7.47	9.32	7.33
Blunham	,,		8.38	12.17	12.31	2.33		5.29	7.53	9.38	7.40
Bedford	,,	7.30	8.51	12.31	12.42	2.47	5.15	5.41	8.05	9.55	7.54
Millbrook	,,	7.41	9.02	12.41	—	2.58	5.26	—	8.16	10.06	8.05
Lidlington	,,	7.46	9.07	—		3.05	5.31	—	8.21	10.11	—
Ridgmount	,,	7.53	9.14	—		3.13	5.38	—	8.28	10.18	—
Woburn Sands	,,	8.00	9.21	12.57		3.20	5.45	—	8.35	10.25	8.18
Fenny Stratford	,,	8.07	9.28	—		3.26	5.52	—	8.41	10.31	—
Bletchley	arr.	8.10	9.31	1.05		3.30	5.55	6.03	8.45	10.35	8.25

Weekdays

Bletchley	dep.	8.25 a.m.	9.05		11.40	1.40	2.10	4.10	6.25	9.25
Fenny Stratford	,,	8.27	—		—	1.43	—	4.13	6.28	9.28
Woburn Sands	,,	8.33	9.12		11.47	1.49	—	4.20	6.35	9.35
Ridgmount	,,	8.39	—		11.52	1.57	—	4.27	6.42	9.42
Lidlington	,,	8.44	—		—	2.03	—	4.33	6.48	9.49
Millbrook	,,	8.48	—		—	—	—	4.39	6.54	9.54
Bedford	,,	9.00	9.34	11.50	12.07	2.18	2.45	4.52	7.08	10.05
Blunham	,,	9.11	9.44	12.01	12.17	—	2.55	5.04	7.20	——
Sandy Junc.	,,	9.16	9.49	12.09	12.23	—	3.00	5.16	7.26	
Potton	,,		9.55	—	12.32		3.08	5.26	7.37	
Gamlingay	,,		10.00		12.38		3.15	5.34	7.45	
Old North Road	,,		10.10		12.48		3.26	5.45	7.56	
Lords Bridge	,,		10.20		12.58		3.37	5.56	8.07	
Cambridge	arr.		10.30		1.10		3.49	6.10	8.19	

Sundays

Bletchley	dep.	11.35 a.m.
Fenny Stratford	,,	—
Woburn Sands	,,	11.42
Ridgmount	,,	11.49
Lidlington	,,	11.56
Millbrook	,,	12.01
Bedford	,,	12.14
Blunham	,,	12.26
Sandy Junction	,,	12.32
Potton	,,	12.43
Gamlingay	,,	12.51
Old North Road	,,	1.02
Lords Bridge	,,	1.13
Cambridge	,,	1.25

[Note: trains between Sandy Junction and Bedford only; Willington station was not opened until 1903 for passengers.]

A.5   *July 1850   London & North Western Railway*

Weekdays only

Euston Square	dep.	9.00 a.m. (Express)	5.30 p.m. (1st & 2nd only)
Leighton Buzzard	arr.	10.00	7.00
Dunstable	arr.	10.45	7.45

Bletchley	dep.	9.35 a.m. (1st & 2nd only)	6.50 p.m. (1st & 2nd only)
Leighton Buzzard	arr.	9.50	7.05
Dunstable	arr.	10.45	7.45

A.6   *July 1890   London & North Western Railway*

Weekdays only

Euston	dep.	6.00	8.00	9.30	10.15	11.45	3.15	6.00	7.10
Leighton Buzzard	,,	7.57	9.30	10.27	12.20	2.45	4.45	7.15	9.35
Stanbridgeford	,,	8.06	Sig.	10.37	Sig.	Sig.	Sig.	Sig.	Sig.
Dunstable	arr.	8.12	9.45	10.44	12.35	3.00	5.00	7.30	9.50

Dunstable	dep.	7.25	9.00	10.05	11.23	1.28	3.05	6.05	8.20
Standbridgeford	,,	7.32	9.05	10.10	11.30	1.34	3.10	6.12	8.27
Leighton Buzzard	arr.	7.42	9.15	10.20	11.40	1.43	3.20	6.22	8.37
Euston	,,	9.35	10.25	—	1.55	4.10	5.25	7.35	11.15

[As regards Down Trains the word 'Sig' means that the train stops only to set down passengers if prior notice is given to the guard, and to pick up passengers provided a clear signal is given to the engine driver.]

Appendix B

Timetables for M.R. and branches

B.1

May 1857   Midland Railway

		Weekdays				Sundays	
Leicester	dep.	6.00	8.00	1.00	5.35	—	—
Bedford	dep.	8.15	10.36	3.15	8.06	10.06 a.m.	8.06 p.m.
Cardington	arr.	—	10.46	—	8.16	10.16	8.16
Southill	,,	—	10.58	—	8.28	10.28	8.28
Shefford	,,	8.30	11.06	3.40	8.35	10.36	8.36
Henlow	,,	—	11.15	—	8.45	10.45	8.45
Hitchin	,,	9.00	11.30	4.00	9.00	11.00	9.00
King's Cross	arr.	10.15	12.45	5.05	10.25	—	—

King's Cross	dep.	—	6.30	10.00	5.00	—	—
Hitchin	,,	6.00	8.15	11.00	6.00	7.30	5.30
Henlow	arr.	—	8.27	—	6.12	7.42	5.42
Shefford	,,	6.19	8.35	11.19	6.20	7.50	5.50
Southill	,,	—	8.43	11.27	6.28	7.58	5.58
Cardington	,,	—	8.55	—	6.40	8.10	6.10
Bedford	,,	6.42	9.05	11.47	6.50	8.20	6.20
Leicester	,,	9.00	11.45	2.05	9.36	—	—

[Note the poor service at Henlow and Cardington.]

B.2

September 1860.   Midland Railway

Class		Weekdays					Sundays	
		1 & 2	1, 2 & 3	1 & 2	1, 2 & 3	1 & 2	1, 2 & 3	1, 2 & 3
Leeds	dep.	3.00	—	8.30	12.30	4.25	—	7.00
Sheffield	,,	4.05	—	9.35	1.10	5.15	—	8.15
Derby	,,	6.00	8.10	11.50	2.25	6.40	—	11.30
Nottingham	,,	6.00	8.05	11.45	2.30	6.35	—	11.30
Burton	,,	—	7.55	11.25	1.45	5.40		
Leicester	,,	7.10	9.35	12.55	4.00	7.45	7.30	5.30 p.m.
Market Harborough	,,	7.38	10.19	1.27	4.44	8.11	8.19	6.19
Kettering	,,	7.55	10.48	1.44	5.13	8.20	8.52	6.52
Wellingborough	,,	8.08	11.10	1.56	5.35	8.43	9.16	7.16
Irchester	,,	*	11.17	—	5.42	—	9.24	7.25
Northampton	,,	—	9.20	11.30	4.30	7.05	—	10.35
Peterborough	,,	—	9.00	11.40	3.40	5.45	—	12.45
Sharnbrook	,,	8.26	11.32	2.11	5.57	—	9.41	7.41
Oakley	,,	—	11.42	—	6.06	—	9.53	7.53
Bedford	,,	8.40	11.55	2.25	6.18	9.08	10.06	8.06
Cardington	,,	*	12.03	—	6.25	—	10.16	8.16
Southill	,,	8.53	12.17	—	6.38	—	10.28	8.28
Shefford	,,	8.58	12.24	2.42	6.44	—	10.36	8.36
Hitchin	,,	9.15	12.50	3.05	7.10	9.35	11.05	9.05
Cambridge	,,	10.55	—	4.30	9.00	—	9.05 p.m.	
King's Cross	arr.	10.05	1.35	3.50	8.00	10.20	11.50	9.50

*Stops to take up only.
[The above timetable appeared as an advertisement in the *Bedfordshire Mercury* for 1st September 1860. The railway is referred to as 'The Midland Counties Railway' although this title was dropped in 1844.]

B.3   *July 1867   Midland Railway*

Class		1 & 2	1, 2 & 3	1 & 2	Weekdays 1 & 2	1 & 2	1 & 2	,1 2 & 3	
King's Cross	dep.	6.25 a.m.	7.20	9.10	11.00	11.30	3.00 p.m.	3.40	5.35
Hitchin	,,	—	8.18	—	11.45	—	—	4.27	—
Henlow	,,	—	8.28	—	—	—	—	4.38	—
Shefford	,,	—	8.35	—	11.57	—	—	4.45	—
Southill	,,	—	8.42	—	12.03	—	—	4.51	—
Cardington	,,	—	8.51	—	—	—	—	5.02	—
Bedford	,,	7.32	9.00	10.13	12.18	12.40	4.08	5.09	6.41
Oakley	,,	—	9.08	—	—	—	—	5.20	—
Sharnbrook	,,	7.45	9.19	—	12.31	—	—	5.30	—
Northampton	arr.	8.40	10.15	11.50	—	1.40	5.05	6.40	7.40
Irchester	dep.	—	9.33	—	—	—	—	5.45	—
Wellingborough	,,	8.01	9.39	10.40	12.45	1.05	4.33	5.52	E
Kettering	,,	8.13	9.59	10.55	12.57	—	4.45	6.14	—
Market Harborough	,	8.33	10.26	——	—	—	5.03	6.39	E
Leicester	,,	9.00	11.10		1.16	—	5.03	6.39	E
Burton on Trent	arr.	10.40	1.30 p.m.		1.45	1.55	5.28	7.30	7.50
Nottingham	,,	10.25	12.55		3.10	4.15	6.30	—	9.25
Derby	,,	10.20	1.15		3.15	—	6.30	—	8.40
Sheffield	,,	11.55	3.35		4.25	—	8.10	—	8.50
Leeds	,,	12.30	5.05		5.15	—	9.35	—	10.00
									10.45

Class		Weekdays 1 & 2	1 & 2	1, 2 & 3	Sundays 1, 2 & 3	1 & 2
King's Cross	dep.	6.30 p.m.	8.48	6.45 a.m.	5.55 p.m.	8.48
Hitchin	,,	7.23	—	7.33	6.43	—
Henlow	,,	A	—	7.47	6.55	—
Shefford	,,	7.35	—	7.54	7.01	—
Southill	,,	7.41	—	8.00	7.07	—
Cardington	,,	7.49	—	8.12	7.18	—
Bedford	,,	7.57	9.53	8.22	7.27	9.53
Oakley	,,	—	—	8.36	7.38	—
Sharnbrook	,,	8.12	—	8.45	7.49	—
Northampton	arr.	9.25	—	10.20	8.40	—
Irchester	dep.	8.24	—	9.01	8.03	—
Wellingborough	,,	8.32	10.17	9.08	8.09	10.17
Kettering	,,	8.48	10.29	9.28	8.28	10.29
Market Harborough	,,	9.09	10.45	9.59	—	10.45
Leicester	,,	9.45	11.10	10.50	—	11.10
Burton on Trent	arr.	—	12.53 p.m.	7.35 p.m.	—	12.53 a.m.
Nottingham	,,	12.15	12.15	6.10	—	12.15
Derby	,,	12.18	—	8.15	—	12.18
Sheffield	,,	2.10 a.m.	—	5.35	—	2.10
Leeds	,,	3.00	—	6.55	—	3.00

Note: A or E stops to set down only.

B.4 *July 1868 Midland Railway*

		Weekdays						Sundays	
Bedford	dep.	—	8.45	12.12	3.07	5.35	7.05	8.14	7.30 p.m.
Ampthill	,,	—	9.01	12.28	3.23	5.51	7.21	8.30	7.46
Harlington	,,	—	9.12	12.39	3.34	6.02	7.32	8.41	7.57
Leagrave	,,	—	9.24	12.51	3.46	6.14	7.44	8.53	8.09
Luton	,,	8.05	9.33	1.00	3.55	6.23	7.53	9.02	8.18
Chiltern Green	,,	8.12	9.41	1.08	—	6.31	8.01	9.10	8.26
Harpenden	,,	8.18	9.48	1.15	4.06	6.38	8.08	9.17	8.33
St Albans	,,	8.28	10.00	1.27	4.18	6.50	8.20	9.29	8.45
Radlett	,,	8.37	10.11	1.38	—	7.01	8.31	9.40	8.56
Elstree	,,	8.44	10.19	1.46	4.33	7.09	8.39	9.48	9.04
Mill Hill	,,	8.52	10.27	1.54	—	7.17	8.47	9.56	9.12
Hendon	,,	8.58	10.33	2.00	4.44	7.23	8.53	10.02	9.18
Finchley Road	,,	—	10.41	2.08	4.52	7.31	9.01	10.10	9.26
Haverstock Hill	,,	—	10.45	2.12	4.56	7.35	9.05	10.14	9.30
Kentish Town	,,	—	10.50	2.17	5.01	7.40	9.10	10.19	9.35
Camden Road	,,	—	10.53	2.20	5.04	7.43	9.13	10.22	9.38
King's Cross	,,	9.15	10.57	2.24	5.08	7.47	9.17	10.26	9.42
Farringdon St	,,	9.19	11.01	2.28	5.12	7.51	9.21	10.30	9.46
Aldersgate St	,,	9.21	11.03	2.30	5.14	7.53	9.23	10.32	9.48
Moorgate St	arr.	9.23	11.05	2.32	5.16	7.55	9.25	10.34	9.50

Note: The main line through trains will continue to run to and from the Great Northern station at King's Cross until further notice.
[Trains on this timetable refer only to stations between Bedford and Moorgate Street.]

Moorgate St	dep.	—	9.10	1.22	4.16	5.10	7.10	8.33	8.05	7.00
Aldersgate St	,,	—	9.12	1.24	4.18	5.12	7.12	8.35	8.07	7.02
Farringdon St	,,	—	9.14	1.26	4.20	5.14	7.14	8.37	8.09	7.04
King's Cross	,,	—	9.18	1.30	4.24	5.18	7.18	8.41	8.13	7.08
Camden Road	,,	—	9.22	1.34	4.28	5.22	7.22	8.45	8.17	7.12
Kentish Town	,,	—	9.25	1.37	4.31	5.25	7.25	8.48	8.20	7.15
Haverstock Hill	,,	—	9.31	1.43	4.37	5.31	7.31	8.54	8.26	7.21
Finchley Road	,,	—	9.35	1.47	4.41	5.35	7.35	8.58	8.30	7.25
Hendon	,,	—	9.43	1.55	4.49	5.43	7.43	9.06	8.38	7.33
Mill Hill	,,	—	9.50	2.02	—	5.50	7.50	9.13	8.45	7.40
Elstree	,,	—	9.58	2.10	5.00	5.58	7.58	9.21	8.53	7.48
Radlett	,,	—	10.05	2.17	—	6.05	8.05	9.28	9.00	7.55
St Albans	,,	—	10.17	2.29	5.15	6.17	8.17	9.40	9.12	8.07
Harpenden	,,	—	10.27	2.39	5.25	6.27	8.27	9.50	9.22	8.17
Chiltern Green	,,	—	10.34	2.46	—	6.34	8.34	9.57	9.29	8.24
Luton	,,	7.35	10.44	2.56	5.39	6.44	8.44	10.07	9.39	8.34
Leagrave	,,	7.44	10.54	3.06	5.49	—	8.54	—	9.49	8.44
Harlington	,,	7.53	11.03	3.15	5.58	—	9.03	—	9.58	8.53
Ampthill	,,	8.04	11.14	3.26	6.09	—	9.14	—	10.09	9.04
Bedford	arr.	8.20	11.30	3.42	6.25	—	9.30	—	10.25	9.20

[Notice that Cricklewood, West Hampstead and Flitwick stations are missing. Flitwick was opened in 1870.]

B.5 *July 1890 Midland Railway*

						Weekdays					
St Pancras	dep.	5.15 a.m.	6.10	7.55	9.05	10.00	11.10	12.30 p.m.	1.15	2.05	4.00
Kentish Town	,,	—	6.14	7.59	9.09	10.04	11.14	—	1.20	2.09	—
Hendon	,,	—	6.37	8.10	9.19	—	—	—	1.39	—	—
Mill Hill	,,	—	6.44	8.16	9.24	—	—	—	1.45	—	—
Elstree	,,	—	6.52	8.23	9.30	—	—	—	1.51	—	—
Radlett	,,	—	6.58	—	9.36	—	—	—	1.57	—	—
St Albans	,,	—	7.07	8.34	9.44	—	11.40	—	2.05	2.36	—
Harpenden	,,	—	7.54	8.46	9.55	—	11.51	—	2.16	2.49	—
Chiltern Green	,,	—	8.00	—	—	—	—	—	2.24	—	—
Luton	,,	—	8.07	8.55	10.04	Slip	12.00	1.09	2.40	2.59	—
Leagrave	,,	—	8.16	—	10.13	—	—	—	2.48	—	—
Harlington	,,	—	8.25	—	10.35	—	12.14	—	2.56	—	—
Flitwick	,,	—	8.32	—	10.42	—	—	—	3.06	—	—
Ampthill	,,	—	8.37	9.16	10.47	—	12.23	—	3.11	3.20	—
Bedford	,,	6.15	9.00	9.32	10.59	11.09	12.38	1.37	3.23	3.38	5.05
Wellingborough	,,		9.32	10.00	—	—	1.01	—	—	4.04	—
Kettering	,,		—	10.16	—	—	1.16	—	—	4.17	—
Market Harborough	,,		—	—	—	—	1.32	2.20	—	—	—
Leicester	arr.		—	—	—	12.12	2.02	2.45	—	—	6.07
			A					B			C

continued.

St Pancras	dep.	4.20 p.m.	5.00	5.43	6.05	6.30	8.30	9.15	12.00 midnight
Kentish Town	,,	4.24	5.04	5.48	6.09	6.35	8.34	9.20	12.06 a.m.
Hendon	,,	—	—	—	—	6.54	—	—	—
Mill Hill	,,	—	—	—	—	7.00	—	—	—
Elstree	,,	—	—	—	6.27	7.07	—	—	—
Radlett	,,	—	—	—	6.33	7.14	—	—	—
St Albans	,,	4.51	Slip	6.15	6.41	7.22	9.03	—	12.35
Harpenden	,,	5.01	—	6.26	6.50	7.34	9.12	—	—
Chiltern Green	,,	5.07	—	6.32	—	7.40	—	—	—
Luton	,,	5.13	—	6.38	7.01	7.47	9.22	—	12.51
Leagrave	,,	5.22	—	—	—	7.57	—	—	—
Harlington	,,	5.31	—	6.51	—	8.06	—	—	—
Flitwick	,,	5.38	—	—	—	8.13	—	—	—
Ampthill	,,	5.43	—	7.00	—	8.18	—	—	—
Bedford	,,	5.55	6.07	7.12	7.32	8.30	9.54	10.27	1.20
Wellingborough	,,	—	—	—	7.59	—	10.16	—	—
Kettering	,,	—	—	—	8.20	—	10.30	—	—
Market Harborough	,,	—	—	—	8.38	—	10.47	—	—
Leicester	arr.	—	7.10	—	9.13	—	11.12	11.32	2.26
							D	E	F

Note: A — Newspaper train
B — Matlock and Buxton express
C — Drawing room saloon car in train
D — Mail train
E — Scotch Express
F — Sleeping saloon cars, London to Manchester.
[Note also the importance of Kentish Town as an exchange station. The slip coach services to St Albans and Luton. Harlington (then known as Harlington for Toddington) and Ampthill have a better service than Flitwick.]

B.5 *July 1890 Midland Railway*

Sundays

St Pancras	dep.	7.30 a.m.	9.30	2.30 p.m.	3.15	5.40	8.30	9.15	12.00 midnight
Kentish Town	,,	7.38	9.37	2.34	3.19	5.44	8.34	9.19	12.06 a.m.
Hendon	,,	7.58	9.59	—	—	5.57	—	—	—
Mill Hill	,,	8.07	10.06	—	—	6.04	—	—	—
Elstree	,,	8.15	10.14	—	—	6.12	—	—	—
Radlett	,,	8.21	10.20	—	—	6.18	—	—	—
St Albans	,,	8.30	10.29	3.02	—	6.27	9.03	—	12.35
Harpenden	,,	8.43	10.41	3.11	—	6.39	9.12	—	—
Chiltern Green	,,	8.50	10.48	—	—	6.46	—	—	—
Luton	,,	8.56	10.55	3.20	—	6.52	9.22	—	12.51
Leagrave	,,	9.05	11.04	—	—	7.00	—	—	—
Harlington	,,	9.15	11.14	—	—	7.10	—	—	—
Flitwick	,,	9.22	11.22	—	—	7.17	—	—	—
Ampthill	,,	9.27	11.27	—	—	7.22	—	—	—
Bedford	,,	9.48	11.45	3.52	4.23	7.42	9.54	10.27	1.20
Wellingborough	,,	10.22	—	4.14	—	8.16	10.16	—	—
Kettering	,,	10.45	—	4.29	—	8.38	10.30	—	—
Market Harborough	,,	11.09	—	4.44	—	9.02	10.47	—	—
Leicester	arr.	11.55	—	5.13	5.27	9.47	11.12	11.32	2.26
					A	**B**	**C**		**D**

A — Liverpool & Manchester express
B — Mail
C — Scotch Express; sleeping cars London to Edinburgh & Glasgow
D — Sleeping cars, Liverpool and Manchester.

Sundays

Leicester	dep.				2.46 p.m.		7.32	
Kettering	,,				—	6.25	—	
Wellingborough	,,		—	10.03	—	6.42	—	8.33
Bedford	,,	7.27 a.m.	7.50	10.40	3.52	7.25	8.38	9.00
Ampthill	,,	—	8.03	—	—	—	—	—
Flitwick	,,	—	8.08	—	—	—	—	—
Harlington	,,	—	8.14	—	—	—	—	—
Leagrave	,,	—	8.26	—	—	—	—	—
Luton	,,	—	8.33	11.07	—	—	—	9.26
Chiltern Green	,,	—	8.40	—	—	—	—	—
Harpenden	,,	—	8.46	—	—	—	—	9.38
St Albans	,,	—	8.54	11.25	—	—	—	9.46
Radlett	,,	—	9.04	—	—	—	—	—
Elstree	,,	—	9.10	—	—	—	—	—
Mill Hill	,,	—	9.17	—	—	—	—	—
Hendon	,,	—	9.23	—	—	—	—	—
Kentish Town	,,	—	9.42	12.05	4.52	—	9.38	10.12
St Pancras	arr.	8.30	9.50	12.15	5.00	9.35	9.45	10.20
					E			

E — Drawing Room Saloon Cars, Liverpool and Manchester to London.

B.5

July 1890   Midland Railway   Weekdays

Station		1	2	3	4	5	6	7	8	9	10	11
Leicester	dep.	1.50 a.m.	—	—	—	7.15	—	—	—	—	12.24 p.m.	2.06
Market Harborough	"	2.14	—	—	—	7.44	—	—	—	—	—	—
Kettering	"	2.40	—	—	—	8.09	—	—	—	—	1.40 p.m.	—
Wellingborough	"	3.09	—	—	—	8.20	—	—	—	—	1.50	—
Bedford	"	—	7.27	—	8.10	8.57	10.42	11.27	—	1.29 p.m.	2.17	3.10
Ampthill	"	—	—	7.03	—	9.09	—	11.45	—	—	—	—
Flitwick	"	—	—	7.15	—	9.14	—	12.24	—	—	—	—
Harlington	"	—	—	7.20	8.37	9.21	—	12.37	—	—	—	—
Leagrave	"	—	—	7.26	—	—	—	12.42	—	—	—	—
Luton	"	—	—	7.38	—	9.35	—	12.49	—	—	—	—
Chiltern Green	"	—	—	8.00	8.48	9.47	—	12.58	—	—	2.42	—
Harpenden	"	—	—	8.07	8.57	9.59	—	1.04	—	—	2.54	—
St Albans	"	—	—	8.13	9.05	—	—	1.13	—	—	3.02	—
Radlett	"	—	—	8.22	9.11	—	—	1.20	—	—	—	—
Elstree	"	—	—	8.30	9.17	—	—	1.28	—	—	—	—
Mill Hill	"	—	—	8.36	9.23	—	—	1.38	—	—	—	—
Hendon	"	—	—	8.42	—	—	—	1.44	—	—	—	—
Kentish Town	"	—	—	8.53	9.31	10.22	11.42	1.51	2.15	2.28	3.26	4.09
St Pancras	arr.	—	8.30	9.00	9.38	10.30	11.50	1.58	2.23	2.35	3.35	4.15
										A		B

Continued

Station		1	2	3	4	5	6	7
Leicester	dep.	4.42	6.14	7.37	—	—	—	—
Market Harborough	"	5.11	—	—	—	—	—	—
Kettering	"	5.35	—	—	7.45	8.30	—	—
Wellingborough	"	5.45	—	—	—	8.44	—	—
Bedford	"	6.25	7.18	8.43	8.55	10.08	4.08 p.m.	—
Ampthill	"	6.40	—	—	9.28	10.16	4.20	—
Flitwick	"	6.52	—	—	9.40	10.26	4.25	—
Harlington	"	6.57	—	—	—	—	4.32	—
Leagrave	"	7.04	—	—	—	10.33	4.41	—
Luton	"	7.13	7.44	—	—	10.40	4.47	6.55
Chiltern Green	"	7.18	—	—	—	10.46	—	—
Harpenden	"	—	—	—	9.56	11.04	—	7.07
St Albans	"	—	—	—	—	—	—	7.15
Radlett	"	—	—	—	—	—	—	—
Elstree	"	—	—	—	—	—	—	—
Mill Hill	"	—	—	—	—	—	—	—
Hendon	"	—	—	—	—	—	—	—
Kentish Town	"	—	—	—	—	—	—	7.41
St Pancras	arr.	—	8.25	9.45	—	11.12	—	7.50
			C	D				

A — Luncheon Saloon Car.
B — Drawing Room Saloon Car, Liverpool to London.
C — Drawing Room Saloon Car, Manchester to London.
D — Dining Saloon Car, Manchester to London.

[Note the excellent service from Bedford; 14 trains to London of which 6 are non-stop.
Harlington is referred to in the timetable as 'Harlington for Toddington'.
Cricklewood and West Hampstead stations are not yet included.
Finchley Road, Haverstock Hill and Camden Road stations were served by the Moorgate Street trains.
Ampthill still had a slightly better service than Flitwick.]

B.6   *May 1872   Midland Railway*

Weekdays only

Bedford	dep.	8.46	9.59	4.12	6.50
Northampton	arr.	9.50	2.10	5.00	9.40

Northampton	dep.	7.10	10.40	2.30	4.50
Bedford	arr.	8.10	11.52	3.31	6.18

[Passengers had to change at Wellingborough in each
direction. This was before the opening of the Bedford &
Northampton Railway.]

B.7   *August 1872   Bedford & Northampton
Railway* (worked by the Midland
Railway)

Weekdays only

Bedford	dep.	8.40	11.15	1.07	4.17	6.55
Turvey	,,	8.52	11.26	1.19	4.28	7.07
Olney	,,	9.02	11.36	1.29	4.38	7.17
Horton	,,	9.12	—	1.39	—	7.27
Northampton St John's	arr.	9.25	11.55	1.59	4.57	7.40

Northampton St John's	dep.	7.25	10.00	12.45	4.37	6.20
Horton	arr.	7.36	—	12.57	—	6.32
Olney	,,	7.45	10.18	1.07	4.56	6.42
Turvey	,,	7.55	10.27	1.17	5.06	6.52
Bedford	,,	8.07	10.38	1.30	5.17	7.05

[Timetable as advertised in the *Bedfordshire Times*. Midland trains
ran into their own terminus at Northampton. Horton (later
Piddington & Horton) always had a poor service.]

B.8   *July 1890   Midland Railway*

Weekdays only

Bedford	dep.	7.45	12.27	5.05	7.32
Cardington	,,	7.56	12.36	5.13	7.41
Southill	,,	8.05	12.44	5.21	7.49
Shefford	,,	8.11	12.50	5.27	7.55
Henlow	,,	8.23	12.56	5.33	8.03
Hitchin	arr.	8.35	1.07	5.45	8.15

Hitchin	dep.	7.00	9.53	2.56	6.05
Henlow	,,	7.09	10.02	3.05	6.17
Shefford	,,	7.15	10.08	3.10	6.23
Southill	,,	7.21	10.14	3.17	6.29
Cardington	,,	7.29	10.22	3.27	6.37
Bedford	arr.	7.35	10.28	3.33	6.43

B.9

July 1890

Weekdays only

Northampton	dep.	8.05	9.45	2'15	5.20	7.50
Piddington	,,	8.16	9.56	2.26	5.31	8.01
Olney	,,	8.26	10.06	2.36	5.41	8.11
Turvey	,,	8.35	10.15	2.45	5.50	8.20
Bedford	arr.	8.45	10.25	2.55	6.00	8.30

Bedford	dep.	8.30	11.15	1.25	5.10	7.37
Turvey	,,	8.41	11.26	1.36	5.21	7.48
Olney	,,	8.50	11.35	1.45	5.30	7.57
Piddington	,,	9.00	11.45	1.55	5.40	8.07
Northampton	arr.	9.10	11.55	2.05	5.50	8.17

Appendix C

Timetables for G.N.R. and branches

C.1

July 1850
Eastern Counties Railway
Weekdays only

London (Shoreditch).	dep.	11.30 a.m.
Cambridge	arr.	1.38 p.m.
Cambridge	dep.	2.00
Huntingdon	arr.	2.55

Huntingdon	dep.	12.40 p.m.
Cambridge	arr.	1.33
Cambridge	dep.	3.06
London (Shoreditch)	arr.	5.20

[The above timetable shows the train service between London and Huntingdon just before the opening of the Great Northern Railway. Huntingdon has been selected so as to show the train services both north and south of the Bedfordshire towns and villages.]

C.2

July 1860   Great Northern Railway
Weekdays

Class		1, 2 & 3	1, 2 & 3	1 & 2	1 & 2	1 & 2	1 & 2	1 & 2	1 & 2	1 & 2	1 & 2
King's Cross	dep.	6.30 a.m.	7.40	10.05	12.00	12.25 p.m.	1.45	4.05	5.00	5.05	8.00
Holloway	,,	6.35	—	10.10	—	12.30	—	—	—	—	8.05
Hornsey	,,	6.45	—	10.20	—	12.38	—	4.17	—	—	8.15
Wood Green	,,	6.48	—	—	—	—	—	4.20	—	—	8.18
a Southgate	,,	6.53	—	10.27	—	12.45	—	4.25	—	—	8.23
Barnet	,,	7.00	—	10.35	—	12.52	—	4.33	—	5.25	8.32
Potters Bar	,,	7.09	—	10.43	—	1.01	—	4.42	—	—	8.42
Hatfield	,,	7.20	—	10.53	—	1.13	—	4.52	—	5.40	8.53
Welwyn Junction	,,	—	—	10.58	—	—	—	—	—	5.47	8.58
Welwyn	,,	7.30	—	11.03	—	1.23	2.23	5.00	—	5.52	9.04
Stevenage	,,	7.42	—	11.15	—	1.35	2.35	5.12	—	6.03	9.14
Hitchin	,,	8.00	8.40	11.27	—	1.46	2.50	5.21	—	6.15	9.28
b Arlesey	,,	8.10	—	11.36	—	1.55	3.00	—	—	6.24	9.38
Biggleswade	,,	8.20	—	11.45	—	2.04	3.09	5.34	—	6.32	9.48
c Sandy	,,	8.28	—	11.50	—	2.12	3.17	5.40	—	6.39	9.54
St Neots	,,	8.40	—	12.05	—	2.25	3.30	5.53	—	6.51	10.08
Offord	,,	8.52	—	12.15	—	2.34	3.39	—	—	—	—
Huntingdon	arr.	9.00	9.20	12.25	1.20	2.45	3.50	6.07	6.40	7.04	10.22

Sundays

Class		1, 2 & 3 & Gov.	1, 2 & 3
King's Cross	dep.	7.30 a.m.	8.00 p.m.
Holloway	,,	7.35	—
Hornsey	,,	7.45	8.10
Wood Green	,,	7.48	—
a Southgate	,,	7.53	8.17
Barnet	,,	8.00	8.25
Potters Bar	,,	8.10	8.34
Hatfield	,,	8.22	8.45
Welwyn Junction	,,	8.31	8.50
Welwyn	,,	8.34	8.55
Stevenage	,,	8.40	9.05
Hitchin	,,	9.00	9.20
b Arlesey	,,	9.13	9.32
Biggleswade	,,	9.26	9.42
c Sandy	,,	9.35	9.48
St Neots	,,	9.48	10.02
Offord	,,	10.02	—
Huntingdon	,,	10.13	10.18

FARES from King's Cross.
Single Journey. To::

	1st	2nd	3rd
Arlesey	7s	5s	3s 1d
Biggleswade	7s 6d	5s 6d	3s 5d
Sandy	8s	6s	3s 8d
St Neots	9s 6d	7s	4s 3½d
Offord	10s	7s	4s 7½d
Huntingdon	10s 6d	8s	4s 10½

[Note: (a) The station is referred to in *Bradshaw* as 'Southgate & Colney Hatch'.
(b) The station is referred to in *Bradshaw* as 'Arlesey & Shefford Road.'
(c) The station is referred to in *Bradshaw* as 'Sandy for Bedford'.]

C.2   *July 1860   Great Northern Railway*

Class		1 &2	1 & 2	1 & 2	Weekdays 1 & 2	1, 2 & 3	1 & 2	1 & 2	Sundays 1, 2 & 3
Huntingdon	dep.	8.43	10.38	1.21	2.28	3.00	6.10	9.04	5.20
Offord	,,	—	10.45	1.29	—	3.06	6.18	—	5.30
St Neots	,,	8.55	10.57	1.40	—	3.15	6.31	9.16	5.45
a Sandy	,,	9.08	11.10	1.52	—	3.27	6.43	9.29	6.00
Biggleswade	,,	9.15	11.20	2.10	—	3.33	6.53	9.36	6.10
b Arlesey	,,	A	11.30	2.20	—	3.41	7.05	9.46	6.22
Hitchin	,,	9.35	11.45	2.35	3.13	4.00	7.25	10.00	6.40
Stevenage	,,	9.43	11.55	—	—	4.10	7.35	10.10	—
Welwyn	,,	9.55	12.10	2.55	—	4.22	7.47	10.20	—
Welwyn Junction	,,	10.00	—	—	—	4.26	7.52	—	—
Hatfield	,,	10.09	12.25	—	—	4.35	8.02	10.30	7.10
Potters Bar	,,	—	—	—	—	4.47	8.13	10.37	—
Barnet	,,	—	—	—	—	4.55	8.23	10.47	—
c Southgate	,,	—	—	—	—	5.05	8.29	10.55	—
Wood Green	,,	—	—	—	—	5.11	8.34	—	—
Hornsey	,,	—	—	—	—	5.15	8.40	11.00	—
Holloway	,,	—	—	—	3.35	5.25	8.55	11.10	7.40
King's Cross	arr.	10.40	1.00	3.40	4.00	5.30	9.00	11.15	7.45

Note: A — stops to set down passengers only.
    a — In *Bradshaw* 'Sandy for Bedford'.
    b — In *Bradshaw* 'Arlesey & Shefford Road'.
    c — In *Bradshaw* 'Southgate & Colney Hatch'.

[Note also the poor service for 3rd class passengers.
Tempsford station not opened until 1862.
Arlesey Siding station not opened until 1866 and renamed Three Counties twenty years after.
There is no mention in 1860 of Knebworth, Brookmans Park, Hadley Wood, Oakleigh Park, Harringay and Finsbury Park stations.]

C.3 *July 1890 Great Northern Railway*

						Weekdays					
King's Cross	dep.	5.25 a.m.	7.45	8.45	10.32	11.45	1.25 p.m.	3.00	4.20	5.00	5.30
Finsbury Park	,,	5.30	7.54	8.51	10.45	11.51	1.35	—	4.27	—	—
Hatfield	,,	5.52	8.23	9.15	11.17	12.16	2.02	—	4.53	5.25	—
Welwyn	,,	—	—	—	11.25	—	2.10	—	—	—	—
Knebworth	,,	—	—	—	11.31	—	2.17	—	—	—	—
Stevenage	,,	—	—	—	11.39	—	2.24	—	—	—	—
Hitchin	,,	6.15	8.52	9.35	11.48	12.39	2.41	3.44	5.16	5.48	—
Three Counties	,,	6.25	8.59	—	11.56	—	2.48	—	—	5.55	—
Arlesey	,,	6.29	9.02	—	12.00	—	2.51	—	—	5.58	—
Biggleswade	,,	6.39	9.11	—	12.09	—	3.00	—	5.30	6.07	—
Sandy Junction	,,	6.47	9.18	—	12.18	12.55	3.07	—	5.37	6.13	—
Tempsford	,,	6.55	9.24	—	12.24	—	3.13	—	—	6.30	—
St Neots	,,	7.05	9.32	—	12.33	—	3.21	—	5.49	6.38	—
Offord	,,	7.15	9.39	—	12.41	—	3.29	—	—	6.44	—
Huntingdon	arr.	7.26	9.46	10.06	12.49	1.14	3.36	—	6.03	6.50	Slip

		Weekdays continued			*Sundays*	
King's Cross	dep.	5.50 p.m.	7.00	9.35	8.35 a.m.	6.30 p.m.
Finsbury Park	,,	5.57	7.07	9.42	8.46	6.40
Hatfield	,,	6.22	7.30	10.04	9.36	7.24
Welwyn	,,	6.30	—	—	9.47	7.33
Knebworth	,,	6.36	—	—	9.54	—
Stevenage	,,	6.42	7.46	—	10.00	7.45
Hitchin	,,	6.51	7.54	10.27	10.10	7.56
Three Counties	,,	6.58	8.01	10.34	10.17	8.03
Arlesey	,,	7.01	8.04	10.37	10.20	8.06
Biggleswade	,,	7.10	8.13	10.46	10.29	8.15
Sandy Junction	,,	7.16	8.19	10.52	10.38	8.22
Tempsford	,,	7.22	8.25	—	10.45	—
St Neots	,,	7.30	8.33	11.04	10.55	8.34
Offord	,,	7.36	8.40	—	11.03	—
Huntingdon	arr.	7.45	8.48	11.16	11.12	8.47

[Note: Huntingdon is served by one Slip Coach from the 5.30 p.m.]

FARES

From King's Cross	*Single*			*Return*		
to:	*1st*	*2nd*	*3rd*	*1st*	*2nd*	*3rd*
Three Counties	5s 6d	4s 3d	2s 11½d	11s	8s 6d	5s 11d
Arlesey and Shefford Road	6s	4s 3d	3s 1d	11s 9d	8s 6d	6s 2d
Biggleswade	6s 6d	4s 9d	3s 5d	12s 6d	9s 3d	6s 10d
Sandy	7s	5s	3s 8d	13s 6d	10s	7s 4d
Tempsford	7s 6d	5s 6d	3s 11d	14s 3d	11s	7s 10d

First, Second and Third Class coaches now on all trains.

C.3   *July 1890   Great Northern Railway*

Weekdays

Huntingdon	dep.	8.02 a.m.	9.45	10.54	1.25 p.m.	2.42	4.46	6.30	7.23	7.42	10.29
Offord	,,	8.08	—	11.00	1.31	2.48	4.52	—	—	7.48	—
St Neots	,,	8.15	9.56	11.07	1.39	2.55	4.59	—	7.34	7.58	10.41
Tempsford	,,	8.23	—	11.15	1.46	3.03	5.08	—	—	8.03	—
a Sandy Junction	,,	8.34	10.08	11.22	1.53	3.10	5.42	—	7.50	8.10	10.53
Biggleswade	,,	8.41	10.14	11.28	2.00	3.17	5.49	—	7.57	8.17	10.59
b Arlesey	,,	8.48	—	11.35	2.07	3.24	6.08	—	8.04	8.24	—
Three Counties	,,	8.52	—	11.38	2.10	3.27	6.12	—	8.08	8.28	—
Hitchin	,,	8.58	—	11.44	2.17	3.34	6.19	7.03	8.15	8.35	11.12
Stevenage	,,	—	—	11.55	3.03	3.56	—	—	—	8.53	—
Knebworth	,,	—	—	12.01	3.10	4.02	—	—	—	8.59	—
Welwyn	,,	—	—	12.08	3.17	4.09	—	—	—	9.06	—
Hatfield	,,	—	—	12.17	3.26	4.17	6.45	—	8.45	9.15	—
Finsbury Park	,,	9.44	11.04	12.29	3.55	4.39	7.18	—	9.06	9.49	11.54
King's Cross	arr.	9.50	11.10	12.45	4.00	4.45	7.23	7.45	9.13	9.55	12.00

Sundays

Huntingdon	dep.	5.40	8.47
Offord	,,	5.46	—
St Neots	,,	5.53	—
Tempsford	,,	6.02	—
a Sandy Junction	,,	6.10	—
Biggleswade	,,	6.17	—
b Arlesey	,,	6.25	—
Three Counties	,,	6.30	—
Hitchin	,,	6.38	9.20
Stevenage	,,	—	—
Knebworth	,,	—	—
Welwyn	,,	—	—
Hatfield	,,	7.11	—
Finsbury Park	,,	7.36	10.04
King's Cross	arr.	7.50	10.10

[Note: a. Sandy for Bedford now called Sandy Junction in *Bradshaw*
b full name of station—Arlesey and Shefford Road.]

C.4   *July 1890*   *Great Northern Railway*

							Weekdays				
Dunstable (L.N.W.)	dep.	6.00 a.m.	7.10	8.12	8.20	9.25	10.12	10.45	12.45 p.m.	2.05	3.35
Dunstable Church Street	,,	6.05	7.15	8.16	8.28	9.30	10.17	10.50	12.50	2.10	3.40
Luton	,,	6.15	7.32	8.25	8.40	9.40	10.32	11.40	1.07	2.20	3.35
New Mill End	,,	—	7.39	—	8.47	—	10.39	11.47	1.14	—	4.00
Harpenden	,,		7.44		8.52		·10.44	11.52	1.19		4.05
Wheathampstead	,,		7.49		8.57		10.49	11.57	1.24		4.10
Ayot	,,		7.55		9.03		10.55	12.04	1.31		4.16
Hatfield	arr.		8.05		9.12		11.04	12.12	1.40		4.25

								Sundays			
Dunstable (L.N.W.)	dep.	5.05 p.m.	5.50	7.32	7.42	8.31	9.55	—	—	—	—
Dunstable Church Street	,,	5.10	5.55	7.37	7.50	8.35	10.00	8.05 a.m.	10.50	5.55	8.35
Luton	,,	5.30	6.05	7.47	8.07	8.45	10.10	8.15	11.00	6.05	8.45
New Mill End	,,	5.37	—		8.14	—	—	8.23	—	6.13	—
Harpenden	,,	5.42			8.19			8.28		6.18	
Wheathampstead	,,	5.47			8.24			8.33		6.23	
Ayot	,,	5.53			8.30			8.39		6.29	
Hatfield	arr.	6.02			8.39			8.50		6.40	

[Note: New Mill End renamed Luton Hoo in 1892.]

							Weekdays					
Hatfield	dep.				8.25	9.57				12.20		3.18
Ayot	,,				8.35	10.06				12.29		3.27
Wheathampstead	,,				8.41	10.12				12.35		3.33
Harpenden	,,				8.53	10.17				12.40		3.38
New Mill End	,,				8.58	10.22				12.45		3.43
Luton	,,	6.45 a.m.	7.50	8.40	9.09	10.30	11.08	12.20 p.m.		2.45	4.00
Dunstable Church St.	,,	6.56	8.00	8.50	9.19	10.40	11.18	12.30	1.02	2.55	4.11
Dunstable (L.N.W.)	arr.	7.00	8.05	8.55	9.24	10.44	11.22	12.35	1.16	2.59	4.16

Hatfield	dep.	4.53		6.26		7.33		10.10
Ayot	,, ·	5.03		6.36		7.43		10.20
Wheathampstead	,,	5.09		6.42		7.49		10.26
Harpenden	,,	5.14		6.47		7.54		10.31
New Mill End	,,	5.19		6.52		7.59		10.36
Luton	,,	5.29	6.30	7.04	8.00	8.10	9.23	10.47
Dunstable Church Street	,,	5.39	6.40	7.14	8.10	8.20	9.33	10.58
Dunstable (L.N.W.)	arr.	5.45	6.50	7.19	8.15	8.25	9.38	11.02

			Sundays			
Hatfield	dep.		9.42		7.20	
Ayot	,,		9.52		7.40	
Wheathampstead	,,		9.58		7.47	
Harpenden	,,		10.03		7.52	
New Mill End	,,		10.08		7.57	
Luton	,,	7.35 a.m.	10.25	5.25 p.m.	8.10	
Dunstable Church Street	,,	7.45	10.35	5.35	8.20	
Dunstable (L.N.W.)	arr.	—	—		—	

C.5   *Sandy & Potton Railway   July 1860   Weekdays*

The Sandy & Potton Railway appeared in *Bradshaw* probably from January 1858, the last entry being in December 1861. Instead of the usual tables the services were mentioned in a paragraph in the corner of the page applying to the Great Northern Railway main line. The following is to be found on page 68 of the *Bradshaw* for July 1860.

POTTON & SANDY

From Potton at 8.10 and 10.50 morning; 3 and 6.20 afternoon.
From Sandy at 9.10 and 11.55 morning; 3.30 and 6.55 afternoon.
Distance 3 miles; Time on journey—10 minutes
Fares Potton-Sandy: First class 9d; second class 6d; third class 3d.
Day tickets 1s 9d.
Fares to London First class 8s 9d; second class 6s 6d; third class 3s 11d.
Day tickets to London First class 13s; second class 9s 9d.

There is no mention of Sunday services.

The following table has been prepared to show connecting trains.

S. & P.R.					
Potton	dep.	8.10 a.m.	10.50	3.00 p.m.	6.20
Sandy	arr.	8.20	11.00	3.10	6.30
G.N.R.					
Sandy	dep.	9.08	11.10	3.27	6.43
King's Cross	arr.	10.40	1.00 p.m.	5.30	9.00
Class		*1 & 2*	*1, 2 & 3*	*1, 2 & 3*	*1 & 2*

S. & P.R.					
Potton	dep.	8.10 a.m.	10.50	3.00 p.m.	6.20
Sandy	arr.	8.20	11.00	3.10	6.30
G.N.R.					
Sandy	dep.	8.28	11.50	3.17	6.39
Huntingdon	,,	9.00	12.25	3.50	7.04
Peterborough	,,	9.40	2.15 p.m.	4.30	7.35
Grantham	arr.	—	3.20	5.45	8.33
Class		*1, 2 & 3*	*1 & 2*	*1 & 2*	*1 & 2*

G.N.R.					
Class		*1 & 2*	*1, 2 & 3*	*1, 2 & 3*	*1 & 2*
Grantham	dep.	7.15 a.m.	8.50	—	4.15 p.m.
Peterborough	,,	8.10	10.05	—	5.35
Huntingdon	,,	8.43	10.38	3.00 p.m.	6.10
Sandy	,,	9.08	11.10	3.27	6.43
S. & P. R.					
Sandy	,,	9.10	11.55	3.30	6.55
Potton	arr.	9.20	12.05	3.40	7.05

G.N.R.					
Class		*1, 2 & 3*	*1 & 2*	*1 & 2*	*1 & 2*
King's Cross	dep.	6.30 a.m.	10.05	1.45 p.m.	5.05
Sandy	,,	8.28	11.50	3.17	6.39
S. & P.R.					
Sandy	dep.	9.10	11.55	3.30	6.55
Potton	arr.	9.20	12.05	3.40	7.05

Appendix D

Railways in Bedfordshire for which Plans were deposited, but which were never built

Year	Names	Length	Reason
1844	Ely & Bedford	44 miles	withdrawn
,,	Eastern Counties, extension to Hertford and Biggleswade	10 ,,	Rejected Standing Orders
,,	Direct Northern, first route	177 ,,	Amalgamated with London & York to become G.N.R.
,,	London & York	186 ,,	See above
1845	Great Northern Railway extension to Luton and Dunstable	19 ,,	Hatfield-St Albans passed; rest deferred to 1860
.,	Leicester & Bedford	63½ ,,	Rejected in Lords
,,	Northampton Bedford & Cambridge	20½ ,,	Wound up
,,	Wolverton Newport Pagnell & Bedford	11 ,,	Withdrawn
,,	Ely & Huntingdon, extension to Bedford	20½ ,,	Withdrawn
,,	London & Nottingham	69 ,,	Wound up
,,	Cambridge & Oxford	73 ,,	Royston-Hitchin 18 miles, built
	South Midland Railway	46 ,,	Rejected by House of Commons
.,	Midland & Eastern Counties	53 ,,	Wound up
,,	Direct London & Manchester	175 ,,	Wound up
,,	Bedford & Cambridge	26½ ,,	Defeated Standing Orders
,,	Bedfordshire, Hertfordshire & Essex Junction	55 ,,	Abandoned
.,	Eastern Counties Railway, extension to Bedford from Cambridge (Shelford)	27½ ,,	Powers lapsed
.,	Eastern Counties Railway, extension to Huntingdon and Bedford	44 ,,	Rejecetd by Parliament
	Direct Northern Railway, second route	177 ,,	Amalg. with Ldn & York to form Great Northern
,,	London & Birmingham extension to Luton, Watford and Dunstable	20 ,,	Rejected by House of Commons
1846	Midland extension to Hitchin	63 ,,	Act obtained but deferred
1852	Great Northern, Bedford branch	8 ,,	Act obtained but postponed
1858	Bedford, Potton & Cambridge	29 ,,	Rejected by Commons
1860	St Albans & Shefford	24 ,,	Abandoned
1864	East & West Junction extension to Bedford	26 ,,	Bankrupt
,,	Bedford, Northampton & Leamington	47 ,,	Abandoned
1865	East & West Junction extension to Hitchin	38 ,,	Bankrupt
1871	Towcester & Hitchin	37 ,,	Abandoned
1885	Bedford & Peterborough	31 ,,	Withdrawn
1910	Leagrave & Luton Light Railway	1½ mile	Unable to comply with Luton R.D.C.

Appendix E

Excursions

Midland Railway

Horticultural and Floral Fete and Balloon Ascent at Wellingborough

On Tuesday, 11th September, 1860 a special train will leave Hitchin, Bedford and the undermentioned stations for Wellingborough.

Fares there and back and Times of Starting

Hitchin	10.30 a.m.	1s 6d
Henlow	10.40	1s 6d
Shefford	10.47	1s 6d
Southill	10.57	1s 6d
Cardington	11.08	1s
Bedford	11.15	1s
Oakley	11.25	1s
Sharnbrook	11.35	9d

Children under 3, free; above 3 and under 12, half fares
Tickets not transferable.
The special train will leave Wellingborough in returning at 6.30 the same day.
Tickets will be available to return by this train only.

James Allport, *Derby*

Great Northern Railway

International Exhibition   29th July 1862

Huntingdon	dep.	5.40 a.m.
St Neots	,,	6.00
Sandy	,,	6.20
Biggleswade	,,	6.30
King's Cross	arr.	8.15

Fare 3s.   Return train 7.20 p.m.

Seymour Clarke

Midland Railway

International Exhibition

Leicester	dep.	4.15 a.m.	Fare	1st class	9s	Covered carriage	4s 6d
Kettering	,,	5.32		,, ,,	8s	,, ,,	4s
Bedford	,,	6.30		,, ,,	6s	,, ,,	2s 6d
Shefford	,,	6.52		,, ,,	6s	,, ,,	2s 6d
King's Cross	arr.	8.40					

Return at 8.30

James Allport, *General Manager*

Midland Railway

Kingsbury and Hendon Summer Races
Thursday 23rd July 1868

A cheap excursion train will run to Hendon by the Midland Railway's new route as under:

Bedford	dep.	10.00 a.m.	Fare	1st class	5s	Covered carriage	2s 6d
Ampthill	,,	10.16		,, ,,	5s	,, ,,	2s 6d
Harlington	,,	10.27		,, ,,	4s	,, ,,	2s
Leagrave	,,	10.39		,, ,,	4s	,, ,,	2s

Children under 3, free; above 3 and under 12, half fare.
Tickets not transferable. No luggage allowed.
The return train will leave Hendon at 7.15 p.m. the same day and the tickets will be available for return by this train only.

James Allport, *General Manager*

Great Northern Railway   *Cheap Day Trip to the Seaside*
Monday 10th August 1868

A cheap excursion will run to Ramsgate, Margate and Broadstairs as under:

Huntingdon	dep.	5.33 a.m.	Fare	1st Class	12s	Covered carriage	6s
Offord	,,	5.41		,, ,,	12s	,, ,,	6s
St Neots	,,	5.50		,, ,,	12s	,, ,,	6s
Tempsford	,,	5.58		,, ,,	12s	,, ,,	6s
Sandy	,,	6.07		,, ,,	12s	,, ,,	6s
Biggleswade	,,	6.14		,, ,,	11s	,, ,,	5s 6d
Arlesey	,,	6.23		,, ,,	11s	,, ,,	5s 6d
Arlesey Siding	,,	6.27		,, ,,	11s	,, ,,	5s 6d
Hitchin	,,	6.40		,, ,,	10s	,, ,,	5s
Margate	arr.	10.15					
Broadstairs	,,	10.25					
Ramsgate	,,	10.30					

Return from Ramsgate at 6.45, Broadstairs 6.50 and Margate 6.55, same day only.

Seymour Clarke, *General Manager*

Appendix F
Railway Accidents
Extracts from the Coroner's Inquest Book for Bedfordshire, 1854–86

Extracts from the Coroner's Inquest Book for Bedfordshire, 1854-86

Date		Name	Place	Cause	Age
24th February	1854	Thomas Haining	Biggleswade	Knocked down by train	21
27th December	1856	Richard Street	Souldrop	(navvy)	26
24th May	1860	W. S. Clarke	Biggleswade	Standing on top of engine and striking a bridge	24
19th March	1861	James Cherry	Stratford	Run over	37
5th December	1861	Alf. Eddington	Biggleswade	Jumped out of carriage	28
10th July	1862	Wm. Hatton	Shefford	Run over	62
4th October	1862	John York	Biggleswade	Knocked down	47
17th January	1866	Charles Bell	Luton	Navvy in Ampthill tunnel: run over	22
1st September	1868	H. Darnell	Sharnbrook	Run over	65
17th October	1868	J. Rainbow	Biggleswade	,, ,,	41
14th May	1869	Joseph Dixey	Sandy	,, ,,	75
14th June	1870	Thomas Baston	Biggleswade	,, ,,	32
		Kim Larman	,,	,, ,,	30
8th August	1870	Mary Roberts	Luton	,, ,,	74
22nd September	1870	Fred Howkins	Arlesey	,, ,,	28
22nd May	1871	David Winch	East Hyde	,, ,,	22
17th October	1871	Robert Barcock	Sharnbrook	Crushed between wagons	40
3rd August	1872	Silas Smith	Chiltern Green	Run over	30
10th December	1872	Georgina Smith	Sharnbrook	,, ,,	21
30th April	1873	Jonathan Dunt	Luton	,, ,,	46
17th September	1873	Geo. Kefford	Tempsford	,, ,,	11
7th March	1874	Wm. Bosworth	Turvey	,, ,,	40
12th October	1874	Benj. Watson	Luton	,, ,,	26
2nd December	1874	Jas. Wagstaff	Biggleswade	Fell from platform	64
11th March	1875	Wm. Edwards	Sharnbrook	Run over	47
25th March	1875	James Barnet	Luton	Jumped from train	31
10th July	1875	Benj. White	Moggerhanger	Run over	49
23rd December	1876	Thos. Pepper	Arlesey Siding	Collision	49
		John Lovell	, ,,	,,	25
,,		Maurice Mitchell	,, ,,	,,	21
,,		Lucy Thompson	,, ,,	,,	34
,,		Abergail Longstaff	,, ,,	,,	29
30th September	1880	George Rose	Totternhoe	Struck by wagon	8
1st April	1881	Benjamin Franklin	Luton	Run over	21
		Thomas Hawkins	,,	,,	22
15th June	1882	William Clarke	Wymington	Killed by fall of earth	34
12th December	1882	Joseph White	Sharnbrook	Run over	40
27th March	1883	Mary Ann Gardner	Luton	,, ,,	26
7th July	1883	Charles Truett	Sharnbrook	,, ,,	54
4th August	1883	James Smith	Souldrop	,, ,,	53
6th November	1883	Jas. Partridge	Wymington	,, ,,	26
25th June	1884	James Pratt	Biggleswade	,, ,,	44
3rd October	1885	Wm. Baldwin	Sandy	,, ,,	13
11th January	1886	F. O. Tofield	Luton	,, ,,	17
14th January	1886	Albert Bunker	Oakley	Run over	16
9th June	1886	George Barley	Sharnbrook	,, ,,	55
5th November	1886	A. L. Graham	,,	Fell from train	56

Appendix G

Summary of Bedfordshire lines

London & Birmingham Railway
Engineer: Robert Stephenson
Contractors: Grissell & Peto (Buildings at Euston and much of the track)
                  - Pritchard   (Weedon contract)
                  J. Nowell   (Kilsby tunnel)
                  R. Diggle   (Birmingham district)
                  J. Bramah   (Buildings at Curzon Street, Birmingham)
                  and others
Act: 1833
Opening: 17th September 1838 (throughout)
Note: Name changed to London & North Western Railway in 1846 after amalgamation with the Grand Junction Railway and others.

Bedford & London & Birmingham Railway
Engineer: Robert Stephenson
Contractor: T. Jackson
Act: 1845
Opened: 17th November 1846
Note: Absorbed by the L.N.W.R.

Dunstable Railway
Engineer: Robert Stephenson
Contractors: T Jackson '
Act: 1845
Opened: 1st June 1848
Closed: 2nd July 1962
Note: Chairman—George Stephenson; a director Richard Gutteridge
                  Absorbed by the L.N.W.R.

Great Northern Railway
Engineer: William Cubitt
Contractor: Thomas Brassey
Act: 1846
Opened: 7th August 1850
Note: Original terminus Maiden Lane, London. King's Cross opened 1852. Direct line through Newark opened 1st August 1852.

Midland Railway
                  Extension from Leicester (Wigston Junction) to Hitchin
Engineer: Charles Liddell
Contractor: Thomas Brassey
Act: 1855
Opened: 8th May 1857
Note: Reduced from main line to branch status on 13th July 1868
Closed: 1st January 1962.

Midland Railway
                  Extension from Bedford to St Pancras
Engineers: Liddell & Barlow
Contractors: Thomas Brassey, A .Ritson, Waring Bros and others
Act: 1863
Opened: To Moorgate Street 13th July 1868; to St Pancras 1st October 1868
Note: Tracks quadrupled from 1880

Luton Dunstable & Welwyn Junction Railway
Engineer: J. C. Birkinshaw
Contractors: Jackson & Bean
Act: 1856
Opened: Dunstable to Luton 3rd May 1858; Luton to Welwyn Junction 1st September 1860
Closed: April 1965
Note: The section opened in 1860 was under the name of the Hertford Luton & Dunstable Railway.

Sandy & Potton Railway
Engineer: Brundell (of Doncaster)
Contractor: Culshaw (of Biggleswade)
Act: None required
Opened: 9th November 1857
Note: Absorbed by the Bedford & Cambridge Railway 1862. The locomotive 'Shannon' has been fully restored to working order.

Bedford & Cambridge Railway
Engineer: (1) Liddell & Gordon
                   (2) Charles Liddell
Contractor: Joseph Firbank
Act: 1860
Opened: 7th July 1862
Closed: 1st January 1968.

Bedford & Northampton Railway
Engineer: Charles Liddell
Contractors: Clark & Punchard
Act: 1865
Opened: 10th June 1872
Closed: 31st March 1962.

INDEX OF NAMES

Assizes, 92.
Atmospheric Railway, 48.

Board of Trade, 50, 87, 88, 90, 94, 95, 100, 105, 114.
Bradshaw's Guide, 35.
Brakes, Barker's, 91; Westinghouse, 90, 105.

Canals, 1; Grand Junction, 2, 5, 30.
Cattle Plague, 110.
Chancery, Court of, 5.
Coaches, Edinburgh stage, 2; postchaise, 2; 'Times', 3.

Excursions, 79, 109.

Great Exhibition, 40.

Heating systems, 74.
Hunt, Oakley, 110.

Insurance Companies, County Fire Office Ltd., 106; Railway Passengers, 113.

Litigation, Priestley v. Fowler, 97.
Locomotives, 'Little England', 35; 'Shannon', 34, 35, 38, 59.

Militia, Beds., 58.

Navvies, 1, 4, 56, 65, 68.
Newspapers, Beds Merc., 42, 60, 68, 74, 79, 81, 91, 98, 101, 103, 107, 109, 112, 114; Beds Times, 10, 37, 53, 56–62, 80–82; Herts & Beds. Refmr., 45, 46; Northants Merc., 47; Railway Record, 66; Railway Times, 86; Times, 83.

Packhorses, 2.
Parliament, Bills and Acts of, Carriers' Act, 97; Employers' Liability, 99, 100; Railway (Gds & Pssgrs Commctn), 102; Reform, 100; Regulation of Railways, 88, 95, 101; Trade Union, 100; Workmen's Cmpstn., 101.
Preservation Societies, Great Western, 35.
Pullman coach, 42, 81, 104.

Quarter Sessions, 66, 80, 102, 110, 111.

Railways, Bedford & Cambridge, 35, 37, 59, 62, 80, 112; Bedford & Northampton, 43, 62, 63, 66, 68; Boston Bedford & London, 44; British Rail, 88; Buckinghamshire, 107; Cambridge & Bedford, 26; Cambridge & Oxford, 51, 56; Chester & Holyhead, 87; Direct Independent London & Manchester, 17, 18, 47; Direct London & Manchester, 7, 16–18, 45, 50; Direct Northern, 7, 13–15, 25, 30; Eastern Counties, 6 13, 25, 30, 56, 95, 108; Ely & Bedford, 8, 9, 14, 15, 45; Ely & Huntingdon, 65; Great Eastern, 107; Great Northern, 7, 13, 14, 18, 20–25, 31, 32, 40, 57, 60, 88, 89, 93, 103, 107, 111, Great Western, 87, 104, 114; Hertford Luton & Dunstable, 32, 59; Hertford & Welwyn, 32; Leeds & Bradford, 3; Leicester & Bedford, 17, 18, 25, 26, 55; Leicester & Swannington, 24; Liverpool & Manchester, 4, 97; London & Birmingham, 3, 5–8, 30, 45, 49, 50, 86, 87, 97, 108; London & Brighton, 4; London Brighton & South Coast, 71, 95, 99; London & Croydon, 95; London & North Western, 12, 13, 24, 27, 31, 32, 53, 68, 74, 91, 95, 98, 103, 107, 109, 111–114; London & Nottingham, 25; London & South Western, 103, 107, 109, 114; London & York, 13–18, 25, 31; Luton & Dunstable, 26; Luton Dunstable & Welwyn Junction, 31, 32; Manchester Sheffield & Lincolnshire, 105; Metropolitan District, 95; Midland, 13, 24, 25, 28, 40, 42, 57, 59, 60, 66–68, 90, 91, 98, 103, 104, 107, 108, 111, 114; Midland Counties, 24, 108; Midland & Eastern Counties, 56; North Eastern, 107; North Staffordshire, 107; Northampton Bedford & Cambridge, 15, 16, 49, 63; Northern & Eastern, 6; Sandy & Potton, 34, 38, 59; Somerset & Dorset Joint, 107; South Eastern, 95, 103; South Midland, 25; Stockton & Darlington, 4; Turin & Novara, 18; Wantage Tramway, 35.
Railway, Mania, 7, 24, 87; Orphanage, 100, 101; Temperance Union, 101.

Signals, 23.
Sunday Travel, 109.

Trade Unions, Amalgmtd Soc. Railway Servants, 92, 94, 100, 101; Assoc. Society Loco. Engrs. & Firemen, 100; General Railway Workers', 101; Loco. Steam Engine Drivers' etc. Society, 98, 100; Railway Clerks' Assn., 99, 100; Transport Salaried Staffs Assn., 99.
Transport Users' Consultative Cttee, 39.

Wages, 67, 99.
Wyvern, 24.

BEDFORDSHIRE Historical Record Society

Have you ever thought of joining the Bedfordshire Historical Record Society?

Founded in 1912 by the indefatigable Dr Herbert Fowler with a group of notable Bedfordfordhire historians, the Society's purpose is to publish documentary material relevant to the county's history. Under Dr Fowler, Secretary and Editor from 1912 to 1940, it gained a high reputation for scholarship. Later editors were Joyce Godber, author of *History of Bedfordshire,* and Patricia Bell, both of them also County Archivists. By 1993 the Society had published 72 volumes, which serve many purposes. They give members an opportunity to engage in historical and editorial work and, by printing Bedfordshire documents, they make these more accessible to students who perhaps don't read Latin or cannot travel to see original manuscripts.

Members receive each year's publication as it appears and have the chance of buying back volumes at reduced prices. The 1994 volume is the first of three on 'Bedfordshire churches 1820-1865', and will cover parishes from A to G. An annual meeting is held in Bedford, with a distinguished speaker on a subject connected with the current year's publication, and members can meet and talk over tea afterwards. The subscription for private members is £10 from 1 April 1994 and for institutional members £14. The price of each volume to non-members is at least £15, so there is a considerable financial advantage in joining.

For more details of membership, contact the Secretary, Betty Chambers, 50 Shefford Road, Meppershall, Beds SG17 5LL

BEDFORDSHIRE HISTORICAL RECORD SOCIETY PUBLICATIONS LIST: VOLUMES IN PRINT

The Bedfordshire Hearth Tax Return for 1671, edited by Lydia M Marshall. Vol. 16 (1934), reprinted with new introduction 1990.

Miscellanea. Vol. 49 (1970).

Samuel Whitbread's Notebooks 1810-11, 1813-14, edited by Alan F Cirket. Vol. 50 (1971)

Some early Nonconformist Church Books, edited by H G Tibbutt. Vol. 51 (1972).

The Inhabitants of Cardington in 1782, edited by David Baker. Vol. 52 (1973).

Elementary Education in Bedford, 1868-1903 *and* Bedfordshire Ecclesiastical Census, 1851, by D W Bushby. Vol. 54 (1975).

The Minutes of The First Independent Church (now Bunyan Meeting) at Bedford 1656-1766, edited by H G Tibbutt. Vol. 55 (1976).

Worthington George Smith and other studies. Vol. 57 (1978).

Bedfordshire Wills proved in the Prerogative Court of Canterbury, 1383-1548, edited by Margaret McGregor. Vol. 58 (1979).

Miscellanea. Vol. 59 (1980).

The Bedfordshire Farm Worker in the Nineteenth Century, by Nigel E Agar. Vol. 60 (1981).

Law and Order in Georgian Bedfordshire, by Eric Stockdale. Vol. 61 (1982).

Printed Maps and Town Plans of Bedfordshire, 1576-1900, by Betty Chambers. Vol. 62 (1983).

Court of Augmentations accounts for Bedfordshire, edited by Yvonne Nicholls. Vols. 63 and 64 (1984 and 1985).

Law and Local Society in the time of Charles I: Bedfordshire and the Civil War, by Ross Lee. Vol. 65 (1986).

The Diary of a Bedfordshire Squire, edited by Richard Morgan. Vol. 66 (1987).

The Bedfordshire Schoolchild; elementary education before 1902, by David Bushby. Vol. 67 (1988).

The Bedford Moravian Church in the Eighteenth Century, edited by Edwin Welch. Vol. 68 (1989).

Hundreds, Manors, Parishes & the Church: a selection of early documents for Bedfordshire, edited by John S Thompson. Vol. 69 (1990).

Bedfordshire Clock & Watchmakers, 1352-1880, by Chris Pickford. Vol. 70 (1991).

Bedfordshire Muster Rolls, 1539-1831, edited by Nigel Lutt. Vol. 71 (1992).

Bedfordshire Historical Miscellany: Essays in Honour of Patricia Bell. Vol. 72 (1993).

Bedfordshire Churches in the Nineteenth Century: Parishes A-G, edited by Chris Pickford. Vol. 73 (1994)

Publications may be obtained through booksellers or ordered direct from the Publications Officer,
Mrs M Budek, 10 Kimbolton Avenue, Bedford, MK40 3AD.

Books Published by THE BOOK CASTLE

JOURNEYS INTO HERTFORDSHIRE: Anthony Mackay.
Foreword by The Marquess of Salisbury, Hatfield House. Nearly 200 superbly detailed ink drawings depict the towns, buildings and landscape of this still predominantly rural county.

JOURNEYS INTO BEDFORDSHIRE: Anthony Mackay.
Foreword by The Marquess of Tavistock, Woburn Abbey. A lavish book of over 150 evocative ink drawings.

NORTH CHILTERNS CAMERA, 1863–1954: From the Thurston Collection in Luton Museum: edited by Stephen Bunker.
Rural landscapes, town views, studio pictures and unique royal portraits by the area's leading early photographer.

LEAFING THROUGH LITERATURE: Writers' Lives in Hertfordshire and Bedfordshire: David Carroll.
Illustrated short biographies of many famous authors and their connections with these counties.

THROUGH VISITORS' EYES: A Bedfordshire Anthology:
edited by Simon Houfe.
Impressions of the county by famous visitors over the last four centuries, thematically arranged and illustrated with line drawings.

THE HILL OF THE MARTYR: An Architectural History of St. Albans Abbey: Eileen Roberts.
Scholarly and readable chronological narrative history of Hertfordshire and Bedfordshire's famous cathedral. Fully illustrated with photographs and plans.

LOCAL WALKS: South Bedfordshire and North Chilterns:
Vaughan Basham. Twenty-seven thematic circular walks.

LOCAL WALKS: North and Mid-Bedfordshire:
Vaughan Basham. Twenty-five thematic circular walks.

CHILTERN WALKS: Hertfordshire, Bedfordshire and North Buckinghamshire: Nick Moon.
Part of the trilogy of circular walks, in association with the Chiltern Society. Each volume contains thirty circular walks.

CHILTERN WALKS: Buckinghamshire: Nick Moon.

CHILTERN WALKS: Oxfordshire and West Buckinghamshire:
Nick Moon.

OXFORDSHIRE WALKS: Oxford, the Cotswolds and the Cherwell Valley: Nick Moon.
One of two volumes planned to complement Chiltern Walks: Oxfordshire and complete coverage of the county, in association with the Oxford Fieldpaths Society.

LEGACIES: Tales and Legends of Luton and the North Chilterns:
Vic Lea. Twenty-five mysteries and stories based on fact, including Luton Town Football Club. Many photographs.

ECHOES: Tales And Legends of Bedfordshire and Hertfordshire
Vic Lea. Thirty, compulsively retold historical incidents.

ECCENTRICS and VILLAINS, HAUNTINGS and HEROES.
Tales from Four Shires: Northants., Beds., Bucks. and Herts.:
John Houghton. True incidents and curious events covering one thousand years.

MURDERS and MYSTERIES, PEOPLE and PLOTS:
A Buckinghamshire, Bedfordshire and Northamptonshire
Miscellany: John Houghton. This fascinating book of true tales roams around three counties and covers three centuries.

THE RAILWAY AGE IN BEDFORDSHIRE: Fred Cockman.
Classic, illustrated account of early railway history.

BEDFORDSHIRE'S YESTERYEARS: The Family, Childhood and
Schooldays: Brenda Fraser-Newstead.
Unusual early 20th century reminiscences, with private photographs. Three further themed collections planned.

WHIPSNADE WILD ANIMAL PARK: 'MY AFRICA': Lucy Pendar.
Foreword by Andrew Forbes. Introduction by Gerald Durrell. Inside story of sixty years of the Park's animals and people – full of anecdotes, photographs and drawings.

FARM OF MY CHILDHOOD, 1925–1947: Mary Roberts.
An almost vanished lifestyle on a remote farm near Flitwick.

A LASTING IMPRESSION: Michael Dundrow. An East End boy's wartime experiences as an evacuee on a Chilterns farm at Totternhoe.

EVA'S STORY: Chesham Since the Turn of the Century: Eva Rance
The ever-changing twentieth-century, especially the early years at her parents' general stores, Tebby's, in the High Street.

DUNSTABLE DECADE: THE EIGHTIES: – A Collection of
Photographs: Pat Lovering.
A souvenir book of nearly 300 pictures of people and events in the 1980s.

DUNSTABLE IN DETAIL: Nigel Benson.
A hundred of the town's buildings and features, plus town trail map.

OLD DUNSTABLE: Bill Twaddle.
A new edition of this collection of early photographs.

BOURNE AND BRED: A Dunstable Boyhood Between the Wars:
Colin Bourne. An elegantly written, well-illustrated book capturing the spirit of the town over fifty years ago.

ROYAL HOUGHTON: Pat Lovering.
Illustrated history of Houghton Regis from the earliest times to the present.

THE CHANGING FACE OF LUTON: An Illustrated History:
Stephen Bunker, Robin Holgate and Marian Nichols.
Luton's development from earliest times to the present busy industrial town. Illustrated in colour and monochrome. The three authors from Luton Museum are all experts in local history, archaeology, crafts and social history.

THE MEN WHO WORE STRAW HELMETS: Policing Luton, 1840–1974: Tom Madigan.
Meticulously chronicled history; dozens of rare photographs; author served Luton Police for nearly fifty years.

BETWEEN THE HILLS: The Story of Lilley, a Chiltern Village:
Roy Pinnock.
A priceless piece of our heritage – the rural beauty remains but the customs and way of life described here have largely disappeared.

THE TALL HITCHIN SERGEANT: A Victorian Crime Novel based on fact: Edgar Newman.
Mixes real police officers and authentic background with an exciting storyline.

COUNTRY AIR: SUMMER and AUTUMN: Ron Wilson.
The Radio Northampton presenter looks month by month at the countryside's wildlife, customs and lore.

COUNTRY AIR: WINTER and SPRING: Ron Wilson.
This companion volume completes the year in the countryside.

Specially for Children

VILLA BELOW THE KNOLLS: A Story of Roman Britain:
Michael Dundrow. An exciting adventure for young John in Totternhoe and Dunstable two thousand years ago.

ADVENTURE ON THE KNOLLS: A Story of Iron Age Britain:
Michael Dundrow. Excitement on Totternhoe Knolls as ten-year-old John finds himself back in those dangerous times, confronting Julius Caesar and his army.

THE RAVENS: One Boy Against the Might of Rome:
James Dyer. On the Barton Hills and in the south-each of England as the men of the great fort of Ravensburgh (near Hexton) confront the invaders.

Further titles are in preparation.

All the above are available via any bookshop, or from the publisher and bookseller

THE BOOK CASTLE
12 Church Street, Dunstable, Bedfordshire, LU5 4RU
Tel: (0582) 605670

2/95. ST	